# The Baby Planner Profession:

## What You Need to Know! The Ultimate Guide and Resource for Baby Planner Professionals

# The Baby Planner Profession:

What You Need to Know! The Ultimate Guide and Resource for Baby Planner Professionals

## Mary Oscategui

Cover photography by Arina
Borodina
www.arinabphotography.com

Cover Model Heather Newton
magnificentmamas.tumblr.com

*For Bella Luna*

# Contents

# Introduction

Welcome to The Baby Planner Profession, What You Need To Know! The Ultimate Guide and Resource for Baby Planner Professionals. I am honored to present you with the second edition of the first official book about the baby planning industry. This book marks the conception and the birth of your very own baby planning business. The intention of this book is to provide you with all the tools and support necessary to get started in the fabulous new industry of baby planning. The book defines the role of a baby planner, establishes a scope of practice, and covers a wide variety of topics: birthing basics, breastfeeding basics, sleeping basics, product basics, and much more. It is a very exciting time to become involved, and it is a great opportunity to begin a career in baby planning. I'm sure you will learn some fun things about life, health, and babies along the way.

## My Story

It was during my pregnancy with my daughter 'Bella Luna' that I first discovered the importance of having a strong support system. I had always been very independent, yet when I suddenly found myself pregnant and living on the West Coast far away from my family, I suddenly realized that I was going to need to find a network of support as soon possible. There were so many services, products, and decisions to ponder. I was exhausted by the amount of energy and time spent researching all the information on pregnancy. I knew that I needed to reach out for additional support to navigate me through the process. I was blessed to come across an amazing mid-wife named Mary Jackson, who helped me find the support and guidance I needed. Through her close network of friends and practitioners I had full-time support and guidance throughout my beautiful and challenging journey into motherhood.

The entire experience stirred up in me a passion to help and support expecting moms throughout their pregnancy. I realized I had found my calling. A few months after Bella was born, I committed myself to becoming a "baby planner" extraordinaire. Prior to this I had been in the health and fitness industry for more than fifteen years. Since I already had extensive training in consulting, business, management, and as a health practitioner, I saw the perfect way to combine this with my passion for motherhood.

As I allowed my dream to blossom, I spent countless hours creating the specifics of my vision. I developed and designed the website, created the services, floated a blog, and developed marketing and advertising tools. It was an amazing and extremely rewarding adventure! Along the way, my relationship with Bella's father went through a big change....and suddenly I was faced with the challenge of being a single parent of a one year old baby girl. I never lost sight of my dream and continued moving forward.

Along the way I met and socialized with other women and men who were passionate about pregnancy, motherhood, and fatherhood...not to mention their beautiful babies who really welcomed and encouraged me to reach for the stars. I knew in my heart that my business was something many expecting parents could truly benefit from, and I was not going to give up.

Being a single mom, and arriving to Northern California to settle with my daughter, presented some challenges, but after spending some time reflecting and meditating, I came up with a new way to involve families with The Baby Planner....I could share the business! Why not help others start businesses all over the country? They could share the workload, create a community, and partake in the joy of this industry, and at the same time we could have the support that we all need to continue caring for our children. Thus, I began to reach out to friends, clients, and fans, and received an overwhelming positive response for my ideas.

I gave birth to my book in August of 2009 as I saw the clear need to establish a written set of standards and credentials in the new and emerging industry of baby planning. There continues to be a considerable amount of confusion when it comes to the role of a baby planner, their scope of practice, and credentials, so I knew it needed to be established through a well written book.

I also formed the International Academy of Baby Planner Professionals (IABPP) in September 2009, where I introduced a training and certification program that is presented through a webinar to prepare women (and men) for a new career in baby planning. Having a standardized education process by where a credible certification is earned will help build the respect and credibility that our industry deserves. We became the first baby planning organization to offer a formal baby planner certification, where we educate  future  baby planners through evidence based facts, creative and effective professionalism, business management, strong leadership, sales, and communication in order to provide their clients with exceptional service. In 2010 we expanded into the International Maternity Institute, offering the following additional certification programs: Maternity & Child Sleep Consultant, Greenproofer and Greenbirth Educator, Maternity Stress Management Coach, and Maternity Product Specialist. Today, we are a leader in birth and maternity professional education providing online cutting edge, evidenced based educational programs, products and services for the maternity professional and are currently represented in twenty-two countries around the globe.

To find our current students and certified graduates, visit MaternityInstitute.com where you will find their names and links to their business listings under our Members tab.

The response has been incredible and my dream is now becoming a reality. With that said, I am delighted and I feel extremely fortunate to introduce you to this book as a baby planner's ultimate guide and resource for what you need to know when starting a business or enhancing the one you already have. In the follow pages I share my tips, formulas, advice, struggles, and successes, as well as providing the encouragement for you to realize your own dreams in this exciting and emerging new industry.

## Additionally

I'd like to give special thanks and acknowledgement to the following individuals who have contributed and supported the "The Baby Planner Profession: What You Need To Know, The Ultimate Guide and Resource for Baby Planner Professionals" in order to bring awareness to new and expecting clients, as well as future baby planners:

Michele Roeder Mahoney, Mira Murphy, Katherine Nelson, Mattheau Faithauer, Deirdre Clark, Josie Quinto, Victor Oscategui Sr, Patricia Oscategui, Esther Oscategui, Gail Montemayor, Iveta Barinow, Rachel Macias, Ana Anselmo, Ingrid Prueher, Isabelle Lacarce-Paumier, Laura Maher, Barbara Moore, Georgia Montgomery, Charles Schwartz, Angelique Millette, Emily Schaffer, Kristin Nemzer, Eden Somberg, Beth Greer, Dr. Rama Golen, Chalita Photikoe, Charles Schwartz, Diana Stobo, Sue Baelen, Joseph Lizio, Diana from Best Baby Organics, Mary E Jackson, Neliana Wagter and the wonderful nannies at Sun Valley Park, Jens and Carrie Hillen, Dr. Catherine Darley, Anne Montgomery, Linn Walsh, Britt Rodriguez, Kristie Morris, Mike and Paola Dias, Lisa Malley, Sarah Cohen, Harry Young, Glenn Ebersole, Robin Brown, Jennifer Smith, Katrina Ball, Sunnie Bae, Mary Lopez, Nicole Kaduson, Julie Tupler, Diana Paul, Molly Arthur, Michelle LaRowe, Lisa Malley, Tim Ettus, Colleen Driscoll, Linda Woody, Stefanie Antunes, Dayna Landry, Catherine Beier, Cindy Bailey, Elizabeth Dameron-Drew, Pat Cascio, Joy Rose, Julie Tupler, Julie Elkshen, Emily Genevish, Mike Stigliano, Martin Simenc, Nicole Bohorad, Tammy Romer, Debra Flashenberg, Gabriela Rosa, Dr. James McKenna, Ronald Goldman, Pamela Paul, Denise Spatafora, Jen Aliano, Gea Meijering , Melissa Bartick, Beth Salerno, Rob Fisher, and Mark Wood.

Wishing you love and success,

Mary Oscategui
The Baby Planner
thebabyplanner.com

Founder
International Maternity Institute
Maternityinstitute.com

# History of Baby Planning:
# An exciting new career

Although the origins of baby planning can be traced to a few different sources, "Baby Planner" as a profession was first formally established and recognized in the media in September 2006, when a woman by the name of Keely Paice launched her business in the UK.

Her story is as follows:

*"I was editing a magazine and regularly traveling overseas when I was pregnant with my first child. I did everything to prepare for the birth of my baby myself and - after hours of research and far too many shopping trips - I was exhausted before that first proper sleepless night had even happened.*

*"I imagined how wonderful it would be to get advice on what works and what doesn't from people who weren't trying to sell me anything - especially if they turned up at my front door in order to do it. The idea for Babyplanners was born. Independent, straightforward and practical support to help women, and men, make the most of this amazing life-stage.*

*"By coupling an insight into your personal wants and needs with our personal experience and knowledge of the best products and services for new and expectant parents, we hope to make your experience of preparing for that most important of visitors go as smoothly as possible."*

*--Keely Paice, founder, Babyplanners - September 2006*

Since that first sprout, the baby planning industry has taken hold in America and has sprouted all across the country at an ever-growing pace. The first media recognition of the baby planning industry in the US was in 2007. Baby planners first popped up on the west coast, beginning in California and Oregon, followed by the east coast with Boston and New York, and then Florida. Now just about every major city has a baby planner: Los Angeles, San Diego, San Francisco, Portland, Seattle, Las Vegas, Boston, Westport, Chicago, NYC, Atlanta, Austin, Dallas, Washington DC, Denver, Philadelphia, and smaller towns such as St Louis, Maple Grove, Columbus, Canton are also sprouting baby planners. Internationally, baby planners have sprung up in Great Britain, Canada, Australia, South Africa, New Zealand, The Netherlands, and France.

It's an extremely exciting time to be a baby planner.

There are approximately six million pregnancies in the US per year; four million of them are live births. There are approximately 10.4 million single moms in the US and this number is steadily growing. Adoption has undergone enormous changes over the last few decades including open adoption, gay adoption, international adoptions and trans-racial adoptions. There are also millions of women who are going through infertility treatments.

Below are a few statistics from the American Pregnancy Association:

## EVERY DAY IN AMERICA

- ☐ 16,438 women become pregnant
- ☐ 11,018 women give birth
- ☐ 4,780 women endure a pregnancy loss
- ☐ 8,219 women experience an unplanned pregnancy
- ☐ 1,172 women become pregnant while uninsured
- ☐ 5,479 couples begin to struggle with infertility issues

Additionally, many expecting parents today are both working full-time jobs and do not have the extra time or energy to fully prepare for their new arrival. It is becoming more common for expecting parents to live away from their extended family, not having an extra hand available.

There is an overabundance of services and products, making it more difficult to know what's best. Moms are also returning back to work early, making it hard to cope with the many discomforts of post pregnancy including leaving their babies. As a result, new moms and dads can find themselves tired, stressed, limited on time, and spending more money than necessary.

Thanks to the birth of the baby planning industry, preconceiving, expecting, and new parents have the opportunity of hiring a baby planner to help make their journey less stressful, and more enjoyable.

## Benefits of being a baby planner

A baby planner is one of the few jobs that offers so many benefits. As a baby planner you will have a job that is empowering, fulfilling, creative, intimate, and worthwhile. By starting your own baby planning business, you have the freedom to be your own boss, while participating in the most miraculous journey of expectant parents' lives.

Below is a list of other benefits:

- ☐ Bringing awareness and education to clients.
- ☐ Offering care and non-judgmental presence.
- ☐ Preparing customized programs and services tailored specifically to address client's needs.
- ☐ Networking with practitioners and vendors whom share the same passion as you.
- ☐ Developing strong partnerships with clients, practitioners, and vendors.
- ☐ The opportunity to constantly learn and grow in many fields such as health and fitness, green living, new parent education, product and service knowledge, coaching, design, event planning, organization, and so much more.
- ☐ The flexibility of making your own schedule and working from home when needed.
- ☐ Earning an income anywhere from $35,000 to over $100,000 depending on the demographics and your interpersonal skills.
- ☐ The ability to specialize in areas such as single parenting, adoption, infertility, multiples, and corporate programs for business.
- ☐ Exposure to various forms of media, press, and online/offline networks.
- ☐ Working in an ever-changing and dynamic industry.

# What exactly is a Baby Planner?
## Scope of Practice

*"**My mission** is to empower you to know all your options,
so that you can confidently make the most suitable
decisions for you and your baby."*

**–Mary Oscategui, The Baby Planner**

Below are some additional examples of how a variety of other baby planners have described their businesses:

"From the kit you need to practitioners you can trust, we put you on the inside track. We advise on all aspects of pregnancy and new parenthood so you can make informed choices –and enjoy the experience- at every step of the way." - **Baby Planners UK**

"Taking on whatever maternity sends your way." –**Birthful**

"Empowering families; Honoring birth; Changing lives..." –**Mindful Mothering BDA**

"Be conscious, Be amazing, Be you." –
**Serendipity Birthing**

"The DC Baby Planner provides guidance and resources for expectant and new parents to help prepare for the arrival of baby and beyond. We determine the best solutions to make life's greatest adventure stress-free." –**DC Baby Planners**

"Helping new and expecting parents one baby step at a time." – **Bassett Baby Planning**

*"To educate and assist parents as they sail into their new lives, to de-stress this very changing time with help and guidance in preparing their homes, their minds, and getting ready for the new small package that needs hundreds of parts!..... (It is shipped from the factory with only one small part, a loving heart)"* – **The Houston Baby Planner**

"My mission  is to offer myself in service to families in guiding them to a place of balance, inspiration and empowerment. As they become more aware and connected with their intuition they blossom into confident, conscientious and compassionate beings."--- **Emily Schaffer, Baby Planner**

"Belle Jour Baby Planning is here to support and guide you in preparing for your upcoming birth and easing the transition into parenthood."---- **Belle Jour Baby Planning**

## What is a baby planner?

A certified baby planner is a maternity consultant that provides support, information, education and resources to new and expecting parents. By evaluating their clients specific needs and providing them with the appropriate information, education and resources, baby planners empower their clients to make the best decisions for their growing family.

Baby planners tailor their services to suit their clients specific needs, lifestyle and preferences and help them to determine the types of resources, services and products that will be essential for them to utilize on their journey towards parenthood and beyond.

Baby planners are also concerned with educating their clients. By introducing their clients to a variety of options on pre-conception, pregnancy, post-partum and parenting topics, baby planners empower their clients to make informed and educated decisions. Baby planners may introduce their clients to various options regarding birthing, feeding, sleeping, health, fitness, nutrition, eco-friendly living, safety, post-partum support, budgeting, baby gear and more.

Additionally certified baby planners serve as a matchmakers, coordinators, and specialists. As a matchmaker, a baby planner pairs their clients with the most suitable and reputable services and products based on their specific needs and lifestyle. As a coordinator, a baby planner may organize special events such as a baby shower, baby moon, or maternity retreat or may arrange for photo shoots and birth announcement design. As a specialist, a baby planner can offer additional expertise if licensed or accredited in a particular field relating to maternity.

## Who would need a baby planner?

Below are a few examples:

- ☐ Preconceiving parents who want to prepare and know all their options.

- ☐ Infertile women or men (couples) who need encouragement and assistance.

- ☐ Expectant parents who want to learn, know all their options and receive a tailored and customized program to match their specific needs.

- ☐ Expectant parents who are working full-time jobs and can barely find any time for leisure.

- ☐ Expectant parents that feel stressed and overworked.

- ☐ Expectant parents that do not have relatives living close by to assist.

- ☐ An expectant parent who already has children, or is having multiples.

- ☐ A single, expecting mom.

- ☐ Expecting moms on bed rest.

- ☐ New parents who want a tailored and customized program to match their specific needs.

- ☐ New parents who may need assistance and support in transitioning to life with baby.

- ☐ Adoptive parents who need support.

- ☐ Businesses wishing to establish new parent education for their employees.

## What are the characteristics of a good baby planner?

Below are a few:

- ☐ Enjoys working with expecting and new families
- ☐ Well versed and knowledgeable in both the service and product side of the baby planning industry.
- ☐ Objective
- ☐ Great listener
- ☐ Communicates well
- ☐ Personable
- ☐ Educator
- ☐ Organized
- ☐ A master at handling finances
- ☐ Establishes great connections
- ☐ Refers when necessary
- ☐ Professional
- ☐ Provides quality customer service
- ☐ Dependable
- ☐ Trustworthy

## What is a baby planner's scope of practice?

The role of a baby planner is to empower clients by offering support and education in a non-biased fashion that is tailored for meeting the unique needs of each individual family during preconception, pregnancy and beyond. A Baby Planner is committed to advising their clients of all their options so that they may make informed decisions. A baby planner also offers consultations with general knowledge relating to all aspects of preconception, pregnancy and newborn care. This includes a wealth of service and product knowledge as well as expertise in specific areas.

I personally feel that baby planners should not try to be experts at everything and should take the time to pursue the proper credentials, experience, and insurance required for each additional specialty they decide to offer. You do not need to be a baby gear expert, a car seat installer, a nursery interior designer, or baby proofer in order to be a baby planner. Each of these areas involves an extensive amount of training, education, and experience. They are considered specialties. Regard these added services as areas of expertise that you may already have in your background or may decide to offer in addition your main role as a consultant.

Unless you hold an additional license or certification in a specific area of practice, it is not legal to give medical advice, diagnose, or treat your clients. In addition you should remain cautious in attempting to perform for a client the following: exercise programs/plans, diets or nutritional programs, therapy, pre/post natal massage, pre/post natal yoga/pilates, personal training, doula services, midwifery, cpr, etc. Even matters such as postpartum depression and lactation consulting are best left to specialists.

Some examples of what a baby planner is NOT:

- ☐ A medical advisor
- ☐ A therapist
- ☐ A nutritionist
- ☐ An exercise coach
- ☐ A psychologist

☐   A masseuse

*Please note: If a baby planner is trained, experienced, licensed or certified in any of the areas above, she or he may perform these additional services outside of the main role as a baby planner.

## Connecting

Your foundation as a baby planner is your network of talented practitioners who specialize in pre and post natal services. This is especially important for the times when you encounter situations outside your scope of practice.

Also take note, that at times it may be very important for you to introduce yourself to your client's birthing practitioner, (midwife or obstetrician), in the case certain medical conditions appear that are not within your scope of practice. This will help to establish a relationship and understanding of each other's role throughout your client's pregnancy and beyond.

## Products

When dealing with products, it is wise to consider current standards of safety and it is highly recommended that you maintain an up-to-date list of recall items. From a legal standpoint it is highly recommended that you suggest products, but not recommend them. It is also up to you to work closely with additional product experts who review products as a full-time job in order to stay current, up to date, and informed.

## Consulting

Because pregnancy is such an intimate and sensitive time, you may find yourself in a challenge to fully understand the boundaries between knowing how to, and how not to, advise your clients. When in doubt, you should refer out or seek advice from a qualified professional, who can help. A baby planner is the "go to" person to find the best of everything during and after pregnancy. You wouldn't ask a concierge to write you up an exercise plan, or make you a nutritious meal, but you do ask a concierge to find you the best people to do it for you. Similarly, this is how a baby planner works (unless a baby planner has additional certifications, degrees, or licenses to perform additional services for the client).

Below are a couple examples of what to do and what not to do:

## Case scenario one:

Let's say a pregnant client feels sick during your consult and asks you to advise her on what supplements or herbs she can take to relieve her symptoms. The appropriate response is to point her to her doctor or midwife, or refer her to a nutritionist or naturopath specializing in pre and post natal nutrition. You *do not* tell her what supplements to take, even though you may have some knowledge in this area. That would be moving out of your scope of practice.

## Case scenario two:

Let's say a pregnant client asks your advice on which sleeping pillows she could use to improve her quality of sleep. This is certainly within your scope of practice to do so because it is assumed that as a baby planner you have done your research and either you have tested various pillows or worked with a sleep expert who has done so. You may even decide to have a sleep consultant work directly with your client to provide additional assistance if needed.

## Case scenario three:

If your client asks you the best way to safety proof their home, you can discuss various options to do so, and provide them with educational resources.. However, unless you are a certified baby proofer, you do not handle the installation. The best response is to recommend an experienced baby proofer from the IAFCS, who will provide the service for the client.

## Case scenario four:

As for birth consulting, if your client is not sure which birthing classes are suitable for her, it is your job to educate her and assist her in finding the best class for her needs.

**Does an expecting parent need a baby planner, when they have many parenting resources online or local support groups?**

The best comparison I can relate this to, are the services offered in a health club. In a health club, for example, you have a Group Exercise department, where groups of members gather to attend a fitness class, and you also have a Personal Training department, where members go to receive individual attention to address their individual fitness needs.

Similarly, in the baby industry, you have centers and online resources that offer groups of people information, for example a parent's center or local support group, and now you have baby planners, whom offer individualized support and customized services. Both are necessary.

Some expecting families enjoy a group or online setting, and other expecting families enjoy the individualized care and attention. For me, a baby planner really focuses on specializing and catering to the specific tastes and needs of each family they are working for. If a prospective client came to me, for example, and asked me to recommend them a good stroller, I would have to consult with them first to find out their lifestyle, tastes, budget, and so on. The truth is that there are many strollers, meeting safety and quality standards; hence you are a matchmaker, matching the needs of your clients with the appropriate services and products.

## Controversy

There has been some controversy and skepticism surrounding the role of a baby planner and whether it is a viable and sustainable career. There is a certain misconception that a baby planner is somehow taking away from a parent's personal journey into parenthood, almost as if the baby planner is doing all the thinking for the parents. This is not the case. The fact is that there is an overwhelming and continuous stream of services and products being introduced into the pregnancy world, as well as new medical research constantly pouring in. This was not the case fifty years ago. Since most parents today are working full-time, usually the husband *and* the wife, they can find themselves overwhelmed. A baby planner can be a tremendous help in lessening the burden of today's fast paced world. Also with an estimated 750,000 mothers on bed rest each year, a baby planner can be a valuable resource and support for them.

A baby planner, is essentially a 'one stop shop', organizing and presenting all the available options (both services and products) to new and expecting families in order to empower them to make the best decisions for themselves and their baby. A good baby planner enables parents to have more time to learn about parenthood, while efficiently supporting all their needs.

A baby planner also plays an extremely important role as an objective provider, offering their clients the opportunity to make informed decisions they feel good about. Most times expecting and new parents are receiving an overwhelming amount of opinions from friends, family, colleagues, books, magazines, tv, and radio shows. Helping a client connect with what they truly feel is best for them is a great gift.

What credentials and
background are necessary?

Since baby planning is a non-government regulated industry, just like personal training, yoga, sleep consulting, lactation consulting, childbirth education consulting, etc.....having credentials are important.

It is important to note that being a mom or dad does not automatically make one a baby planner. There is a fair amount of work and preparation involved in order to provide a high quality service to your clients. This includes: experience working one on one with clients, excellent listening skills, being objective, research and knowledge of all services and products in the world of pregnancy, networking and partnering with practitioners and businesses that serve new and expecting moms, business management, communication, sales, and marketing skills.

### What Makes a Certification Valuable?

Certification programs ensure the competence of Baby Planner professionals. Certification programs establish standards for baby planner education and play an important role in developing a qualified professional. The certification of a baby planner affirms a knowledge and experience base in their field, their employers, and the public at large. Certification represents a declaration of a particular individual's professional competence.

Certified Baby Planners are maternity consultants whose role extends beyond that of a typical baby planner/maternity concierge. By evaluating their clients specific needs, introducing their clients to a variety of options on pre-conception, pregnancy, post-partum and parenting topics, and providing them with the appropriate information, education and resources, certified baby planners empower their clients to make the best decisions for their growing family.

Certified baby planners take their careers to the next level by completing an accredited and reputable educational program that equips them to launch, operate, and manage their own baby planning business. Earning a certification blended with personal experience is a priceless asset baby planners can use to build their credibility and stand out in the baby planning market.

Steps to becoming a Certified Baby Planner involve:

- Research
- Education
- Support
- Course attendance
- Completion of course assignments and a final exam
- Preparation
- Time Management
- Practicum Hours

Another approach for gaining credibility and expertise when starting out in the baby planning industry is to intern for a distinguished baby planner or participate in a training program such as a baby planner certification. It will set you apart from other baby planning businesses, help you connect with your mission and goals, help you gain support and understanding of how you can collaborate with your competitors, and increase your level of confidence.

Additionally, all major and respected industries have standards that provide and require education. Most clients also want to know what formal experience, training, and qualifications you have before they pay for your services, so it helps to have gone through a formalized training course, via a certification or to have worked with a reputable baby planner.

Clients will understand the value of your services when they see how you can successfully address their needs. Your experience, knowledge, and reputation play an integral role. This is the very reason that I was very compelled about developing an organization with a formal system of qualifications and education in the form of a three month training program, which includes a certification for upholding the highest standards as a baby planning professional.

I am often asked, "Do I need to have children of my own in order to be a baby planner?" No, not at all. However, you certainly should have a fair amount of experience working with pregnant women, nursing mothers, or babies in general, in order to be seen as credible. Your background may include being a nanny, baby nurse, doula, or even baby product expert; all of which will compliment your role as a baby planner. What if you do not have experience, but are very interested in pursuing this business? Then I highly recommend working as an intern for an established baby planner, or going through a standard form of education that ensures you go through various forms of practical applications to prepare you.

There is a constant stream of new products, services, and education being introduced into the maternity and newborn market, so even if you are starting your business with a firm foundation, it is wise to stay open and be prepared to explore, learn, and discover more.

Your background can also be used to your advantage by turning it into an area of specialty or expertise within the baby planning field. For example, you may have had twins, or triplets, or you may be an adoptive parent, or a same sex parent, or a single parent, or a parent who has dealt with infertility. All of these can be used to your advantage as a 'specialty', when setting up your business.

I also recommend networking, partnering, forming an advisory board, and even working with international, national, and locally established professionals, companies, and organizations.

Some examples of well-respected and established professionals and companies include:

- ☐ Midwives
- ☐ OB/GYN's
- ☐ Chiropractors
- ☐ Lactation Consultants
- ☐ Baby and Maternity Retailers
- ☐ Sleep Consultants
- ☐ Birthing Doulas
- ☐ Postpartum Doulas

- ☐ Child Proof Experts
- ☐ Child Care Experts
- ☐ Product Demonstrators & Safety Experts
- ☐ Green Experts
- ☐ Pre/Post Natal Yoga Instructors
- ☐ Pre/Post Natal Massage therapists
- ☐ Birthing Class Educators
- ☐ Infant CPR instructors
- ☐ Acupuncture

# Before you begin: Necessary Factors

Before embarking on your new journey as a baby planner it is extremely important to consider the following factors which can support or slow down your business:

- ☐ Taking the Small Business Readiness Assessment
- ☐ A healthy environment
- ☐ Overcoming negative relationships and welcoming positive relationships
- ☐ Support from friends, family, and co-workers
- ☐ A well equipped home office set-up
- ☐ A daily planned work schedule
- ☐ Organization
- ☐ An EIN number and fictitious business name certificate
- ☐ A business bank checking account

## Small Business Readiness Assessment Tool

The US Small Business Administration provides a wonderful assessment to help you determine whether you are ready to start a small business. You can find the Small Business Readiness Assessment Tool by visiting http://www.sba.gov or by typing the following URL to your internet browser: http://web.sba.gov/sbtn/sbat/index.cfm?Tool=4. Your responses will be scored automatically and an assessment profile provided, when you click the submit button. You will also receive, based on your score, a statement of *Suggested Next Steps*, directing you to the most appropriate SBA resources to help improve your business preparedness.

## A healthy environment

A healthy environment is essential to your health and productivity. A healthy environment includes: getting enough sleep, relaxation, implementing a balanced exercise routine, making better food choices, using non-toxic products for your home, and being conscious those around you as a whole.

In preparation for your business, make a list of ways that you can improve upon your current environment. Celebrate the healthy choices you are already making and note the challenges. Devise a plan that will help you overcome those challenges.

## Negative and Positive Relationships

Negative relationships, whether they be with your partner, family, or friends, can challenge the success of your business and even lead to its' demise. I cannot stress this enough. Running a business successfully takes a lot of energy, time, and support from all those around you. When a negative relationship is accepted into your space, it is easy to lose sight of your passion, dream, and goals. Negativity takes a glass from half full to half empty. Rather than approaching challenges with an opportunity for productive solutions, you get stuck focusing on the problems. This leads you to second guess your choices and decisions. Doubt becomes your friend. I learned this the hard way. Take it from me when I tell you that if you want your business to succeed, there is no room for negativity.

Here are some ways you can deal with negative relationships and welcome positive ones:

The first step is to acknowledge and recognize the negative relationship. The next step would be to develop a strategy to overcome it.

Most times these relationships involve intimate partners or family, whom are not easy to avoid, so the key is to be blunt and strong. Make it clear that this is your passion, and there is no room for doubters. Baby planning is a very positive and supporting role, it is one that supports motherhood and fatherhood, and it is a beautiful career.

Other ways to handle negative people and environments:

- ☐ Offer a positive perspective
- ☐ Take extra care of yourself, and create some space. Leave for the weekend, or just take a nice bubble bath, treat yourself to a massage, or take a long walk.
- ☐ Keep a list of the reasons why you love this business
- ☐ Set up a daily phone call with a positive friend or family member.
- ☐ Re-evaluate your boundaries.
- ☐ Remain as optimistic as possible.

## Support from Family, Friends, Co-workers

Gladly receive or ask for support. Most people, especially close friends and family, want to see you succeed, and as a result are more than happy to assist you with your needs. As an entrepreneur it may seem weak to ask for help. It's natural to feel this way because we think we show our strength and success by somehow managing everything ourselves. However, if we observe many models of success, they involve a network of people working together for a greater cause. Be clear as to why this is a great business, and why you love it. When others see you have a love for what you do, they will want to support you however they can.

Support can come to you in many ways. It could be as simple as a family member or friend offering to take care of your child to a business partner offering to promote your services.

Here are a few examples of how others can support for you or your business:

- ☐ Delegating work to co-workers or business partners, so you relieve yourself of some of the workload.
- ☐ Asking for an additional 2-4 hours of extra childcare per week so you may use this time to rejuvenate, relax, and pamper yourself.
- ☐ Networking with local businesses and mother's groups to help spread the word about your business.
- ☐ Asking a friend or group of friends for ideas or suggestions to improve upon your business.
- ☐ Hiring a cleaning service to come by once a week to do the hard stuff, so you can give yourself a few extra hours to work, relax, or play.
- ☐ Have your partner or a family member help you prepare meals or snacks to have ready for the work day.
- ☐ Host a local new and expecting moms meet-up to introduce yourself and services to new and expecting moms. Ask for their feedback, ideas, and interests.

## A well-equipped home office setup

A home office should be well equipped with the following:

- ☐ An up-to-date computer and printer
- ☐ An ergonomic friendly working space(ergonomic chair, keyboard etc ) with natural lighting
- ☐ A fast internet connection
- ☐ An unlimited long distance calling plan
- ☐ Hands free phone

## A daily planned work schedule

If you want to succeed, you absolutely MUST keep a daily planned work schedule. Otherwise you may be finding yourself managing your time and business very poorly. Once you have a planned work schedule, it can always be changed. At what time does your day begin? At what time does it end? When is your lunch break? At what time do your respond to emails? What times are your consultations? When do you return phone calls? At what time do you prepare for new and existing clients? When do you update your blog, write a review, send out a newsletter? These are just a few questions. There are a lot more, so you can see why having a daily planned work schedule is necessary and helpful.

## Organization

Organization is a must for your business if you want to succeed. Below are ten useful tips to get totally organized.

1. If you are currently working with more than one client create an in-box for each person.
2. Keep only essential items on your desktop.
3. Create a separate drawer for personal paperwork, items, etc.
4. Purchase Magazine boxes to store booklets, magazines, and catalogs you want to keep.
5. Tear out magazine articles and put them in their own file.

6.  Create a simple filing system that is easy to use, and color coded.

7.  Return calls in batches. Leave specific messages and the time you called if they aren't available.

8.  Empty workspace of everything but the project you're working on to cut down on distractions.

9.  At the end of each project or event, organize paperwork and file or store it.

10. Straighten-up your desk at the end of the day and especially at the end of the week so that you can start each morning with a clean space.

## EIN number and fictitious name business certificate

Before you open up a bank account you will need to provide them with an employee identification number (EIN) for your business and in some states a fictitious name business certificate.

If you claim your business as a sole proprietor you can use your social security and do not need an EIN number, however I recommend it. You can find out more information and apply for your EIN number at http://www.irs.gov/businesses/small/index.html.

The fictitious name business certificate is defined as: *A legal document showing the operating name of a company, as opposed to the legal name of the company. In the case of a corporation, a fictitious business name is any name other than the corporate name stated in its articles of incorporation.*

Source: Entrepreneur.com

If your bank requires a fictitious name business certificate, they will tell you where you can register.

## Business Bank Checking Account

The Internal Revenue Service requires that you open a separate bank checking account for your business. It helps to identify your business, keep your business finances apart from your personal finances, and it can help you establish credit for your business. It also helps you manage how you are handling your cash flow and investments in a very organized and effective manner. Without a business bank check account, keeping track of your profits and losses can get pretty messy in your personal account. I also recommend keeping additional records via invoices, receipts, or financial software which you can use to double check your banking records.

# Specifying your area of
# expertise and role

Your role as a baby planner is to essentially educate, support and coach your clients through the labyrinth of services and products in a non-biased fashion so they can make the best choices for themselves and their baby. I always get asked questions regarding the length of time one should spend with a client. "Do you start with them during the first trimester, second, or third?" "If they call only to use your services regarding a specific product or a single event, is it worth your time?"

The answers to these questions become clear when you define your ideal client, which we cover in chapter six. You may decide to work with clients as a consultant from the beginning of pregnancy until a few months after they have given birth, or you may decide to work as a concierge, or do both. There are some adjustments and modifications to be made when dealing with special cases such as adoption, surrogacy, and infertility. What's most important is to be clear about your mission and who you want to service; otherwise you'll find yourself overworked and compromising the quality of your business.

Now, let's examine the four main roles that fall under the baby planner umbrella:

## Consultant

As a consultant, part of your job is to sharpen your skills in communication, listening, coaching, and organization. You will be arranging consultations with your potential clients, and during this time, you'll be assessing and clarifying your client's major concerns and needs. You are primarily a listener, offering objectivity so that your client can connect with their vision and goals. This will also give you the opportunity to fully understand how to tailor your services for them.

Having a background or understanding of parent coaching can be a huge asset for baby planners. Coaches help clients to come up with their own solutions and help to keep them motivated towards achieving great results. A coach is not a counselor in that the focus is not on the problem, but on the solution. Coaches also contribute their own expertise and knowledge around a variety of topics. Giving parents advice is one thing, and parent coaches help their clients discover their own answers, providing the ultimate in support and guidance that results in positive changes for the entire family. Having a background in coaching can also help you clarify who you are, what you want, what's blocking you, and how you can communicate more effectively with your clients.

Questionnaire and assessment forms are also very helpful tools in determining exactly what your client's needs are. (These forms are provided in chapter seven) Since there are so many factors involved in the planning of a baby, you will want to spend some time after you have consulted with your client to ensure that all areas have been appropriately covered and addressed. This will give you some space to be creative and adaptable to your client's needs.

## Service Expert

As a service expert you are extremely knowledgeable of all the services, support, and education available during and after pregnancy your client's pregnancy. You are aware of all your client's birthing options and co-sleeping choices. You know the difference between a Lamaze class, Bradley Method, Birthing From Within, and a Hypnobirthing class. You can define the differences between a nanny, doula, and night nurse. Be it a prenatal massage, acupuncture, nutrition, or yoga, you recognize which services will be most appropriate for your clients. You also know where all the parent centers are located in your client's area and which forms of education may be most beneficial to them. This also includes knowledge of birthing center locations, fitness classes, yoga classes, infant cpr dates and times, baby proofing experts, going green resources, support groups, doulas, midwives, doctors, photographers, nutritionists, therapists, spa and salon, sleep consultants, lactation consultants, baby sign language, baby shower prep, baby registry, and much more.

## Product Expert

Being a product expert for some baby planners, has become the most identifiable role within the baby planner community. A product expert means that you have done countless hours of research and are extremely knowledgeable of the following: strollers, car seats, baby carriers, nursing covers, nursing pillows, baby bottles, baby co-sleepers and cribs, mattresses, diapers and wipes, diaper bags, feeding products, baby and mom apparel, bouncers, high chairs, swings, potty training products, pads and covers, play yards, pads and covers, safety products, gates, footwear, educational products, books, dvd, blankets, going green, organic products, natural foods, bassinets, bibs, play mats, bath care products, skin care products, changing tables, home décor, accessories, and toys. It also means that you are aware of not only what products are best sellers, but more importantly which products rank highest in safety, quality, and function.

Additionally, you will have reviewed and tested the products to guarantee their safety and will be able to demonstrate them. <u>Be careful not to marginalize yourself as a product expert</u>, otherwise the more important aspects of a woman's pregnancy, health and safety, will be overshadowed. It is very easy to cross boundaries in this area and if you are not careful, you may find yourself reviewing products all the time, which will compromise the quality of your role in other key areas. Keep in mind that there are product experts whose full time job is to review products. Connect and work with them so you can stay informed and free up some of your time to work with clients.

When I first became involved in the baby planning industry I noticed how many mommy bloggers and websites were already offering product expertise. What would make a baby planner any different? More importantly, how is a baby planner able to service many clients, if they are spending most of their time reviewing products? Products are necessary and an integral part of baby planning, however for me, the services and support offered throughout a woman's pregnancy is the higher priority.

There is also the possibility that you may be held liable for the recommendation of products, since the legal aspects in this area are grey, so I suggest working very closely with a full-time product demonstrator who can advise you and keep you up to date. Keep in mind that product expertise is only one of many categories falling under the umbrella of a baby planner.

## Concierge/Coordinator

As a concierge and coordinator you are prepared to deliver the very best throughout all stages of pregnancy at any given time. You assist clients with various tasks and events including setting up a registry, preparing for a baby shower, booking appointments, arranging for spa services, suggesting a photographer or birth class.

## Specifying your expertise

Specifying your expertise involves examining all your current interests, qualifications, strengths, and weaknesses. On the one hand, you may find that you enjoy focusing in one area of baby planning such as preparing for baby showers or setting up a registry. In that case, you will spend most of your time developing and integrating this area into your business, while delegating the other areas to your network of partners and practitioners. On the other hand, you may find yourself to be an expert in two or three areas, in which case you would handle more work and delegate less to your network of partners and practitioners. Is one approach better than the other? No. What matters most is how you are managing yourself, your workload, time, and energy. It is very easy to get stuck or cornered into one area of baby planning, so my advice is to re-evaluate your services and examine whether you are effectively marketing all of them and serving the needs of your clients. At the end of the day, your primary job is to address your client's needs and ensure that they are being met.

It is not uncommon for doulas, nurses, midwives, lactation consultants, childbirth educators, parent coaches, nursery designers, maternity fashion experts, and baby gear consultants to pursue a career as a baby planner. Let's take a look at some backgrounds of a baby planner which can be considered an area of specialty or expertise; giving you the ability to offer additional services. I highly recommend that you pursue the proper credentials, qualifications, experience, licenses, or certifications, in order to offer additional specialty services. Not only does it protect your business, but it also protects your client.

More in depth information in each of these areas can be found very easily. For example: online or through contacting a local practitioner. Below are brief explanations of each.

## Parent and Baby Coach

Baby Planners with a parent/baby coaching background can use many of their coaching skills to support their clients. Coaching creates a powerful on-going relationship between two people. However, rather than instruct, advise or problem solve, the job of the coach is to ask questions, listen, and empower. Coaching can help to conquer fears and anxieties, play an active role in the decision making process so parents to be do not feel helpless, develop intuitive powers, and release creative abilities. This is very useful for couples and singles transitioning into the role of parenthood and for baby planners who want to establish a deeper connection with their clients.

## Parent Coaching Certifications:

### Parent Coaching Institute
http://www.parentcoachinginstitute.com/

### Academy for Coaching Parents International
http://www.academyforcoachingparents.com/

## Lactation Consultant

A baby planner, who is also certified as a lactation consultant, would be considered to have a specialty and expertise in the area of breastfeeding. Lactation consultants educate consumers and professionals in all aspects of breastfeeding. A breastfeeding expert easily blends well with all the other aspects of baby planning, especially because this is a subject matter that does not need to be fully addressed till post pregnancy; allowing you the time and energy to focus on other skills and areas in your craft.

## Certifications to become a lactation consultant:

### International Board of Lactation Consultant Examiners
http://www.iblce.org/

### Lactation Education Resources
http://www.leron-line.com/

### Lactation Education Consultants
http://www.lactationeducationconsultants.com/

### Childbirth and Postpartum Professional Association
http://cappa.net/

## Baby Nurse/Nanny Care

A Baby Nurse is a trained infant/newborn specialist who assists mom and dad with the day-to-day care of their new baby. Similarly, a nanny is someone who is hired by a private family to care for the family's children. The advantage one has as a baby planner with a background as a baby nurse or nanny is that she will automatically anticipate and prepare for the items, support, and services that the mom-to-be needs, based on her experiences working with moms in the past. They will find that most of the planning happens naturally. However, because of her direct experiences with mom and baby, it may be easy to have formed strong opinions about products, services, and even parenting styles, so it is highly advisable that she remain objective when dealing with each client.

## Baby Nurse and Nanny Certifications:

### Infant and Childcare Training Center
http://www.infantcaretraining.com/

### International Nanny Association
http://www.nanny.org/

## Doula

DONA international defines a doula as such:

*The word "doula" comes from the ancient Greek meaning "a woman who serves" and is now used to refer to a trained and experienced professional who provides continuous physical, emotional and informational support to the mother before, during and just after birth; or a woman who provides emotional and practical support during the postpartum period.*

A baby planner with a doula background can be a tremendous support for their clients. They offer many benefits and are very helpful with the physical and emotional challenges of pregnancy, labor, and post pregnancy.

## Birth and Postpartum Doula Certifications:

DONA International
http://dona.org/

CAPPA
http://cappa.net/

International Childbirth Education Association
http://www.icea.org/

Child Birth International
http://www.childbirthinternational.com/

## Baby Proofer

Infant and child safety is a major concern for most if not all expecting parents. A baby planner with a background in babyproofing can be extremely helpful for their clients. A babyproofing expert is naturally aware of child safety matters, which will come very handy when evaluating your client's home and environment. Please note that babyproofing is not an easy job and involves extensive knowledge and training in general home safety, choking, suffocation, entrapment, burn, fire, electrical, drowning, falls, poison, tipovers, and industry trends. There is currently only one organization who provides the babyproofing industry with a certification program, IAFCS.

## ChildProofer Certification:

International Association for Child Safety
http://iafcs.org/

## Health and Fitness

A baby planner with a health and fitness background will certainly keep busy. Health continues to be one of the top priorities of new and expecting families. Personal Trainers, Yoga Instructors, Pilates Instructors, Physical Therapists, and Wellness Coaches are a few examples of health and fitness professionals. This can be a real plus, as there is nothing that improves the overall experience of pregnancy more than good health. Within every profession of the health and fitness industry, there are a variety of methods and techniques. There are many different kinds of pre/post natal health and fitness certifications available.

Below are a few:

## Prenatal Yoga Certification:

http://www.prenatalyogacenter.com/

## Prenatal Pilates

http://www.thecenterforwomensfitness.com/

## Prenatal Fitness

http://www.healthymomsfitness.com/training.htm

http://www.afpafitness.com/store/prepost-natal-exercise-certification-p-674.html

http://www.afaa.com/

## Diastasis Rehab

http://diastasisrehab.com/

## Nutrition

Nutrition plays a key role in all areas of pregnancy, from preconception to breastfeeding. A baby planner with a background specializing in prenatal nutrition can help families dealing with fertility issues, pregnancy discomforts, breastfeeding issues, postpartum depression and common discomforts of a newborn such as colic, gas, and problematic sleep.

There are different degrees of nutritionists, ranging from registered dieticians to holistic health counselors. A registered dietician has completed a 4 year degree from a university, is licensed by the state, and has participated in an internship program. A nutritionist usually has a bachelor's degree in nutrition and dietetics, and a holistic health counselor completes a 6 month- 1 year program. The main differences within each role are defined by their limited abilities to treat and diagnose. There are a variety of certifications to choose from. Below are a few:

## Nutrition Certification

### Institute for Integrative Nutrition
http://www.integrativenutrition.com/

### Bauman College
http://www.baumancollege.org/

### Global College of Natural Medicine
http://www.gcnm.com/

## Sleep

A baby planner with a background as a sleep consultant plays a very beneficial role for an expecting mom during her pregnancy and once her baby is born. Sleep challenges experienced by both mom and baby are very common. Most sleep consultants are certified and trained to work with children. The International Maternity Institute is the first to introduce a program that also addresses sleep issues during pregnancy. Currently there are a few sleep consultant certifications available in both Maternity & Child Sleep:

International Maternity Institute
http://maternityinstitute.com

Naturally Nurturing
http://www.naturallynurturing.co.uk

Sleep Sense Coach
http://www.sleepsense.net

Gentle Sleep Coach
http://www.gentlesleepcoach.com/

## Going Green/Greenproofing Expert

Being an expert in the realm of green living for mom and baby involves well rounded knowledge of all products and services that are eco-friendly, organic, non-toxic, safe, and natural. This also includes an in depth understanding of the harmful chemicals and ingredients that exist in commercial household products, baby products, and mommy products.

Just as babyproofing is designed to prevent children from injuring themselves or doing damage around the home, a certified greenproofer™ is a maternity eco-consultant that meets with expecting or new families to provide education, support, and resources in order to protect families and their children from unsafe exposure to potentially toxic substances in their home, on their body, and in their environment.

To become a Greenproofer visit:

International Maternity Institute
http://maternityinstitute.com


## Fertility

Dealing with fertility issues can be a very frustrating and emotional time for couples, especially if they have been trying to conceive a child for years without positive results. There are so many factors involved: medical, genetics, nutrition, age, smoking, being overweight or underweight, too much exercise, or too much caffeine intake, bacterial infections, etc. Most baby planners usually work with clients after conception, however they may decide to start beforehand and help their clients find the best practitioners on their journey toward conception. There are many resources available that have produced outstanding results. Below are a few:

### Natural Baby Pros
http://www.naturalbabypros.com/

### Fertile Kitchen
http://www.fertilekitchen.com/

### Gabriela Rosa
http://naturalfertilitybreakthrough.com/

## Baby Gear/Product Expert/Car Seat Technician

Although some baby planners spend a good portion of their time reviewing products, a baby planner with a background as a product demonstrator, gear expert, or car seat technician has a tremendous amount of helpful knowledge and experience to share with expecting and new families. There are so many different brands of strollers, car seats, carriers, high chairs, cribs, that it can be extremely overwhelming for parents to try to figure out which product is safest and most suitable for them and their baby. For example: The National Transportation Safety Board estimates that 80 percent of child safety seats are incorrectly installed. This is why car seat technicians play such an important role. It is vital for baby planners to educate parents to be aware of local car seat inspectors and technicians. Safekids.org provides The National Child Passenger Safety Certification Training Program to certify individuals as child passenger safety technicians and instructors.

## CPS Certification
http://cert.safekids.org/

The International Maternity Institute offers a Maternity Product Specialist Course for those that want to specialize as a baby product expert.
http://maternityinstitute.com

## Maternity Fashion & Beauty

Women and men who have backgrounds in maternity fashion and beauty products may enjoy acting as personal shoppers for their baby planning clientele. Many clients enjoy receiving advice about fashion and beauty and there is no better time than a woman's pregnancy to make her feel absolutely gorgeous. Baby Planners who want to specialize in this area will need a working knowledge of maternity wear, baby wear, skin care products, a variety of spa treatments, salon services, designers, style, make-up, trends.

# Childbirth Educators

Below is a great article about childbirth educators by Jen Aliano, of NaturalBabyPros.com

## What is a Childbirth Educator?

Childbirth educators teach expectant parents how to prepare for labor, birth, and the postpartum period. They teach techniques to help with relaxation and pain in labor, methods to use throughout the childbirth process, as well as information on late pregnancy, labor, breastfeeding, postpartum, and newborn care.

There are many different types of Childbirth Educators and class options. Below are just a few.

## The Bradley Method

Also known as Husband Coached Childbirth, the Bradley Method is based on information about how the human body works during labor, and it emphasizes the husband's role for support of the birthing mother. Couples are taught how they can work with their bodies to reduce pain and make their labors more efficient, as well as methods to use to avoid medication, natural breathing, and guided imagery. There is a strong emphasis on pre-natal nutrition throughout the class.

American Academy of Husband-Coached Childbirth
Box 5224
Sherman Oaks, CA 91413-5224
1-800-4-A-BIRTH | (818) 788-6662

## Lamaze

This is one of the most well-known and widely used methods. It teaches the laboring mother to birth with confidence using several different techniques, including movement and positioning, labor support, massage, relaxation, hydrotherapy, the use of hot and cold, as well as incorporating focused breathing techniques to ease through labor.

Lamaze Administrative Office
2025 M Street, NW, Suite 800
Washington, DC 20036-3309

1-800-368-4404 | (202) 367-1128
Fax: 202-367-2128

## Birth Works

One of the unique factors of this method of childbirth is its focus on both the emotional as well as physical aspects of the birthing woman. Birth Works takes into account that a woman's emotions and beliefs around birth have a huge effect on birth's outcome, and that any issues must be addressed prior to the birthing time. The method incorporates preparation of body, mind, and spirit in a way that helps the mother to gain a higher trust in herself and her innate ability to give birth. Other areas of focus include nutrition, exercise, birth plans, breastfeeding, and postpartum issues, as well as traditional topics such as components of labor, pelvic body work, labor positions, comfort measures for labor, etc..

Birth Works© Inc.
P.O. Box 2045
Medford, NJ 08055
1-888-TO-BIRTH (888-862-4784)

## Birthing from Within

This form of childbirth education utilizes projects such as artwork and journalism to approach any fears, emotions or concerns surrounding labor and birth. It focuses on experiencing birth as a rite of passage, opening the body-mind connection before and during labor and birth using self-hypnosis and visualization, and on methods to overcome specific fears surrounding birth and the pain associated with it.

Birthing from Within
P.O.Box 4528
Albuquerque, NM 87106
1-505-254-4884

## International Childbirth Education Association (ICEA)

This group lives by the philosophy "the freedom of choice based on knowledge of alternatives in family-centered maternity and newborn care." They educate about all options in childbirth, help prepare for labor, birth, and parenthood, encourage individualized care with minimal medical intervention, and promote the development of safe, low-cost alternatives in childbirth. They emphasize the importance of birth as an event that forms new relationships and connections within the family. Other specialists certified by ICEA include postnatal educators and perinatal fitness educators.

ICEA
1500 Sunday Drive, Suite 102
Raleigh, NC 27607
1-800-624-4934 | (919) 863-9487

## Hypnosis for Childbirth

Hypnotherapy has become an increasingly popular method of managing fear, anxiety, and pain in labor. This method of preparation for childbirth focuses on mental and physical relaxation during labor. It is based on the notion that increased tension leads to increased pain, and by practicing to decrease tension in the body, the sense of pain can be controlled or diminished. Hypnosis can also work with fears and emotions stemming from previous birth experiences. Some methods incorporate other areas of focus including breathing, visualization, nutrition, and perennial massage.

Below are some of the more popular forms of hypnosis used in childbirth.

**HypnoBirthing®**
5640 E. Bell Rd. #1073
Scottsdale, AZ 85254
1-602-788-6198

**Hypnobabies**
7108 Katella Avenue #241
Stanton, CA 90680
1-714-952-BABY (2229)

**The Leclaire Method**
The Mind Body Center
Attn: Michelle Leclaire O'Neill, Ph.D., R.N.
855 Via de la Paz, Suite 1
Pacific Palisades, CA 90272
1-310-454-0920

Jen Aliano is the Co-Owner and Creator of Natural Baby Pros. She is first and foremost, a wife and mother of two wonderful baby boys who take up the majority of her time and attention. She loves them more than she has ever loved anything in her life, and it is because of them that she started her website and adventure. "The births that we experienced together, and the time we spent together before and after those births, are what motivated me to take on this amazing project. If it weren't for them, this website would not be here, nor would I have found my life's calling…", says Jen.

Jen is also also an acupuncturist, nutritionist, and holistic health practitioner, specializing in the care and treatment of fertility issues, pregnancy, and the post-partum period. She smiles when she thinks of the babies that she has helped bring into this world, but then is reminded of how many women and couples are still struggling with just becoming pregnant, and many of them are unaware of all the different therapies available to help before, during, and after their own journeys into motherhood. For more information visit: http://www.naturalbabypros.com

## Additional Specialties:

## Adoption

Adoption can be a lengthy and trying process that could use a lot of help and support. A baby planner who has had experience adopting a child, may have been adopted, or who has previously worked with adoption, may want to specialize in this area. I advise baby planners who are interested in pursuing this specialty to begin networking with their local community adoption resources to learn more.

## Single Parenting

Being single can introduce a variety of challenges to a new or expecting parent. A baby planner who happens to be a single parent or may have been raised by a single parent may find themselves specializing in this area.

## Multiples

Those of us who are parents of even one child know how much work is involved. So imagine what it must be like to be a new parent to two, three, or more? Having the experience as a parent of multiples will come very handy when working with expectant parents of multiples. They will definitely appreciate a baby planner's experience in this area, and all the advice they can give.

## Business

If a baby planner comes from a corporate background, and enjoys working with businesses, this could be their niche. They can offer a wealth of services to corporate clients. Many top notch companies are interested in specialized health services to keep their employees happy and healthy. Baby Planners specializing in business will most likely work with the company's HR department to offer support and education to their employees.

Who are your clients and
What are their needs?

The three most important business strategies for a baby planner are: a business plan, a marketing plan, and an ideal client profile. We are going to begin by focusing on the ideal client. Creating an ideal client profile can help you target your market effectively and attract more clients.  Many of us make the mistake of starting our businesses without knowing who our ideal clients are. Clearly you want to take into consideration the demographics and the psychographics (which also include geographic and behavior) of your ideal client. The following questions can help you determine your ideal client:

## Demographics

- ☐ How old is your client?
- ☐ What is their gender?
- ☐ Where do they live?
- ☐ What is their occupation?
- ☐ What is their education background?
- ☐ Do they have children?
- ☐ Are they married? Single?
- ☐ What is their income?

## Psychographics

- ☐ What do your clients spend their money on?
- ☐ What do they read?
- ☐ What TV shows do they watch?
- ☐ Do they watch TV?
- ☐ What kind of music do they listen to?
- ☐ What do they eat/drink?
- ☐ How do they dress?
- ☐ What groups do they belong to?
- ☐ What are their interests?
- ☐ What are their needs?
- ☐ Why do they need you?
- ☐ What are their likes and dislikes?

☐  Do they spend time online?

Below are an additional ten useful questions from an article called "How to Recognize Your Ideal Client, Tips From Your Strategic thinking Business Coach" by J. Glenn Ebersole, Jr., (Director of Strategic Marketing & Senior Consultant, LMA Consulting Group):

☐  Who do you really want to work with and what is the compelling reason you want to work with them?

☐  What are the types of problems you want to solve for your ideal clients?

☐  Where is the geographic location of your ideal clients?

☐  What is the minimum revenue/profit that you want to generate from your ideal clients?

☐  What are the socio/demo/psycho graphics of your ideal clients?

☐  What criteria will you use to prioritize the list of ideal clients?

☐  What criteria will you use and how will you "fire" clients that do not fit the ideal client profile?

☐  What types of businesses are your ideal clients in?

☐  What are the core values you will look for in your ideal clients?

☐  What markets do your ideal clients serve?

## J. Glenn Ebersole, Director of Strategic Marketing & Senior Consultant, LMA Consulting Group

J. Glenn Ebersole, a multi-faceted professional, is recognized as a visionary, guide and facilitator in strategic planning and thinking, business coaching, marketing, public relations, management, and engineering. Glenn is the Founder and Chief Executive of The Renaissance Group™, a creative marketing, public relations, strategic planning and business development consulting firm and J.G. Ebersole Associates, an independent professional engineering, marketing, and management consulting firm.

Glenn is the author of "Glenn's Guiding Lines - Thoughts From Your Strategic Thinking Business Coach" newsletter and is known as "Your Strategic Thinking Business Coach," as well as "The PR Doctor" and "Your Strategic Business Connector." Glenn has published more than

350 articles on various business topics and is a top ranked business coach author on EzineArticles.com and the EvanCarmichael.com

A native of Lancaster, PA, Ebersole is also a Registered Professional Engineer in five states, and has a Bachelor of Science Degree in Civil Engineering and a Master of Engineering Degree in Engineering Science from Penn State.

Contact Glenn at 717.509.8889, ext. 243 or via email at jge@lmaconsulting.cc

## Summarizing

When you can answer all the questions listed in this chapter very clearly, you will have successfully created the ideal client(s) to target. You will also find that your company's message is now tailored to be more accurate and specific to reach prospective clients.

## Affordability

Once you have defined your ideal client, there is no reason to be concerned with the question of affordability. You may find that potential clients may come your way that do not match with your ideal client. This is ok. This is your opportunity to decide whether a relationship would be beneficial, or not. Many professional consultants make the mistake of accepting every client that comes their way because they are afraid they will make less or no money otherwise. When you fully understand the power of letting a client go who does not match your needs (or theirs), you will make room for the ones that do, creating a very fruitful and fulfilling environment.

## Choose your clients wisely

Word of mouth travels very quickly. When you surround yourself with clients that match your target, you will enjoy what you do much more, they will be happy to refer you, and come back for more services. If you were to surround yourself with clients who stress you out, weigh you down, or simply do not match each other's needs, the experience will not be enjoyable for either of you. As a result they will not refer you or come back for more services, so it is wise to pass these clients on, leaving space to invite your ideal ones.

## What are your client's needs?

The new client questionnaire provided in the next chapter will help you determine each of your client's immediate and long term needs. Below are some of the questions or concerns our clients have throughout and after pregnancy:

## First Trimester

☐ How can I manage work and pregnancy?

☐ How will this affect my relationship with my partner?

☐ Am I making the right decisions?

☐ Am I doing everything to keep my baby safe and healthy?

☐ Should I have my baby at home, at a birthing center, or hospital?

☐ Am I having the baby naturally or do I opt for drugs?

☐ I am worried and stressed all the time. Is this normal?

☐ What financial changes to I need to make?

☐ Should I start an exercise program?

## Second Trimester

☐ When should I begin preparing for my baby shower?

☐ Should I do an online registry or not?

☐ Which products and services should I purchase? There are so many!

☐ Should I design a nursery now or have the baby co-sleep in my room?

☐ What type of birthing class is best for me? Lamaze? Bradley? Hypnobirthing?

☐ Is my baby safe?

☐ Am I healthy?

## Third Trimester

☐ Am I prepared?

- ☐ Can I do this?
- ☐ Do I need a Doula?
- ☐ Do I have the support I need?
- ☐ Who will be at my birth?
- ☐ Am I returning to work?
- ☐ How long should I breastfeed?
- ☐ Do I have all the necessities for labor and beyond?
- ☐ Should I start looking for a baby nurse, nanny, or daycare?

## Post Natal

- ☐ How can I get my sleep?
- ☐ How do I feel about breastfeeding so far?
- ☐ Can I continue to breastfeed if I return back to work?
- ☐ Have I made a decision on childcare?
- ☐ How am I going to lose this post pregnancy weight?
- ☐ Should I hire a baby proofer?
- ☐ Is my home toxic free and eco-friendly?
- ☐ Should I return to work?
- ☐ How can I cope leaving my baby after three months?
- ☐ How do I handle post partum depression?

# Client Forms

Client Forms can be a great asset to your business. They provide you with valuable information in order to effectively service your client's immediate and long-term needs. I have included three forms that you can use with you clients. Feel free to use them or you can create your own in a way that feels most comfortable and fits with your communication style. Add your own questions or rewrite them.

## New Client Questionnaire

The new client questionnaire provides you with the most relevant information so that you may determine which areas of baby planning will be most beneficial to your clients. It also gives your client the opportunity to share their goals and expectations from you. Rather than communicating the new client questionnaire verbatim, use it as back up tool. Converse with your client as you would converse with a friend or family member. This will help you connect on many levels. Of course you should continue to maintain a level of professionalism throughout.

## Home and Personal Assessment

The second form that I use is a home and personal assessment questionnaire. I keep this one for myself and use it to determine my client's tastes, likes, and interests. This information becomes very handy when you are preparing for a baby shower, choosing products for a registry, or designing a nursery.

## Disclaimer, Waiver, and Liability Form

The last form that I use and give to my clients is a disclaimer, waiver, and liability form. This form is essential and highly significant as it establishes a clear understanding of your role as a baby planner and the voluntary services that you offer.

## The Baby Planner

### New Client Questionnaire
www.thebabyplanner.com

Name

Birthdate

Home Address

Phone number

Email address

Partner's Name                           Phone

Emergency Contact                        Phone

Due Date

Expected location of birth

How are you feeling with your overall pregnancy?

What would you like most support with?

Do you have any concerns or stresses?

Do you feel like you know all your options?

Are you working with an Obstetrician, or Midwife?

Are you working with or do you plan to use a doula?

What kind of family support will be available to you during and after your pregnancy?

How would you describe the involvement and support from your partner?

Is this your first pregnancy?

Do you plan on knowing the sex of the baby before delivery?

Do you plan on breastfeeding and for how long?

Have you thought about your sleeping options with your baby?

Have you set up your registry?

Have you planned or set up a baby shower?

Have you planned or set up a Blessingway?

Have you thought about or set up a baby proof environment?

Are you currently working? If so, how many hours a day are you at work?

What is your profession?

Do you plan on returning back to work? If so, when?

Do you travel often?

On a scale of 1-10, how would you rate your current level of stress?

On a scale of 1-10, how would you rate your overall health?

Are you participating in any form of exercise? If so, how often and for how long?

Are you taking any medication? If so, please provide it.

Are you following a nutrition plan or seeing a nutritionist?

Have you had any injuries in the last three years? If so, please explain.

Please list all the practitioners/doctors you are seeing:

Place a check next to your current interests:

_____ birthing options,     _____ co-sleeping options,
_____ midwife,     _____ lactation consultants
_____ baby proofing     _____ doulas
_____ birthing classes,     _____ going green

_____ fitness and yoga classe _____ nutritionists

_____ personal trainers,    _____ chiropractors

_____ personal chefs,        _____ personal shopper

_____ photographers,         _____ infant cpr classes

_____ spa treatments,        _____ product knowledge

_____ registry set-up,       _____ baby shower

_____ infant massage,        _____ parent education

_____ nursery design,        _____ baby sign classes

_____ maternity fashion,    _____ childcare

On a scale of 1-10, how knowledgeable are you about toxic chemicals in baby products, clothes, food, and the home environment?

On a scale of 1-10, how knowledgeable are you of the available resources for expecting moms in your area?

Have you taken or are you planning to take any child preparation/birthing classes?

Have you prepared a birth plan?

Have you prepared an after-birth plan?

Do you plan on using a nanny or aupair?

Have you thought about or do you have a budget?

What are your top 3 priorities/goals for you throughout your pregnancy? (ex: fitness, nutrition, health, education, maternity wear, setting up registry,etc…)

What are your top 3 priorities/goals for your baby/babies? (ex: safety, health, clothes, products, etc….)

What is your favorite color?

Choose your favorite home environment

____Trendy          ____ Old-Fashioned ____ Classic
____ Modern          ____ Retro          ____ Zen ____ Eco-Friendly

What are, if any, current obstacles or challenges that you would like
to address?

What are your expectations of The Baby Planner?

How can we help you most?

Any additional information that you would like to share with us?

Please do not hesitate to contact us with any additional questions.

We can be reached at (email) or (phone number).

## The Baby Planner

Home and Personal Assessment
to determine tastes, likes, and interests
www.thebabyplanner.com

Client's Name

Home Address

Phone number

How would you describe the home environment?

____Trendy ____Old-Fashioned ____Classic ____
____High End ____Modern____ Retro ____Zen ____Eco-Friendly

Is there a color theme throughout the home?

Which colors stand out most?

How would you describe your client's fashion style?

____Modern ____Old Fashioned ____Classic
____Plain Jane ____Retro

What kind of books are on the shelf?

____Travel ____Fashion ____Parenting ____Self-help ____Other

What kind of decorations (if any) are around the home?

____art ____family photos____collectables ____travel
____souvenirs
____plants ____other

Describe their cleaning products. Are they eco-friendly?

Is their food organic?

Are they playing background music when you arrive?

How big is the home? 2 story? 3 story?

Do they live in an apartment?

Do they have a backyard?

Is the home cluttered?

Do they have plants?

How would you describe your client's energy?

_____fast-paced _____laid back _____stressed _____fun
_____tired/overworked


The liability form listed on the next page should be included in your client contract and reviewed by a professional attorney. I just separated the two for educational purposes, as well as to also give you the flexibility of using the liability portion on your website.

## Disclaimer, Informed Consent, and Waiver of Liability Form

The services that The Baby Planner provides are not intended to replace or supplement the medical advice that you receive before, during, and after the pregnancy, although our employees and representatives have degrees and experience in the medical field. You agree that none of the advice that The Baby Planner provides shall be considered medical advice nor should the advice be relied upon you as medical advice. You should always seek the advice of your medical practitioner. Therefore, you should consult with your personal physician or other health-care professional if you have any healthcare related questions or before embarking on a new diet or fitness program. If a medical problem appears or persists, do not disregard or delay seeking medical advice from your personal physician or other qualified healthcare provider. Accordingly, The Baby Planner expressly disclaims any liability, loss, damage, or injury caused by information provided to the client.

I understand that the services, programs and classes offered by The Baby Planner are voluntary. I acknowledge that injuries, accidents, or other complications associated with products or services may result from my participation. I will consult my physician if I am concerned about any of the risks to my health or well-being that may result from my participation of services with The Baby Planner. I acknowledge that it is my responsibility to follow instructions for any service provided or purchase I make, and to seek help from The Baby Planner if I have any questions. I knowingly and voluntarily agree to waive and release The Baby Planner, its employees and representatives from any and all claims of liability or demands for compensation that I may acquire during my time working with The Baby Planner.

Signature_____

Date_____

[Today's Date]
[Client's Name]
[Partner's Name]
[Address]
[Phone Number]
[Email Address]

# Baby Planner Contract & Letter of Agreement

Dear [Client]

This letter follows our meeting on [Month, Day, Year], during which we discussed your baby planning needs and my professional role in helping you to prepare and plan. It is my understanding that, you will retain me as a Professional Baby Planner Consultant and Concierge during the time agreed: [input the weeks or months agreed upon]

## Description of Services

As a consultant my role includes: -- [# of] consultations with you via in person, telephone/email -- Assistance in budget determination and breakdown as needed -- Discussion of options for services and products suitable throughout and after your pregnancy. [Add any additional and detailed services here as agreed]

Include suggestions and guidance in making the final selections of products, services-- Attendance at [# of] practitioner appointments of your choice -- Up to [# of] hours of professional in-person consultation time throughout the planning process.

If planning a shower, add an addendum contract that will address theme, budget, location, date and time of the event, all the details.

## Addendum Baby Shower:

As a Baby Shower Coordinator my duties include: -- Visit to location site prior to shower -- Development of a detailed baby shower timeline and floor plan for contracted vendors and guests -- Follow up telephone calls to all contracted vendors and guests 1 – 2 weeks before shower day -- Supervision ([#of] hours maximum) -- On-site coordination and supervision at the shower and during the party for up to [# of] hours on [the date of the shower].

- ☐ An additional event manager, on site, the day of the shower. Please note that the services listed above do not include running any baby shower related errands such as picking up or delivering supplies or equipment, catering, etc. As the client, you will rely on me to work as many hours as may be reasonably necessary to fulfill my obligations under this agreement.

## Conditions

- ☐ I understand that my role will be that of consultant and coordinator. You will make the actual selections and final decisions of service providers and I will implement those selections.

- ☐ You will make payments directly to the service providers/vendors and not to me. I do not accept any commissions from recommended vendors and cannot guarantee any service provider's performance or product. If litigation occurs, it occurs in the jurisdiction where my office is located and the winning party will be reimbursed for attorney and legal fees and court costs.

- ☐ It is your responsibility to provide me with contact names, telephone numbers and any scheduled timetables for all service providers involved in the baby shower no later than 14 days prior to the baby shower or upon the signing of this letter.

- ☐ It is also your responsibility to notify me of any changes in a timely manner. I shall not be held liable for any changes made by you.

- ☐ I will use my professional judgment when taking action in regard to changes, weather, tardiness, non-performance, etc. based on the situation, time limitations and/or your wishes.

- ☐ In the event a family member or friend is working to prepare the baby shower, I will work with you and them as needed.

## Fees & Payment Schedule

For my services you will pay me a total of $_____. Payment will be made as follows:

[Include the payment plan in full detail]

A non-refundable retainer in the amount of $_____ - upon signature of this letter of agreement $_____ due on

_____ (Date)  $_____    due  on  _____
(Date)

## Term/Termination

This agreement will terminate automatically upon completion of the services required by this letter of agreement.

## Changes/Cancellations

Any changes made to this letter of agreement must be made in writing and signed by all parties. You may cancel this agreement, in writing, for any reason. If the any services are canceled, refunds are limited to unearned fees, funds in excess of unused or non-refundable fees and out-of-pocket expenses. If you cancel less than [#] days before your delivery– except for the death of a member of your immediate family – there will be no refund.

## Acts of God

If an act of God, such as a fire, flood, earthquake or other natural calamity shall cause you to cancel my services; I will require payment only for the time actually spent planning for your baby. If your understanding parallels mine, please sign one copy of this letter and return it to me along with your payment in the amount of $_____. I wish you all the happiness in the world and look forward to working with you to make your pregnancy the most enjoyable and memorable day of your life.

Sincerely,
Baby Planner's signature Accepted:

Client's signature _____

Partner's signature _____

Date: _____

# Interpersonal Skills

Successful baby planners excel in the area of interpersonal skills. Pregnancy is a very intimate and sensitive time, not only for the woman, but for everyone involved. How you communicate and relate to your client can make or break your business. You may be a marketing whiz or extremely knowledgeable, however if you lack communication skills, you will not get very far with your business. Although earning a good income is a necessary and healthy part of your business, service must always come first. Provide exceptional service and the money will surely follow.

## Communication

The most common ways we communicate are by email, phone, and in person. One of the greatest turn-offs for a potential client, is when you do not respond to their email or phone call in a timely manner. I cannot express enough to you how impressed and happy customers are when you respond to them within a few hours of their initial email or call. I highly recommend responding within a twenty four hour time frame. If you are too busy, hire an assistant. Trust me that this is an easy way to lose clients. Don't do it to yourself.

If communicating by email, be yourself, choose words that come naturally, but maintain your professionalism. If this is the first time a potential client has contacted you by email, welcome them, and keep it brief. My suggestion is to use the email to either set up a phone consultation or in person consultation. Once you have set up a phone or in person consultation, then you can really use your communication skills to win over your potential client.

For a phone consultation you want to be aware of the following:
- ☐ Your tone of voice
- ☐ How fast you talk
- ☐ How well you listen

For an in person consultation, you want to be aware of the following:
- ☐ Eye to eye contact
- ☐ Smile
- ☐ A firm handshake
- ☐ Professional appearance

☐ Friendly tone of voice
☐ Good posture
☐ Positive energy
☐ Listening
☐ Avoid interruptions

## Active listening

Active listening is an important tool you can use to enhance your interpersonal skills. Wikipedia defines active listening as such:

*"Active listening is a structured way of listening and responding to others. It focuses attention on the speaker. Suspending one's own frame of reference and suspending judgment are important in order to fullyattend to the speaker."*

Below is a simple and useful outline on active listening from Taft College:

## Active Listening Skills

### Attending

A: Eye contact
B: Posture
C: Gesture

S.O.L.E.R.

Five steps to attentive listening

**Squarely** face the person
**Open** your posture
**Lean** towards the sender
**Eye** contact maintained
**Relax** while attending

## Paraphrasing

## What is it?

Restating a message, but usually with fewer words. Where possible try and get more to the point.

## Purpose:

1 - To test your understanding of what you heard.

2 - To communicate that you are trying to understand what is being said. If you're successful, paraphrasing indicates that you are following the speaker's verbal explorations and that you're beginning to understand the basic message.

When listening consider asking yourself:

☐   What is the speaker's basic **thinking** message

☐   What is the person's basic **feeling** message

## Clarifying

**What is it:** Process of bringing vague material into sharper focus.

## Purpose:

☐   To untangle unclear or wrong listener interpretation.

☐   To get more information

☐   To help the speaker see other points of view

☐   To identify what was said

## Perception Checking

**What is it:** Request for verification of your perceptions.

## Purpose:

1 - To give and receive feedback

1 - To check out your assumptions

## Summarizing

**What is it:** pulling together, organizing, and integrating the major aspects of your dialogue. **Pay attention to** various themes and emotional overtones. Put key ideas and feelings into broad statements. **DO NOT** add new ideas.

## Purpose:

- ☐ To give a sense of movement and accomplishment in the exchange
- ☐ To establish a basis for further discussion.
- ☐ Pull together major ideas, facts, and feelings

The three major points of the story are…

## Primary Empathy

**What is it:** Reflection of content and feelings

## Purpose:

1 - To show that you're understanding the speaker's experience

2 - To allow the speaker to evaluate his/her feelings after hearing them expressed by someone else

## Basic Formula:

You feel (state feeling) because (state content)

## Advanced Empathy

**What is it:** reflection of content and feeling at a deeper level.

**Purpose:** To try and get an understanding of what may be deeper feelings

Source: Taft College http://www.taftcollege.edu

## Asking Questions

During your consultation you will begin to discuss with your client the new client questionnaire. I often get asked if I should send the new client questionnaire to my client prior to our first consult or present it during our first consult. I like to present it during the first consult as this gives me the perfect opportunity to see and feel their responses firsthand. Although, your client's answers may speak for themselves, you can also learn so much by their tone of voice and body language. Try not to read the questionnaire verbatim. Use active listening skills. Don't be afraid to ask questions if you are unsure about something. Questions may arise as a natural way of communication at any time during the time spent with your clients. If they seem stressed or concerned at times, do not take it personally. Remember that this is a very sensitive, exciting, and emotional time in their lives. Asking open ended questions can be very powerful and give your clients the opportunity to make empowering choices. Do not be afraid of giving them the space to find the authentic guide within themselves.

## Organization

As a baby planner professional, organization plays a big role in your success. How well you are organized will determine how efficiently and effectively you work. Your clients are very aware when you are not organized and it can discredit your level of professionalism.

## Here are some tips to stay organized:

- ☐ Use a separate file folder or binder for each client.
- ☐ Use tabs and labels to arrange the different areas you wish to address with your client.
- ☐ Use a filing system so if a client calls asking for information, you can get to it right away.
- ☐ Maintain a client contact list including their email and phone number
- ☐ Invest in a good blackberry or iphone
- ☐ Keep clear records of your personal income and expenses from each client

## To summarize:

Always be yourself, be present, non-judgmental, and be fully engaged with your client. If there is something you do not understand or want to clarify ask questions. Be aware of both you and your client's body language. Use active listening skills and give them enough time to answer questions or share their vision with you. Maintain your level of professionalism, by responding to emails and phone calls in a timely manner, and stay organized.

The Baby Planner's mission
statement and developing your own

It wasn't till I became pregnant that I discovered my true purpose. It was then that The Baby Planner was born. I knew that I held the power to create a platform combining my passion for health and fitness along with the resources of education, guidance, and support that I received throughout my pregnancy. What better way could I create a tremendous impact then by empowering families who were preparing to welcome a new baby or child into their lives?

"The Baby Planner's **mission** is to empower you to know *all* your options, so that you can confidently make the most suitable decisions for you and your baby."

## My services include:

## Health and Fitness

I help you prepare for baby pre and post pregnancy through a custom designed exercise and nutrition program; using personal training, yoga, pilates, meditation, and nutrition.

## Birthing Options

I discuss and review the various environments, methods, and care providers used to deliver your baby: homebirth, hospital birth, birthing center, questions to ask your care provider, water birth, hypnobirthing, lamaze, bradley, birthing from within, midwives, doulas, and much more.

## Greenproofing & Going Green

I educate and assist you how to go green with your environment and lifestyle. From your food source to products, I help you to prepare a safe and non-toxic environment for you and your baby.

## Postpartum Care

Once your baby has arrived I support you with the transition and provide you with education and resources on breastfeeding, sleep, postpartum blues, mommy care, childcare, child proofing, car seat safety, essential products, and much more.

## Additional Topics of education, support, and resources include:

Fertility
Postpartum Depression
The best and most needed products for your Baby Registry
Single parenting
Diastasis
Sleep
Breastfeeding
Child Safety
Childcare

Because of the extraordinary impact that health and green living has had in my own personal life, my **philosophy** for The Baby Planner is built on the foundation of green living, healthy natural organic foods, exercise, alternative medicine/techniques, eco-friendly and sustainable services, products, and resources in order to improve upon the quality of your life throughout your pregnancy and beyond.

The health of mom and baby is truly the finest luxury, and that it is why it is my pleasure to support and nurture the important and powerful relationship between mom's physical, mental, and spiritual well-being through the services of The Baby Planner.

I have found that the greatest gift I can offer each of my clients is an objective perspective of all the choices available to them so they can decide what is best for them.  Since they already have so many subjective opinions from family and friends, it can be very confusing and stressful to figure out what is most suitable for them and their baby. This is where a baby planner can be of tremendous help, and how my mission statement was born.

I always continue to work upon improving my services as the needs of my clients change. By listening and acknowledging the needs of each client, I can determine exactly how to tailor my services.

## Developing your own foundation and mission statement

When developing your foundation and mission, take some time to consider the following:

- ☐ What is your mission, and how does this benefit your clients?
- ☐ Does your mission statement attract the clientele you want to service the most?
- ☐ Does your mission convey an understanding to your clients of how you will improve their quality of life?

These questions are essential to the success of your business. Your clients need to relate to your foundation and mission in order to purchase your services. If your foundation and mission are not something your clients can relate to, they will not feel that there is any essential need to hire you.

Put yourself in your client's shoes from all angles: as a pregnant woman, an expecting dad, a soon to be grandparent, same sex or an adoptive parent. Now read your foundation and mission from their perspective. Does it reach them effectively? If you were them, would you want to buy your services?

Mission Statements should answer the following questions:

- ☐ Who are you?
- ☐ Why does your organization exist?
- ☐ What do you do?
- ☐ What is the ultimate result of your work?
- ☐ What does your organization stand for?
- ☐ What makes your organization unique?
- ☐ Who are the beneficiaries of your work?

How long should a mission statement be? Brief. No longer than one page.

# Baby Planner Services

In order for your business to be successful, the services you offer need to be specific and clear. It can be very frustrating for a client to visit a baby planner's website who lists an overwhelming amount of general services, without providing any specific details.

Ask and listen. Review the research and development of your marketing strategy. Have you surveyed perspective clients? Have you tested some of your services on volunteers? These are all great ways to determine what services you offer. As a baby planner, you will have a wide range of services you offer, due to the fact that every woman's needs during her journey will differ slightly. Some women will want to focus on their birthing options, while others want help with their registry, and some may want both.

Be careful not to list too many services on your website. This can be a great turn-off and may even be overwhelming for an expectant parent. As a baby planner, if your main focus is to create a stress free pregnancy for your client, then how can an expectant parent justify hiring you, if they feel overwhelmed by the abundance of services listed on your website? A new client questionnaire and home assessment can be very helpful for you to determine what your client's needs are and customize a plan completely suitable for them. Make your client happy and give them what they want.

## Use a hook and keep it simple

My suggestion is to launch your business by using a simple hook. For example, introduce a brief and affordable package that can be done in two to three consultations. This gives your client the opportunity to get to know you and understand the many services and benefits that you offer. This also gives you the time to get to know them and target their needs effectively.

## The Ultimate Service

The ultimate service is customer service. Without it, you won't get very far. What is considered good customer service? Below are a few examples:

☐   Responding to phone calls and emails in a timely manner

☐   Showing up to your appointments on time

- ☐  Dressing and speaking professionally
- ☐  Being very well-organized
- ☐  Listening and addressing your client's needs
- ☐  Maintaining a positive attitude

## What exactly do you offer?

Offer the services you love to do. If you do not love what you are doing, it shows. Secondly, find out what the needs are of your clients. Ask for volunteers and take a survey. What services do they feel will be most beneficial to them? Be careful not to spread yourself too thin and network with experts who can assist you. Of course, some clients may not resonate with all you offer, but you are not meant to cater to everyone. That is why we have plenty of baby planners to fit into all our client's needs.

Upon understanding your client's specific needs, you can customize your services in various ways.

Below are a few examples of how you may describe some of your services:

## Preparing for Baby

From pregnancy to birth, and beyond, we answer all of your questions and discuss every aspect of pregnancy and the various choices available to you so you can make informed decisions. We also provide you with resources and the latest news so you can be fully prepared.

We determine exactly what your present and future needs are, create a customized plan with you, and cover all areas including:

labor and delivery, weight gain, pregnancy health, safety, birthing classes, nutrition, exercise, style of birth, baby sleeping plans, baby shower, baby registry, photography, breastfeeding, pediatrician, diapers, baby products to buy and avoid, maternity wear, baby wear, infant cpr, etc.

This package can be tailored for the first, second, or third trimester.

## The Baby Planner's Personal Package

My services are custom tailored to suit your individual needs in an objective and supportive environment. I recognize that what is suitable for you, may not be for someone else. I work with you to determine the types of services and products that are essential throughout your pregnancy and which are not. Most importantly I stay focused on the health and safety of you and your baby.

Here is how it works:

## 1st consult (initial home intake)

I begin by coming to your home for an initial consult. I observe your environment, ask you a series of questions, and perform a few to help you determine and decide the areas throughout and after pregnancy that need the most attention.

## 2nd consult

I create a plan based on our first consult, which we will review together. Your plan will include services and products most suitable and essential for your lifestyle and wellbeing. Be it birthing options, exercise, nutrition, parenting education, child care, child safety, breastfeeding, going green, sleep, finding support groups, product demonstration, or safety, we cover it all.

## 3rd consult

I spend time raising awareness and educating you on all your options, the latest service and product information, give you tips, review general basics, and answer questions.

You can choose to end your services here and schedule additional consults as needed, or you can choose to continue with my services and choose from a list of consult topics, classes, or concierge service that I offer.

## Maternity Manager/Personal Assistant

We are available for hire to manage all your household needs throughout your entire pregnancy and beyond. We help to organize, schedule, arrange, coordinate, and oversee all the services, products, and staffing necessary for you and your baby's needs. We schedule and oversee baby nurses, nannies, housekeepers, and additional staff to ensure the healthiest and safest environment for your baby. We are responsible for purchasing the finest items for mom and baby, arranging and preparing healthy meals, personal shopping and running errands, booking and scheduling maternity related appointments, and more.

## Customized A la Carte Concierge Services

Choose from a list of our services that you need. We coordinate and arrange everything for you. From finding the best photographer, to the finest maternity spa, to arranging an eco-friendly baby shower, we're committed to providing you with the very best.

## Baby Shower and Baby Registry

Now let's take a look at two services that may be common with most clients in the United States, baby showers and baby registries. A baby shower is considered cultural and specific to the United States, whereas in France, for example, the celebration of a baby does not happen  till after birth. Setting up a baby registry, on the other hand is quite universal and can be found in just about every country.

## Preparing for Baby Showers

When preparing for a baby shower for your clients, having a handy pre-written check list really helps. There are various themes and fun ways you can prepare for a shower-- everything from eco green, to a traditional baby naming themes. Here are a few questions to sort out before getting started: What is my client's vision for her shower? If it is a surprise shower, what is the vision of the friend, family member, or co-worker involved? How many people will be involved in helping you plan for the shower? Will it be just you or will there be others involved? These questions will be very helpful since (not surprisingly) there tend to be so many opinions and suggestions that arise in the process.

If others are working with you, it will be important to designate roles early on. I have been asked many times, "How far in advance is it best to prepare for a baby shower?" I personally feel that the more time you have to prepare, the better, so I like to give myself nine weeks. You can always make changes along the way. Another question I get asked a lot is, "How many hours on event day do I give myself to prepare?" This is generally determined by the number of people expected at the event. For every twenty people coming, give yourself four hours. Keep in mind that these answers are based upon what has worked best for me. It may differ for you. As long as the quality and service of what you are offering is not being compromised, work how you feel best. Lastly, "How long should a baby shower last?" Typically two to three hours. Virtual Showers are also becoming more common these days in order to connect friends and family who live far away. Below is an example of a simple checklist to help get you started:

## Baby Shower Checklist

Eight to ten weeks before the shower

_____Decide on host/hosts          _____Decide on a theme

_____Co-ed or female               _____Set a date and time

_____Set a budget                  _____Choose a location

_____Prepare a guest list          _____Select invitations

_____Plan a Menu

Four to six weeks before the shower

_____Print map or directions to the event

_____Prepare or purchase decorations and party favors

_____Mail invitations with directions to the baby shower

_____Finalize the menu

_____Place order for cake or treats if applicable

_____Order party rentals if applicable

_____Assist with thank you cards

_____Place order for any special vendors, such entertainment or
    surprises

Two weeks before the shower

_____ Establish an accurate guest count (make follow up calls or
    send email reminders)

_____Prepare and clean location setup

_____Organize and purchase gift for the honoree

_____Purchase or place order for last minute party accessories

_____Place order for catering items or shop for cooking (if
    applicable)

_____If using background music, make sure equipment is working
    properly

_____Prepare goodie bags

_____Determine photographer

One Day before the Event

_____Shop for  H  Hgroceries and prepare platters and/or pick up
    any special catering ordered

_____Purchase beverages     _____Wrap your gift/s

_____Buy flowers     _____Pick up cake

_____Clean house and party area

Day of the Event

_____Decorate     _____ Prepare area for gifts

_____Buy any last minute items     _____Designate clean up crew

_____Choose someone to assist the honoree

_____Determine gift transport

Another helpful option you may want to consider is preparing a timeline of events that occur on the day of the baby shower. You can keep one for yourself or you may decide to create a fun one to hand out to the guests upon arrival.

## Preparing for Baby Registry

It is also helpful to have a checklist when preparing a baby registry for your clients. You can offer them a private tour, help them choose items online, or do both. There are so many options to choose from that it is generally best just to point them where they need to look, and let them take the time to decide which products will work best for them.

One example of a company who offers a unique and effective approach to setting up a registry is AmazingRegistry.com. AmazingRegistry.com is a free service that allows you to register at as many stores as you like through one amazing registry. You can combine your registries from the stores you love into your own registry website, such as www.amazingregistry.com/devereaux, where your friends and family can go to view your selections. Now you are not limited to registering at only one store. If you want to register for two gifts from one store and five from another, do it. All of your registries will show up together on one convenient site. See what was purchased, when, from where, plus many other useful facts about your combined baby registry.

You can also take into consideration that a registry may not be necessary, especially if you are working with an eco-friendly client. They may want to organize their baby shower as a substitute registry and have their family, friends, and co-workers deliver these items. They may also decide to shop for second hand goods, in which case if it is a product, such as a stroller, it is imperative you take all the necessary steps to ensure the safety and quality before making the final purchase.

Below is a sample registry checklist.

## Baby Registry Checklist

## Baby Gear

_____Stroller                              _____Car seat

_____Car seat covers              _____backpack/ carriers/slings

_____activity sets (swings, bouncers, walkers, play yards)

## Feeding

_____Breast pads                    _____nursing pillow

_____breast pump                   _____ nursing cover

_____bib                                 _____high chair

_____BPA free bottles              _____training cups

_____feeding sets                    _____breast milk storage

## Bath Time

_____Organic Shampoo and body wash _____Organic lotion and oil

_____Organic cotton towels      _____Bath toys and
                                                      accessories

_____Wash clothes                  _____Baby tub

## Apparel

_____cap and bootie sets          _____short sleeve one piece

_____long sleeve one piece       _____blankets

_____socks                              _____matching sets

## Diapers

_____Chlorine free or cloth diapers _____Chemical free wipes

_____Diaper bag                      _____Diaper pail

_____Baby changing pads          _____organic diaper rash cream

## Bed Time

_____Organic cotton sheets       _____organic cotton mattress

_____co-sleeper, bassinet,         _____wool mattress pad
   or portable crib

_____decor and accessories       _____receiving blanket

## Safety

_____outlet covers               _____drawer latches

_____corner guards               _____safety gates

_____audio/video monitor         _____smoke and carbon alarm

## Toys

_____rattles                     _____teethers

\_\_\_\_\_soft toys                     _____soothing music

## Parenting Education

\_\_\_\_books    \_\_\_\_dvds    \_\_\_\_cds    \_\_\_\_classes

Below are a few (of many) additional services that can be offered as part of your customized package or a la carte as part of your concierge service.

## Infant Child CPR

Learning CPR for an infant or child is a great service to offer your clients. I highly recommend it to all my clients and to all baby planners. Children can easily choke on a number of objects--even something a simple as lettuce, and they can drown in a very small amount of water in a tub or pool. In an emergency, seconds count. Infants, just like children, have a much better chance of survival if **CPR** is performed immediately. Classes are available at least once a month in your local neighborhood. They are easy to find online, through your local fire department, or parents center.

## Dunstan Baby Language

The Dunstan Baby Language teaches parents or caretakers to hear exactly what their baby is communicating. It can be very discouraging for a parent or caretaker when they are met with the challenge of trying to interpret infant's sounds and cries. Baby Planners can benefit their clients tremendously as a Dunstan Baby Language educator, so they will be able to interpret their infant's sounds and cries – and respond to their needs quickly and effectively.

## Baby Sign Language

Baby sign language is a great communication tool for parents to use with their babies. Most times babies cry out of frustration from not being able to communicate their needs. Since there is a large gap before babies use words to communicate, baby sign language is very helpful. Both parent and baby learn to communicate and bond in a very effective way. Baby sign language instructors can be found online and through parent's centers. It's also extremely cute and adorable!

## Photography

There is nothing like maternity and newborn photographs to capture the most beautiful and amazing moments in your client's journey toward parenthood. There are so many photographers to choose from. Each one has their own unique artsy style so you will have to match their various approaches to your client's tastes. Most photographers offer a number of options to choose from, including: pricing, indoor shots, outdoor shots, black and white, and color. Local photographers are easily found online and through mother's groups.

## Chiropractors

Chiropractors who specialize in pre and post natal services are a good option for some of your clients. My experience has been that some people swear by them while some others don't care for them. This is why it is extremely important as a baby planner that you remain objective and offer these services as needed and requested.

Chiropractic care during pregnancy has been shown to significantly reduce the length of time a woman labors. First time moms averaged a 24 percent shorter labor, while        mothers who have already given birth experienced a 39 percent reduction in the average labor length, compared to controls (Fallon, 1991). Chiropractic adjustments during pregnancy can also reduce the likelihood of experiencing back labor (Diakow, 1991). Regular chiropractic adjustments can safely continue up until the time of birth (Penna, 1989).

## Yoga, Pilates, Fitness Instruction

A large percentage of women find that pre/post natal yoga, pilates, fitness classes, and private training sessions have great benefits both during their pregnancy, and after. There are always a variety of classes and one-on-one training programs offered locally wherever you are. They are a lot of fun and they are a great way to meet other new and expecting moms while helping you improve your health and well-being. Classes and private training can be found in your local gym, yoga studio, pilates studio, or parents center.

## Nutrition Consultations

A good nutritionist or naturopathic physician can help you obtain the knowledge and skills necessary to choose a healthy lifestyle. Having the proper nutrition can really enhance overall quality of life for mom and baby, especially during pregnancy and breastfeeding. Nutritionists can also inform you on which pre and post natal nutrient supplements will work the best in your body, as well as the proper times to start and stop supplementing. Keep in mind, many common herbs can be dangerous during pregnancy, so it's good to let mom's know this, and point them to someone who can advise them on what to avoid.

## Sleep Consultations

Many new parents face a number of sleep challenges and there is no one better than a sleep consultant to give sound advice. Many sleep consultants are also parent coaches who can help with an array of issues that come up during and after pregnancy. Sleep consultants can be found online and at your local parent's center.

## Birthing Coaches and Education

Birth coaches and educators are a great resource in preparing a woman for labor and birth.

There are many types of classes such as:

- ☐ Lamaze classes
- ☐ Bradley Method classes
- ☐ HypnoBirthing classes

☐   Birthing From Within

Classes usually cover the following:

☐   How to know when you are in labor
☐   The various stages and progressions of labor and birth
☐   Techniques for coping with pain as well as reducing pain
☐   How your partner can help you during labor
☐   When to call your doctor or midwife

Birth coaches and educators can be found online, at a parent's center, through a midwife or obstetrician, or through a friend's personal recommendations.

## Prenatal Massage or Infant Massage

Prenatal massage is targeted to the unique needs of mothers-to-be. This therapeutic workout loosens the muscles and joints, improves the circulation, relieves fatigue and elevates the mood, and gives us an overall sense of well-being.

Infant Massage can relieve colic and gas, improve sleep patterns and digestion, help calm and sooth your baby, as well as help form a deep bond.

Make sure to check with your client's doctor or midwife before booking their appointment. Masseuses are best found from personal referrals and through referrals from chiropractors.

## Birthing and Postpartum Doulas

There can be confusion about the differences between postpartum doulas and birth doulas. Although there may be some overlap, especially in the area of breastfeeding, the roles are different. Birth doulas primarily assist mothers during late pregnancy and through birth with a follow-up postpartum visit. Postpartum doulas will often meet parents during their pregnancy, however all of their support comes in right around the time that mother and baby arrive home and for a few weeks later.

## Nursery Design

For parents that opt for a separate sleeping arrangement for their infant, designing a safe, nurturing, and healthy environment for their baby is crucial. An experienced and qualified nursery designer will choose furniture that meets the highest safety standards, choose low voc paint, arrange furniture, chooses colors and imagery, and may work closely with a baby proofer to ensure safety. If they specialize in greenproofing, they can help to improve indoor air quality, reduce electromagnetic exposure, and provide great information and resources for eco-friendly products.

# Business Basics

## Creating a business plan and defining your business

Do you really need a business plan? YES!

Having a written business plan is essential for many reasons:

- ☐ It provides a blue print for your business.
- ☐ It establishes your goals and finances.
- ☐ It will help you compete in the market place.
- ☐ It will help to measure your business performance and track your growth.
- ☐ It is the standard requirement when applying for government grants, loans, or investors.
- ☐ Is helpful when dealing with professionals such as attorneys or accountants

Writing a business plan does take some time and it may seem tedious at first, but it is really worth it. Consider these options before writing your business plan:

### Take a Class

If you are the type of person that does well in a class setting, enroll yourself in a local business plan course. Not only will you end up with a business plan, but you'll have the opportunity to network with fellow colleagues whom you can share ideas and advice with.

### Take an Online Course

If you prefer to write a business plan on your own, there are many online resources offering courses, and business samples.

### Use Software

Business plan software provides an outline, structure, and setup necessary to complete a solid and objective business plan.

### Refer to a Book

There are many books on the market that supply you with the steps and guidance appropriate to create a sound business plan.

## Use a professional to write a business plan for you

Although this seems like the least amount of work, you should spend just as much time thinking your idea and concept through and communicating this to the consultant. You also want to make sure that the consultant is expressing your thoughts clearly.

## What makes a successful business plan?

☐ A strong and well thought out idea
☐ Clear and comprehensive writing
☐ A logical and organized timeline
☐ A unique selling point
☐ Shows increased and continuous revenue

## Business Plan Resources

The US Small Business Administration, Business Know How, and Bplans.com are three great resources that offer complete and invaluable information for your small business, especially when preparing your business plan.

## The US Small Business Administration

The US Small Business Administration is a great resource for small business and for supporting your business plan needs. They even provide a resourceful and free online course on how to prepare a business plan which can be found by visiting the following link:

http://app1.sba.gov/training/sbabp/index.htm.

## Business Know How

The Business Know How provides small business and home business ideas, advice and resources. For more information visit: http://www.businessknowhow.com/

*In addition, there are also a couple of great, free sources of information and help regarding business plan writing - not only will these groups help write business plans but can also help in the research regarding all aspects - like marketing, location, competition, etc. These are the Small Business Development Centers (SBDC) and SCORE ( score.org).

Below is one of many great articles written by Joseph Lizio, CEO of Business Money Today. He offers a different perspective when planning for your business, and reminds us of the importance to consider ourselves and our personal situation.

## When Planning Your Business, Don't Forget About You!

### By Joseph Lizio

Many new entrepreneurs spend a lot of time planning their business. They do this to ensure that once their doors are open things run smooth and that they have a real chance for long-term success.

Most go out and write a business plan. Business plans are great tools in planning your business as well as thinking through all of the small things that business owners have to deal with each and every day. They are very good road maps for a business owner.

But, there is one thing that almost all new business owners miss — and that is their personal situation. They miss it because they get so engrossed in planning the business side. Further, most business plan templates or software just do not cover this issue.

To be a successful entrepreneur, a business owners needs to have the least amount of disruptions (non-business disruptions) possible as well as have the ability to take advance of all opportunities that come their way.

This requires a very solid personal foundation. An entrepreneur must first be mentally ready to put in long hours, make hard decisions and choices and be willing to do what it takes to succeed (take risks). They must also be willing to make personal sacrifices for the business knowing that these scarifies will pay off in the long-term. And, lastly (and most importantly) they must be financially prepared.

This can mean:

1 - Having your personal finances in place so you are not reliant on the business to cover your living expenses. Most businesses take 12 to 18 months just to break even. If the business owner is counting on the business to provide them a salary from day one — they are setting themselves up for a quick failure.

2 - Reducing personal obligations to the lowest level possible by either consolidating debt into one low monthly payment or eliminating personal debt all together.

3 - Lowering living expenses to the most basic of needs. Luxury items are out — stick to just the basics for survival.

4 - Improving credit scores. Regardless of what you may have been told — your personal credit history really, really matters. Should you need working capital or some other type of loan for your business — your personal credit history will come into play. Should you need trade credit or store credit or even insurance — your personal credit history comes into play.

By making yourself the as lean as possible — reducing personal distractions and putting yourself into a position to jump at every opportunity — will go a long way towards your business success.

Every day I come across entrepreneurs who either have great ideas or growing businesses but cannot get them to the next level because their personal situation (bad credit or personal money needs) stands in their way.

Don't be one of them.

Copyright 2009 — BusinessMoneyToday.com

## Joseph Lizio

Joseph Lizio holds a MBA in Finance and Entrepreneurship and has a strong commercial lending background. In his current venture, Mr. Lizio is the founder of - Business Money Today - a site designed to help business owners find and obtain capital to grow their businesses.

http://www.businessmoneytoday.com/

Below is a sample of an expanded business outline:

## Expanded business plan outline

Here's an expanded full business plan outline, with details you might want to include in your own business plan.

**1.0    Executive Summary**
1.1    Objectives
1.2    Mission
1.3    Keys to Success

**2.0    Company Summary**
2.1    Company Ownership
2.2    Company History (for ongoing companies) or Start-up Plan (for new companies)
2.3    Company Locations and Facilities
**3.0    Products and Services**
3.1    Product and Service Description
3.2    Competitive Comparison
3.3     Sales Literature
3.4    Sourcing and Fulfillment
3.5    Technology
3.6    Future Products and Services

**4.0    Market Analysis Summary**
4.1    Market Segmentation
4.2    Target Market Segment Strategy
4.2.1  Market Needs
4.2.2  Market Trends
4.2.3   Market Growth
4.3    Industry Analysis
4.3.1  Industry Participants
4.3.2  Distribution Patterns
4.3.3  Competition and Buying Patterns
4.3.4  Main Competitors

**5.0    Strategy and Implementation Summary**
5.1    Strategy Pyramids

For more information visit http://www.bplans.com/

For a list of sample business plans visit
 http://www.bplans.com/sample_business_plans.cfm

## Business Structure

Upon starting your business, it is necessary to decide which form of business entity you wish to institute. The business form you choose will determine the income tax document that you will need to file. There are five common business structures:

- ☐ Sole Proprietorships
- ☐ Partnerships
- ☐ Corporations
- ☐ S Corporations
- ☐ Limited Liability Company (LLC)

The US Small Business Administration provides a thorough guide of the pros and cons of each structure listed below:

## Forms of Ownership

One of the first decisions that you will have to make as a business owner is how the company should be structured. This decision will have long-term implications, so consult with an accountant and attorney to help you select the form of ownership that is right for you. In making a choice, you will want to take into account the following:

- ☐ Your vision regarding the size and nature of your business.
- ☐ The level of control you wish to have.
- ☐ The level of structure you are willing to deal with.
- ☐ The business' vulnerability to lawsuits.
- ☐ Tax implications of the different ownership structures.
- ☐ Expected profit (or loss) of the business.
- ☐ Whether or not you need to reinvest earnings into the business.
- ☐ Your need for access to cash out of the business for yourself.

## Sole Proprietorships

The vast majority of small businesses start out as sole proprietorships. These firms are owned by one person, usually the individual who has day-to-day responsibilities for running the business. Sole proprietors own all the assets of the business and the profits generated by it. They also assume complete responsibility for any of its liabilities or debts. In the eyes of the law and the public, you are one in the same with the business.

## Advantages of a SoleProprietorship

- ☐ Easiest and least expensive form of ownership to organize.
- ☐ Sole proprietors are in complete control, and within the parameters of the law, may make decisions as they see fit.
- ☐ Sole proprietors receive all income generated by the business to keep or reinvest.
- ☐ Profits from the business flow directly to the owner's personal tax return.
- ☐ The business is easy to dissolve, if desired.

## Disadvantages of a SoleProprietorship

- ☐ Sole proprietors have unlimited liability and are legally responsible for all debts against the business. Their business and personal assets are at risk.
- ☐ May be at a disadvantage in raising funds and are often limited to using funds from personal savings or consumer loans.
- ☐ May have a hard time attracting high-caliber employees or those that are motivated by the opportunity to own a part of the business.
- ☐ Some employee benefits such as owner's medical insurance premiums are not directly deductible from business income (only partially deductible as an adjustment to income).

## Federal Tax Forms for SoleProprietorship

(only a partial list and some may not apply)
- ☐ Form 1040: Individual Income Tax Return
- ☐ Schedule C: Profit or Loss from Business (or Schedule C-EZ)
- ☐ Schedule SE: Self-Employment Tax
- ☐ Form 1040-ES: Estimated Tax for Individuals
- ☐ Form 4562: Depreciation and Amortization

☐ Form 8829: Expenses for Business Use of your Home

☐ Employment Tax Forms

## Partnerships

In a Partnership, two or more people share ownership of a single business. Like proprietorships, the law does not distinguish between the business and its owners. The partners should have a legal agreement that sets forth how decisions will be made, profits will be shared, disputes will be resolved, how future partners will be admitted to the partnership, how partners can be bought out, and what steps will be taken to dissolve the partnership when needed. Yes, it's hard to think about a breakup when the business is just getting started, but many partnerships split up at crisis times, and unless there is a defined process, there will be even greater problems. They also must decide up-front how much time and capital each will contribute, etc.

## Advantages of a Partnership

☐ Partnerships are relatively easy to establish; however time should be invested in developing the partnership agreement.

☐ With more than one owner, the ability to raise funds may be increased.

☐ The profits from the business flow directly through to the partners' personal tax returns.

☐ Prospective employees may be attracted to the business if given the incentive to become a partner.

☐ The business usually will benefit from partners who have complementary skills.

## Disadvantages of a Partnership

☐ Partners are jointly and individually liable for the actions of the other partners.

☐ Profits must be shared with others.

☐ Since decisions are shared, disagreements can occur.

☐ Some employee benefits are not deductible from business income on tax returns.

☐ The partnership may have a limited life; it may end upon the withdrawal or death of a partner.

## Types of Partnerships that should be considered:

1) General Partnership
Partners divide responsibility for management and liability as well as the shares of profit or loss according to their internal agreement. Equal shares are assumed unless there is a written agreement that states differently.

2) Limited Partnership and Partnership with limited liability
Limited means that most of the partners have limited liability (to the extent of their investment) as well as limited input regarding management decisions, which generally encourages investors for short-term projects or for investing in capital assets. This form of ownership is not often used for operating retail or service businesses. Forming a limited partnership is more complex and formal than that of a general partnership.

3) Joint Venture
Acts like a general partnership, but is clearly for a limited period of time or a single project. If the partners in a joint venture repeat the activity, they will be recognized as an ongoing partnership and will have to file as such as well as distribute accumulated partnership assets upon dissolution of the entity.

## Federal Tax Forms for Partnerships

(only a partial list and some may not apply)
☐ Form 1065: Partnership Return of Income
☐ Form 1065 K-1: Partner's Share of Income, Credit, Deductions
☐ Form 4562: Depreciation
☐ Form 1040: Individual Income Tax Return
☐ Schedule E: Supplemental Income and Loss
☐ Schedule SE: Self-Employment Tax
☐ Form 1040-ES: Estimated Tax for Individuals

☐ Employment Tax Forms

## Corporations

A corporation chartered by the state in which it is headquartered is considered by law to be a unique entity, separate and apart from those who own it. A corporation can be taxed, it can be sued, and it can enter into contractual agreements. The owners of a corporation are its shareholders. The shareholders elect a board of directors to oversee the major policies and decisions. The corporation has a life of its own and does not dissolve when ownership changes.

### Advantages of Corporation

☐ Shareholders have limited liability for the corporation's debts or judgments against the corporations.

☐ Generally, shareholders can only be held accountable for their investment in stock of the company. (Note however, that officers can be held personally liable for their actions, such as the failure to withhold and pay employment taxes.)

☐ Corporations can raise additional funds through the sale of stock.

☐ A corporation may deduct the cost of benefits it provides to officers and employees.

☐ Can elect S corporation status if certain requirements are met. This election enables company to be taxed similar to a partnership.

### Disadvantages of Corporation

☐ The process of incorporation requires more time and money than other forms of organization.

☐ Corporations are monitored by federal, state and some local agencies, and as a result may have more paperwork to comply with regulations.

☐ Incorporating may result in higher overall taxes. Dividends paid to shareholders are not deductible from business income; thus it can be taxed twice.

## Federal Tax Forms: Regular or "C" Corporations

(only a partial list and some may not apply)

- ☐ Form 1120 or 1120-A: Corporation Income Tax Return
- ☐ Form 1120-W Estimated Tax for Corporation
- ☐ Form 8109-B Deposit Coupon
- ☐ Form 4625 Depreciation
- ☐ Employment Tax Forms
- ☐ Other forms as needed for capital gains, sale of assets, alternative minimum tax, etc.

### Subchapter S Corporations

A tax election only; this election enables the shareholder to treat the earnings and profits as distributions and have them pass through directly to their personal tax return. The catch here is that the shareholder, if working for the company, and if there is a profit, must pay him/herself wages, and must meet standards of "reasonable compensation". This can vary by geographical region as well as occupation, but the basic rule is to pay yourself what you would have to pay someone to do your job, as long as there is enough profit. If you do not do this, the IRS can reclassify all of the earnings and profit as wages, and you will be liable for all of the payroll taxes on the total amount.

## Federal Tax Forms: Subchapter: S Corporations

(only a partial list and some may not apply)

- ☐ Form 1120S: Income Tax Return for S Corporation
- ☐ 1120S K-1: Shareholder's Share of Income, Credit, Deductions
- ☐ Form 4625 Depreciation
- ☐ Employment Tax Forms
- ☐ Form 1040: Individual Income Tax Return
- ☐ Schedule E: Supplemental Income and Loss
- ☐ Schedule SE: Self-Employment Tax
- ☐ Form 1040-ES: Estimated Tax for Individuals
- ☐ Other forms as needed for capital gains, sale of assets, alternative minimum tax, etc.

## Limited Liability Company (LLC)

The LLC is a relatively new type of hybrid business structure that is now permissible in most states. It is designed to provide the limited liability features of a corporation and the tax efficiencies and operational flexibility of a partnership. Formation is more complex and formal than that of a general partnership.

The owners are members, and the duration of the LLC is usually determined when the organization papers are filed. The time limit can be continued, if desired, by a vote of the members at the time of expiration. LLCs must not have more than two of the four characteristics that define corporations: Limited liability to the extent of assets, continuity of life, centralization of management, and free transferability of ownership interests.

## Federal Tax Forms for LLC

Taxed as partnership in most cases; corporation forms must be used if there are more than 2 of the 4 corporate characteristics, as described above.

In summary, deciding the form of ownership that best suits your business venture should be given careful consideration. Use your key advisers to assist you in the process.

Source: US Small Business Administration; http://www.sba.gov

You'll find that the structure of most baby planners are LLC's or sole proprietorships. You may start out as a sole proprietor like I did and then change your status as your company begins to grow. I highly recommend hiring an attorney or using a business such as BizFilings.com to assist you through the process.

Funding:
How much do I need to get started?

Start-Up Costs for a baby planner are relatively low and can range anywhere from $2,500 to $10,000 depending on the following:

- ☐ Domain name registration
- ☐ Website hosting and maintenance
- ☐ Licenses and permits depending on your state
- ☐ Office equipment
- ☐ Supplies
- ☐ Advertising
- ☐ Marketing Materials
- ☐ Booth rentals at expos and tradeshows
- ☐ Education such as training certifications and conferences

In order to fully give yourself the best chance of starting your company off strong, you will want to effectively handle your cash flow and money management. It is essential that you maintain two separate budgets: one for personal, and one for business. Monitor your spending, and think like a flourishing entrepreneur. Keep a clear and well-noted income and expense sheet. Have a timeline prepared with your expected revenue goals for each month and put a cap on your expenses. So many start-up businesses make the mistake of overspending before earning any income.

Keep in mind that it usually takes a certain amount of time for a new business to break even and start making profits. Many business owners fail or get discouraged because they don't understand why they are not making money from day one to cover their personal expenses. During the start-up phase, make sure not to draw funds out of your business for personal use as those funds can be reinvested in the business for growth. Thus, it is advisable when you start to have at least 18 months of personal cash (capital) to cover personal expenses and debts. Thus, you are not taking needed funds out of your business.

Depending on your start up costs and business plan, you may want to explore sources of capital, especially if you plan on spending a lot of money on marketing, advertising, tradeshows, and education prior to launching your business and servicing customers. You need to be realistic with the financial goals you set for yourself and have a very structured timeline of when those goals need to be met. When starting a business It is very easy to overspend before making consistent profits, so make sure that you invest your money very wisely. Patience is key.

Financing is available through:

- ☐ Government programs
- ☐ Start-up loans
- ☐ Angel investors
- ☐ Partnerships
- ☐ Friends and family

Make sure that you get clear written agreements when borrowing money, even if it is from friends or family.

You may also find that other businesses will try to make money from you before your business had even taken off. Pay caution. These businesses usually offer to promote, market, and advertise your company. Find out all the financial details before agreeing to anything.

## Financing Courses and Programs

Expanding your knowledge in finance will compliment your role as an entrepreneur. There are many courses available through community colleges or business centers. Other resources include books and online courses.

Below is an example of one of the financing programs The US Small Business Administration offers. It is a Financing Basics Course:

## Basic

*While poor management is cited most frequently as the reason businesses fail, inadequate or ill-timed financing is a close second. Whether you're starting a business or expanding one, sufficient ready capital is essential. But it is not enough to simply have sufficient financing; knowledge and planning are required to manage it well. These qualities ensure that entrepreneurs avoid common mistakes like securing the wrong type of financing, miscalculating the amount required, or underestimating the cost of borrowing money. Within Basic Financing Topics we'll review:*

- ☐ Financing Basics
- ☐ Estimating Costs
- ☐ Personal vs. Business
- ☐ Capital for Growth
- ☐ Equity Financing
- ☐ Financial Statements
- ☐ How to Prepare a Loan Package (free online course)

For more information, you can visit this page by using the following link: http://www.sba.gov/services/financialassistance/basics/index.html

# Marketing Basics

Developing a good marketing strategy is an integral part of completing a thorough business plan. A marketing strategy provides specific goals.

This can include the following:
- ☐ Research and Development
- ☐ Planning
- ☐ Communication
- ☐ Evaluation
- ☐ Identifying products and services
- ☐ Defining your ideal client
- ☐ How your company's services and products stands apart from its' competition
- ☐ Price Strategy
- ☐ Promotion
- ☐ Distribution
- ☐ Sales Programs

Let's look at the four key steps.

## Research and Development

This is your opportunity to investigate and find out what interests your clients and what their needs are. You may decide to conduct surveys, web searches, and interviews, or pretest a service you offer, to a volunteer. Feedback is very helpful and can help you determine whether you are on the right track or perhaps need to rethink your strategy.

## Planning

In planning you focus on the challenge, objective, audience, and final goal. Initially for most baby planners the challenge will be to create awareness about this new industry. Most clients will probably have never heard about baby planning until finding you, or some clients may have a perception of baby planning that is slightly skewed. It is at this point that you would set an objective, and plan to meet it. It is important to note that you want to have a clear definition of your clients.

## Communication

Communication is the key to reaching your clients. Put yourself in their shoes. What is on their minds? What are their needs? How do they benefit from your services? When communicating, be as clear and direct as possible Avoid trying to sound like a salesman. Your passion for this industry is one of the reasons they are most likely going to want to work with you.

## Evaluation

An evaluation will help you determine what's working and what's not. Was your strategy effective? Was your message communicated clearly? How did your clients react?

Upon completing your marketing strategy, ask yourself the following questions:

- ☐ Is my strategy measurable?
- ☐ Is my strategy actionable?
- ☐ Does my strategy differentiate my company from the competition?

If you answered yes to all three questions, you have completed your marketing strategy. If not, continue to revise your strategy until you can answer yes to all three questions.

Let's look at different ways to market your business.

## Your Website

Your website will most likely be the first direct marketing your clients will be exposed to, so you want to make sure that you that you take the time to develop an effective one. We will go into more depth in chapter sixteen.

## Business Cards, Post Cards, and Brochures

You'll always want to carry these wherever you go. You may find yourself meeting a potential client at the local market or perhaps you stumble upon a new baby shop. Regardless these will also be very necessary when networking through your local mom-preneur groups, practitioners, vendors, baby fair expos and events.

## Mailing List

Collecting a mailing list is imperative and will help you communicate any news, updates, or invitation to events. There are various ways to collect mailing lists. Some examples include: a mailing form provided through your website, exhibiting your services at an event, or through partnerships.

## Newsletter

Having a monthly newsletter can be very helpful in communicating a lot of information to your clients all at once. This can help to avoid sending your clients too many emails. They will definitely appreciate it.

## Write an article

Writing an article for a local newspaper or mother's group can give you great exposure and credibility. You may also want to submit a guest article to a national magazine or newspaper.

## Guest Speaker

Volunteer as a guest speaker at a local expectant meet up group or event. You can also reach out to various local organizations.

## Press Release

Submitting a press release is a great way to announce and launch your business.

## Pitch Letter

Write a pitch letter for your local tv or radio show. They are always looking for new ideas and trends that will interest their audience. You may also want to offer a business pitch presentation that is about ten to fifteen minutes to investors, partners, or a focus group. Bplans.com has a wonderful pitch center offering many samples, tips, and advice. You can even post a pitch on their site and get feedback!

According to Tim Berry there are five important steps to pitching a business:

- ☐ Be Specific & Concise
- ☐ Sell Yourself
- ☐ Sell Your Offering
- ☐ Close the Deal
- ☐ Nail Your Delivery

Here is an example of a sample pitch letter:

Dear Editor (name)

Many pregnant women these days are stressed, overworked, and overwhelmed. Recent studies have shown how harmful this can be to the developing baby. That's why I thought you might be interested in hearing about the role of a baby planner in order to alleviate these present day challenges during an expectant parents' journey.

I will be the featured speaker at the Parents Center on Wednesday, October 31, 2009, discussing the necessary role of a baby planner in today's society of expectant parents. I will begin speaking at 7 p.m. Beverages and snacks will be served.

I would be honored to have you as our guest. I will call you to confirm your attendance. In the meantime, if you have any questions please call me at 222-888-0000.

Sincerely,

Sally Smith
Baby Planner
Bella Baby Planners of California

## Advertising

Advertising can be purchased from many different sources: blogs, online communities, newspapers, magazines, television, radio, billboards, and much more. Choose your advertising carefully. Make sure it is reaching the audience you want to target and falls within your budget.

## Sponsor

Being a sponsor can involve a high investment. You may decide to sponsor a local event and be offered a booth or to be a guest speaker. You may also decide to find sponsors for your business. There are many benefits in a sponsorship from both sides:

## Some benefits included in sponsorships

- ☐ Logo inclusion on event marketing materials.
- ☐ Right to use event logos.
- ☐ Logo inclusion on the event website.
- ☐ Recognition at all event meetings and ceremonies.
- ☐ Speaking opportunities for company representative at ceremonies.

## Endorsement

Obtaining an endorsement is another notable way to promote your business. An endorsement can come from sources such as high ranked professionals or celebrities. These can include doctors, midwives, celebrities, government officials, or athletes.

## Build your vendor and practitioner network

Just in the same way you create a mailing list building your client and fan database, it is a good idea to do the same thing for vendors and practitioners. They can be very helpful in marketing your business.

In order to be a successful baby planner you need to continuously network to establish very strong relationships with vendors of products and practitioners of services. At the same time you want to manage your time and energy efficiently so that you have plenty of time to work with clients. As vendors and practitioners learn about your business, they will be very eager to contact you and network with you. As a result, you may find yourself overwhelmed with emails/phone calls asking you to sample a product for a review or perhaps meet with a practitioner/educator to learn about their service.

So, how do you handle all this?

The easiest way that I have found in networking with vendors and practitioners is to have designated days and times every week to do so. For example Mon-Wed, I exclusively work with all things related to my clients, consultations, research, preparation, planning, managing, etc….. On Thursday, I dedicate half a day to my clients, and the remainder of the day to interviewing and meeting new practitioners. On Friday, I spend the day learning about new vendors and products, writing a review, or taking a new parenting class offered in the area. This is just an example that has helped me tremendously, however you can arrange and customize your work week to however it suits you best.

## Joint Ventures/Collaboration

You can take your business to another level through joint ventures. Whether you form a partnership, create an advisory board, co-host an event, or co-author a book, collaborating with others can take your business to a whole new level. It can also include your participation in a group that supports entrepreneurs in your industry. You will have the ability to share ideas, make suggestions, and support each other.

## Social Media

Let's look at the various ways in which we can use social media:

## Twitter

It seems like Twitter has taken the world by storm, especially for businesses. It is really a great way to network, reach your target audience, and connect with people whom you normally would never have the chance to by other means. Twitter parties are a fun way to socialize and spread the word about your business. Twitter gives you the opportunity to study your audience and see what your perspective clients are talking about so that you can better serve them. Twitter can also be very addictive and a time waster if you are not careful. You want to make sure that you are using Twitter to network your business, reach clients, and keep it professional. Does that mean you cannot socialize and be yourself? Absolutely not. However, in the same way that you would establish relationships at work, and keep certain things personal, is the same way a Twitter business account should be used. I actually saw a baby planner write about her late night drinking drama one evening, and if I were a perspective client reading this, I am not so sure that I would feel confident or good about hiring her to assist me through my pregnancy. If you must share this type of information with others, use it on a personal Twitter account, not on your business account. It does not reflect well on you or your business.

## Facebook

Facebook is also another very popular platform that has taken the world by storm. It is a bit more intimate and interactive than Twitter, where you have the ability to post articles, files, pictures, videos, link to blogs, post an event, advertise, join groups, and create your own fan page for your business. Facebook also provides additional tools and applications that can be very beneficial for your business.

## Blog

Blogs have become extremely popular and a bit oversaturated, however it is a great way to connect with others and let them get a feel for who you are through your writing. If you are going to start a blog, make sure you update it at least once a month. Imagine what it's like when you visit a service provider's website whose blog was last updated 6 months ago. It may raise doubts for some people.

## Audio

Creating a podcast or an online radio show is a great way to reach an audience, especially busy expecting and new moms.

## Video

Using a video (vlog) is one of the most powerful ways to connect with your audience. Your presence and your voice will quickly allow others to relate to you enough to pursue your services without having met you.

## LinkedIn

LinkedIn exists to help you make better use of your professional network and help the people you trust in return. Their mission is to connect the world's professionals to make them more productive and successful. You can post your resume, job interests, job opportunities, and network with amazing professionals.

## HootSuite

It can be a lot of work to update and log in and out of your different social media accounts. Hootsuite does a wonderful job of making it easier. Hootsuite is an amazing tool that allows you to connect all your social media on one site. You can link your twitter, facebook, linkedin, and wordpress accounts all in one place!

## Visit your local retail stores

It's great to network online, but it's even more fun to do so in person. Take the time to get to know at least one new baby/maternity shop per week. Many retailers enjoy learning about the new industry of baby planning.

## Meet with local service providers and practitioners

Not only will you add to your wealth of resources, but you will learn about the various ways in which these services can help your clients. They will also most times be more than happy to display your marketing materials as well as refer you to their clients.

## Speak at a local event or parent's center

You'd be surprised how many events and parent's centers are looking for people like you to present a new service to their audience. Usually you will be given a fifteen to twenty minute time slot to showcase what you offer.

## Attend a tradeshow, expo, or local networking group

There are so many to choose from and they can be a lot of fun. Baby Fairs, Baby Showers, The Alternative Health Expo, Green Expo, and The NYC Baby Show are just a few of many events offered throughout the year. It is the one stop shop of networking. You have the opportunity to meet and greet vendors, practitioners, and clients all at once.

## Form an Advisory Board

An advisory board is an informal group of mentors who share their knowledge and expertise to help your company be more competitive in the market place. They offer specific advice in key skill areas that can be very beneficial to your business as well as provide essential feedback to determine whether you are on the right track.

## Characteristics of a good Advisory Board may include:

☐ Objectivity

☐ Well-respected individuals or professionals in their industry.

☐ Knowledge and expertise outside your skill set.

☐ Great communicators.

☐ Problem Solvers

## The Ultimate Marketing Tool is YOU: Building your credibility

One of the biggest mistakes you can make as a baby planner is to market your business without showcasing yourself. The biggest asset you have for your business is you. This is what makes you unique. Baby Planning is a personal service. When perspective clients visit your website, they want to know who is the person or persons behind it. They need to relate or connect with who you are and how you communicate before they consider buying your services.

How many times have you visited a website that does not include a personal bio or story about the service provider or company? Are you more likely to purchase services from a website that does not include a story or bio? In most cases, people won't.

So how do you showcase yourself?

Use all your past experiences and work history. Bring attention to your specialties and strengths. Write an ebook, start a video log, host a radio show, submit an article to a national publication, speak at local events or gatherings, pitch your story to a local news channel, or collaborate with other experts. Obtain further education through additional classes, books, research, internships, or certification. Establishing strong relationships, utilizing your strengths, and furthering your education will pave the way for the best marketing tool: YOU!

# Finding a Domain Name

## Choosing a domain name

The first question I get asked when others seek my advice about choosing a domain name is whether they should use the words "baby planner", "baby planners", or "baby planning".

On the one hand using the term "baby planner" in your domain name describes and immediately identifies your business and on the other hand using a unique name without using this term can help your business really stand out. You could make a case for both.

Here are the reasons why I feel using the terms "baby planner", "baby planners", or "baby planning" can be beneficial to your business:

- ☐ The baby planning industry is still new and not yet widely known. Using the term continues to help expand awareness about it.

- ☐ There is an overwhelming amount of pregnancy and maternity websites all using unique names, so it will be hard to identify what you offer unless you spend a good amount of money on marketing and advertising.

- ☐ Having the name baby planner clearly states and defines what you offer.

- ☐ As the baby planning industry gains more popularity, people will be searching for a baby planner online by typing baby planner in the search engine along with their location.

Upon deciding to use any of these terms in your name, the next step would be to decide whether you want to use a unique name or location along with the term; for example "Bella Baby Planners" or "Chicago Baby Planners". Another option would be to do both. Your company may be called Bella Baby Planners based out of Chicago, with the domain name Bella Baby Planners, however you can purchase an additional domain name like "Chicago Baby Planners" and forward this to Bella Baby Planners.

At the end of the day what really matters is which name you like the best and feel the greatest about. After all it is your business and you need to feel good about saying it. Take your time to decide. Imagine your name advertised and on marketing materials. Say your domain name out loud a few times and test it out on others. These are additional ways that can help you decide whether you have made the right choice.

You may also choose to enlist a naming professional, however be prepared to spend a lot of money. They are experts and spend the time researching what name will work best for you. They also are very well-versed in all the legalities involved in naming.

## Do you need to trademark your name?

The first question that arises when considering this matter is: "Does my business name have to be trademarked?" It doesn't. In fact a large percentage of small businesses do not ever register their names. As long as your state laws allow it, you may use an unregistered business name indefinitely—assuming that at no point you are infringing on someone else's trademark.

The thing is, you never really know what direction your business might head, or how successful it may become. Therefore, it makes sense for even the smallest businesses to have their names formally screened. If you know for a fact your business is going to always remain small, and that you have no interest in expanding it down the road, then you really don't need to do a trademark search. However, if you are ambitious and you have a good sense that your "one-man-show" is going to be a big success, then you need to plan accordingly from day one.

The first thing to do is to make sure that your name can be federally registered. This is very important. You will also want to make sure that the primary states you will be doing business in will permit you to do business under the name you desire. For this task, enlisting the services of trademark search firm is something you will want to seriously mull over. The money you spend now doing it right may save you huge costs down the road. Don't get too married to any one name until it has fully cleared the trademark search process. It can be very discouraging to have your name rejected when you have already envisioned your whole future revolving around this name.

## Trademark Classes

When filing for a trademark or service mark there are 45 classes to choose from. Your company can file under a single class or multiple classes, depending on the nature of your service. As a matter of fact, trademarks and service marks operate and are valid under certain classes only. So your mark is only really protected within that class. If you would like a full list of classes you can log onto the "International Schedule of Classes of Goods and Services" at the USPTO website.

There so many misconceptions about trademarks and service marks that getting the right information can be tricky. Most of the misunderstandings revolve around protection issues. Oftentimes people assume that a trademark is universal.

## Conduct A Trademark Search

Here is some advice for you in the case that you decide to tackle the search process on your own. The first place to go is to the Patent and Trademark Depository Libraries, they have an online database of registered marks and also a list of pending registration applications. A good place to search for search for conflicting marks that may still be unregistered, is The U.S. Patent and Trademark Office. They also have a list of patent libraries in your own state.

One important feature on their website is the free database of pending and registered trademarks. These marks are generally entered in the database thirty to sixty days after filing. You can visit their website at http://uspto.gov/ for more information.

I also recommend thoroughly searching your name through a search engine, such as Google, to see if anyone else is using the name. There is a good chance that someone maybe using it unregistered. Try with more than one search engine just to be safe. You may also want to check with domain name companies like                    Network Solutions to see what is available in the marketplace. This will help you narrow down your choices and it can also help you find other businesses using your exact name or similar names. Ideally you will want your business name as a dot com, but if you don't have that option, you will want to consider all the alternative spellings and all the possible domain endings, such as dot net.

# Creating a Logo

Creating a logo to represent your business and brand image is one of the most important tasks in your overall business plan. Your logo is a symbolic representation of everything your company stands for. Most start-up companies tend to underestimate the impact of a great logo, and so they usually spend minimal time in the design.

A logo is a first impression. It is not only a visual representation of everything your company has to offer; it also expresses the soul or essence of the company as well. Over time, your logo will become the most recognizable icon of your business and service. It establishes your identity and simultaneously creates an image of professionalism. Logos can create a sense of comfort, invitation, security, and trust. An ideal logo sends a positive message and conveys the positive aspects of your business. The right logo design can be one of your powerful marketing tools. It sends the message to your potential clients that your company is unique, credible, and professional.

There are three basic logo types: Symbolic, wordmark, and combination.

**Symbolic** logos are like an emblem. They use imagery that conveys an abstract or literal representation of your business. Symbolic logos leave room for a broad interpretation of what your company represents. In order for a symbol to be a truly effective logo, it should conform to these principles: Your symbol should be memorable, crisp, and instantly recognizable.

**Wordmark** logos are primarily font based. They give a sense of formality and refinement. Bold fonts proclaim strength and power, whereas slanted type fonts impart a sense of motion or movement. Thin fonts imply sophistication. It is important when designing a logotype or wordmark that there is legibility and ease of recognition, even when it is reduced to fit on a business card.

**Combination** logos are just what the name implies, a symbol/icon combined with text/font. Combination logos signify the image *and* message that you want to project.

Many good design firms believe that a customer should be able to tell what service or product your company offers just by looking at the logo. That is certainly the ideal. Logos such as the Nike swoosh are only recognizable due to years of savvy marketing and expensive media campaigns.

## Logo--Getting Started

When sketching your logo, first write a one line sentence or a short mission statement to focus your attention. Next, take a look at your competitor's logos to see what their strengths and weaknesses are. You can also get a sense of which logo type you are most attracted to. One key question to ask your self is this: Does my logo portray my company in a manner which implies that I am an expert in this field? This is extremely important.

Before you begin sketching, first articulate the message you want your logo to convey. Try writing a one-sentence image and mission statement to help focus your efforts. Stay true to this statement while creating your logo. Companies that deal with more than one business should have a more generic image.

Decide what aspect of your company you want to emphasize the most: Babies, pregnancy, concierge, motherhood, money saving, time saving, health, education, service, etc. Be clear about the feeling you want to convey and consider whether it comes across as serious, light-hearted, professional, or childish. Be clear as to whether or not it captures your message fully.

Your logo should also be functional and versatile. It should be able to work well on a billboard, on a window, or on a business card. It should also be something that can be photocopied without becoming blurry or losing its essence.

The most effective logos communicate with pictures, not words. A picture says far more than words ever can. If you use your own unique art, you will be seen as more original and creative, than if you use clip art from the internet or something generic, like a smiley face with words. Also, avoid things that are very trendy, because in a few years they may be seen as tacky, or old and overused. Plan to design a logo that is timeless and never needs to be updated.

Design your logo in different color versions, and see how they look. Sit with it for a few days and come back to it. Consider all the places the logo might appear and think about whether or not you want bright or dark tones.

Colors effect viewers in different ways. Red and orange produce excitement, and red tends to also signify danger. Dark blue produces relaxation and comfort, and yellow tends to create a feeling of irritation. If you want your company to portray a professional image, use black, silver, and very dark colors. If you want your company to come across as funky and hip, try bright and vibrant colors.

You can always hire a designer to help you. They will provide an objective view, almost like that of a customer, and they have plenty of experience in empowering logos with specific messages. A good designer will be able to tell you whether or not a logo will transfer easily into print or onto a sign. This could be critical as your business grows. Designers can be very expensive however, ranging from 4,000 to 15,000 dollars. Some charge $15 per hour, and some charge $150. So shop around.

If you are skilled with Photoshop, you probably won't even need to hire a designer. In fact you will probably have fun designing it yourself. Photoshop is the premier computer program for logo design, and it also comes in handy when designing your marketing tools, posters, flyers, and business cards.

On you are finished with your logo make sure you trademark it for protection. You can apply for a trademark at the U.S. Patent and Trademark Office Web site. Once it's protected, you can use it everywhere: on web sites, business cards, stationery, letterhead, brochures, ads, etc. This will create visibility in the marketplace. Creating a logo is a key part of your business design, but also one of the more fun parts. Take your time and enjoy.

Here are some points to take into consideration if you feel that your logo could use improvement:

- ☐ Does your current logo represent at least three of the key elements that make up a credible and high quality logo design?
- ☐ Does the logo express your company in a manner which defines your expertise?
- ☐ Is the logo "modern"?

☐ Does your logo communicate the message that you are trying to convey to your clients clearly and effectively?

If you answered yes to all of these questions, your logo should not be changed.

## Significant points to consider when designing your logo:

Does your logo.........

☐ Attract customers and leave them with an impression?

☐ Deliver a message that stands apart from the rest?

☐ Represent the characteristics of your business?

## Size and Cost

The more intricate and colorful your logo is, the more likely you will be spending more money, so before you finalize your logo, consider the reproduction costs.

Take into consideration the size of your logo. Keep on mind you will be using it for marketing materials such as business cards and postcards. Research a variety of companies and designers to compare packages. Select a logo design company or designer suited to your needs.

## Competition

What style of logo are your competitors using? Trademark your logo. This will prevent competitors from stealing it.

# Developing a Website

Building a web site does not have to be complicated, it is the planning and conceptualization that is most challenging. One could say that most of the hard work is done before you even start. Here are twelve questions to ask yourself before you build your website:

- ☐ **Do I have web hosting?** Web hosting is very inexpensive, usually 8-12 dollars per month. Yahoo is one of the simplest and easiest hosts to use, and is great for beginners. Lonex.com has become very popular. Homestead.com is another good one, for those who know nothing about html.

- ☐ **Are there any websites that I would consider to be my competition?** If so, take note of their key terms and catch phrases.

- ☐ **What are five adjectives that describe what my company does?** This list will help in the overall design and in choosing images.

- ☐ **What are your 5 favorite websites?** Take not of which features stand out, and what you like most about the aesthetics of the site.

- ☐ **What are you least favorite websites?** Take note of what you dislike the most, and specifically what you dislike about the appearance of the site?

- ☐ **What are the top 5 services that you provide?** Make a brief list. This will help you to focus your website on what is important.

- ☐ **Why are your services better than your competitions services?** Make a list an use it to make your site stand above the competition.

- ☐ **Why should people visit your site, and why will they want to come back**? What will bring people back to your site over and over again?

- ☐ **What kind of people do you want to visit your site?** Who is your ideal visitor or target audience? Always know who is going to pay you before you build your website—you are building it for them. We covered this asepct in the "ideal client" section.

☐ **Besides people interested in your services, who else will visit your site?** Advertisers? People selling products? Others in your industry?

☐ **What is the goal of your website? Will it be the primary tool to attract business?** Will you be marketing other ways, or is this your bread and butter? This will determine how much energy and focus to put into it.

☐ **What features would you like to include in on your website?** Contact forms, forum, blog, login, paypal, etc.

## Be sure to include:

Company Logo
Company Tag Line
Phone Number
Fax Number
Address:
Other contact information
Business hours of operation (when phones will be answered, if relevant)

## Additional Tips

Keep your web site clean and simple. Less is more. Many websites try to cram as much as they can on the home page, which can be overwhelming and an instant turn off. If a person is busy or stressed and they come to your web site, the last thing they want to do is be stressed out by all the options and noise. People want a guided tour, so tell them where to click, don't give them 50 options.

Have a friend or partner edit your page and check for mistakes that you may have missed. Having a good editor is important, especially if you have a lot of content.

Last but not least, be creative. Make it your own and make it unique. A website is like art, and it says a lot about whether you are a leader, or a follower. If your web site is fresh and innovative, people will assume that you are as well.

# Sales: Generating profits and preparing for success

Now that you have defined your ideal client, produced a solid business plan, developed a strong marketing strategy, and created a professional website, clients should come to you in droves, right? Well, not necessarily. Here are a few reasons why:

- ☐ Poor time management
- ☐ A lack of organization
- ☐ Spending too much time on product or service reviews
- ☐ Focusing too much on gaining media attention
- ☐ Negative relationships or environment
- ☐ A fear of not getting clients
- ☐ Insufficient communication skills
- ☐ No confidence
- ☐ Uncomfortable asking for money

## Poor time management

Without managing your time wisely you may find yourself overworked and extremely unproductive. As a result, your energy and focus diminish driving potential clients to another baby planner.

## A lack of organization

You may be receiving many emails and phone calls from prospective clients inquiring about your services, but if you lack organization and do not respond in a timely fashion, they may just get discouraged and decide not to work with you.

## Spending too much time on product or service reviews

Many baby planners are currently facing this dilemma. Now that they have successfully networked and spread the word about their business, vendors and practitioners are requesting reviews. Manage your time wisely and remember what your job is as a baby planner. There are already an overwhelming amount of bloggers doing reviews, don't allow yourself to get stuck here. You got into this industry to primarily work with clients, right? That is where most of your focus should be. Limit your reviews to once or twice a week.

## Focusing too much on gaining media attention

Some of us catch what is called the media bug. As soon as you get interviewed by a national news reporter or if perhaps you appear on the local news station, you get hungry for more media attention. This leads you to spend a lot of time working on pitch letters, presentations, press releases, and articles. Yes, it is nice to be recognized, but the most valuable recognition really does come from first and foremost from your clients. You may have all the media attention in the world, but if you're too busy focusing on the media you won't have the room for taking on clients.

## Negative relationships or environment

If you are in an environment or relationship that is negative in your personal life, it will affect your desire to take on clients. You also do not want to carry this energy with you when consulting a perspective client. Remember that pregnancy makes a woman physically sensitive and she will be able to pick up on your energy very easily. Do not be surprised if a client decides not to work with you.

## A fear of not getting clients

If you have a fear that you will not get clients, then you will not get them. The very fear itself is helping to create the outcome. Ask yourself where this fear comes from and whether it holds any validity. Rather than getting stuck in fear, see if you find solutions to your concerns. Perception changes everything.

## Insufficient communication skills

You may have the best looking website and business plan, but if you are a poor communicator, you will not get far with clients. Practice on friends, family, and volunteers.

## No confidence

Without confidence, you have a weak business. Confidence is one of the first impressions your client will pick up on. The last thing a pregnant woman wants is to work with a baby planner that lacks the confidence to get the job done.

## Uncomfortable asking for money

Many business owners and consultants lose a sale very easily because they are just not comfortable asking for money. You need to get comfortable. Asking for money can be made into a fun and very rewarding adventure. Practice asking for money. There is a big difference between asking and begging.

## Steps to getting clients

The first step to getting clients is to become your client. Put yourself in their shoes. Talk their talk. Surround yourself in the environments your clients spend time in. Understand their needs. Secondly, skillfully communicate what you offer and how they will benefit from your services. Lastly, you must be genuine and personable in your approach. Will you face some challenges along the way? Yes, but it's normal and can be easily overcome with sound preparation.

## Timeline

Most business courses and advisors will tell you not to expect to receive a solid income anywhere from 12-36 months of launching your business. I believe this is relative to the approach and management of your clientele. When I get asked how long it takes to get your first baby planning client, my response is as long as it takes you to fully understand your clients needs and address them appropriately. Take a moment and think about what makes you purchase a product or service. It works the same way for your prospective clients. If they feel there is a need, they will have no problem making the purchase.

## Master Keys

Some schools of thought say that the master keys of selling are asking and listening. By asking the right questions to your clients, you can determine what they want most, but in order to do that, you must be a fabulous listener. Most often we spend too much time pushing our products and services, coming from our own self-interest rather than thoroughly understanding what our client wants.

## What do I charge for my services?

You can come up with pricing in a few different ways. First you can look at what other consultants in the area are charging for their services. Second you can discuss with your client their needs and help them develop a budget. Lastly, based on your client's needs and budget, you can offer them different pricing structures and let them choose the most suitable option. In order for your client to justify spending money on your services, they need to understand the value of what you are offering, otherwise they won't spend it. Ask yourself, why do you make purchases on some things and not others? What drives you to make the purchases that you do? This is essentially the way you need to look at the services you offer. There is nothing more frustrating than visiting a website that lists prices without knowing the details of what you are getting or visiting a website that lists general services without specific details or prices. Your perspective client is more likely to hire you when they fully understand the value and benefits from the services you are offering.

## Managing a budget

Professional Baby Planners need to become very comfortable managing a healthy budget for their clients. Create and maintain a spreadsheet which keeps track of your client's expenses which they have agreed upon during their time with you. List products and services purchased; their descriptions, dates, and prices. Keep a clean record at all times. Review it with your client on a regular basis.

## Pricing Structure

It is definitely worth it to take the time to prepare and create your pricing structure. There are a few different ways you can look at pricing structures. Keep in mind that each service you offer must give your perspective clients a clear understanding of the services they are receiving and its' value for them.

Some questions to consider when coming up with your pricing structure:

- ☐ Can you justify the amount you are charging for the services you offer?
- ☐ Would you buy the services you offer?
- ☐ Have you surveyed new and expecting families to get an idea of the services they need and what they feel is reasonable to pay for them?
- ☐ Will your offer a complimentary consultation or not and why?

## Examples of pricing structures:

## Customized Service

With a customized service, prices will vary from client to client based on a number of factors: product and service selection, the number of necessary consultations in person, on the phone, and by email, the amount of time you put in preparing and planning your services.

## Hourly Service

With an hourly service you charge by the hour and decide a set price. This could be used for a new client consultation, when giving advice on a product or service, or when helping your client through a quick issue.

**Take note** that pricing is never set in stone. If you get negative feedback from potential customers regarding your prices, change them. These can be adjusted up as well as down. Prices are always easier to drop then to raise. So, start at the top of the scale then come down if you have too. Also make sure your prices are in-line with competitors, not just other baby planners, but other organizations that may provide similar services (indirect competition companies). Lastly, before dropping prices - you should always run discounts and promotions first. For example, let's say you charge $500 for basic services and are hearing negative feed-back from some customers. Instead of dropping your prices say to $300, run a discount or promotion special - i.e. $200 off the next 20 customers or 40% off for mothers who will give birth around X-mas. This way you can keep your pricing high for those that are not complaining but still attract those customers who are cost adverse. Lastly, the higher the price the better the perceived service or product. If you go too cheap - people will think your service is cheap. Offering your clients discounts will allow those who want your services (but are afraid to pay the price) to believe that they are getting great service at a great deal.

## Packages

Packages can be a useful and even a fun option for some clients. For example you may offer packages such as Setting up a Registry, a Health and Fitness package, or a Pampering Spa package.

## Workshops

If you enjoy educating your clients, you may offer workshops on various topics of interest throughout and after pregnancy. For example you can offer workshops on various birthing options, going green, choosing a doula, or how to maintain a sound budget. You may also choose to partner up with a practitioner or vendor for a workshop.

## Offer Promotions and Discounts for Grand Opening

Offering a promotion or discount upon launching is a nice way to call attention to your business. Many vendors and mommy bloggers will be happy to share your offer with their community.

## My best advice

Be clear on who you are targeting and what services are most suitable for them. Practice and keep practicing your selling technique. Notice what words you use and the tone in which you use them. Friends, family, co-workers, and volunteers can also provide you with valuable feedback.

# Liability and Insurance

## Liability

As baby planners, you must be aware of liability at all times, especially when you are planning for an event like a baby shower, pre labor preparation, or post delivery. Legal issues can also arise in many other circumstances. Some examples include: when advising on a product that may have been recalled, recommending a baby proofer that does not do a good job, and an unsatisfied client with the nursery design. You want to make sure you minimize your risk and increase your safety. Pregnancy is a very emotionally driven time, and unexpected occurrences may happen along the way. It is wise to be prepared. You need to know your boundaries and remember not to cross the line when advising your clients on nutrition, exercise, baby proofing, emotional issues, and so on. There are general aspects in all these areas that are okay to address, but if you are not certified or licensed, keep your advice minimal and general. When in doubt, refer your clients to a professional who is licensed or certified. An attorney can be very helpful in preparing basic contracts or advising you of any legal issues you may have overlooked.

## Due Diligence

Perform due diligence and carefully evaluate the qualifications, experience, and reputation of everyone that you deal with. This ensures that you are taking all the necessary steps to avoid potential problems.

## Disclaimers and Agreements

Your clients need to have a clear understanding of your role and the functions you perform as their baby planner. As presented in chapter seven, a contract including a waiver and liability form signed by your client is of utmost importance. You should also welcome your client to participate or inspect any of the services you agree upon to ensure they are satisfied and clear. The budget discussed and payments your client agrees upon should be noted and signed. You also need to protect yourself should your client decide to terminate their services early or abandon any payment.

## Personal Liability Insurance

As a baby planner consultant it is sensible to purchase personal liability insurance, specifically an errors and omissions insurance.

According to the Insurance Journal

Errors and omissions (E&O) is the insurance that covers your company, or you individually, in the event that a client holds you responsible for a service you provided, or failed to provide, that did not have the expected or promised results. For doctors, dentists, chiropractors, etc., it is often called malpractice insurance. For lawyers, accountants, architects or engineers, it may be called professional liability. Whatever you call it, it covers you for errors (or omissions) that you have made or that the client perceives you have made.

Most E&O policies cover judgments, settlements and defense costs. Even if the allegations are found to be groundless, thousands of dollars may be needed to defend the lawsuit. They can bankrupt a smaller company or individual and have a lasting effect on the bottom line of larger companies.

In short, E&O coverage provides protection for you in the event that an error or omission on your part has caused a financial loss for your client.

Source: InsuranceJournal.com

You can find personal liability insurance that includes errors and omissions online through a local search or through the recommendation of your attorney.

Your insurance cost will depend on a variety of factors that depend on the services you offer. For example: your insurance cost will be higher if you offer baby proofing or car seat installation. You will want cover all of this with your attorney and insurance provider so you are aware of all the benefits and risks of each service you offer.

# Competition

Competing is a normal part of business or is it? Some people say it can be a very healthy way to help you strive to meet the demands of your clients, but shouldn't you be doing that regardless?

Yes, I realize that a business plan and marketing strategy involve studying your competition and competing with them, but I believe only to the extent that you can learn from their mistakes and successes without getting too deeply caught in them.

The dictionary defines competition as a rivalry between two businesses, a struggle, or a winner and loser.

I am going to step out of the standard business model and share with you my own personal take on competition. Please note that this is only my opinion. I encourage you to treat competition as it feels most suitable for you and your business.

I feel competition is needed or comes up only when you are not fully living through your passion and authentic self. When you are not happy with yourself or do not feel satisfied with what you are doing, there is a natural need to be concerned with how others are doing things. When you are fully living out your passion, your uniqueness and authenticity can simply not be matched.

You may experience your "competition" copying your ideas, material, trying to reproduce your creativity, and even trying to discredit your knowledge and expertise. It is easy to feel disappointed and a bit concerned, however, realize that no matter how much another business tries to compete with you, they could never deliver it the way that you do. There is only one Oprah. People can try to imitate her as much as they want, but everyone knows that there is only one Oprah. The same applies to you and me. When a company tries to copy you or even discredit you or your business, welcome the attention they are bringing your way. As the saying goes "There is no such thing as bad publicity." Don't bother giving them your attention, as this can steer you away from your own success. Just continue believing in yourself and keep moving forward.

The other main concern that arises with your baby planner competitors is the "competition" for clients. Because pregnancy is such an intimate experience, I believe that not every client will be the right match for you. If you are a professional, you will immediately accept this fact. The right personality match is extremely important. You would do both you and your clients a huge disservice if you were not the best match for each other. In the same way that a pregnant client finds the best doula to match her personality and needs, is the same way a pregnant client will need to find the best match with a baby planner. Something else to consider is that there is an abundance of clients relative to the amount of existing baby planners. The industry is still so new, so there is more than enough clients for all of us. Just think of the amount of personal trainers, doulas, midwives, doctors, nutritionists in your area. Many of them are earning a great income and have the amount of clients they need. Now think of the amount of baby planners in your area. This should immediately put you at ease.

I'd like to reiterate once again that if you are living through your fullest potential, you will realize that there really is no competition. Try it and you will see.

Competitors could also be great collaborators. Interestingly enough, they can actually turn out to be great friends and allies. Upon understanding each other's strengths and weaknesses, you can learn to work and team up together to increase each other's sales.

Now, will another baby planner business surpass you in sales or popularity at some point or another? Perhaps. But rather than get caught up in comparison and jealousy, take the time to ask yourself if you are satisfied with the way you are running your business. If you are not satisfied with the current state of your business, then revisit the drive and passion that lead you to start your business. Look at obstacles that are currently in your way. Focus on yourself and determine what it will take to live out your dream or passion.

Welcome competition as it ensures the opportunity for our customers to receive the best service. At the end of the day, we are all in business for the greater good of our clientele.

# Green Basics

The term "green" generally refers to sustainable and environmentally friendly products. As a baby planner, we examine and consider all products that are safe, non-toxic, natural, and organic under the following categories:

☐ Skin care products

☐ Bath products

☐ Nail products and salons

☐ Fragrance

☐ Furniture

☐ Clothing

☐ Home Environment

☐ Food

☐ Toys

☐ Bottles

☐ Diapering

☐ Detergents

☐ Sprays and Pesticides

## General Body Care

Below are the chemicals found in most products that your client should be advised to avoid:

## DEA

These chemicals are emulsifiers and foaming agents, widely used in cosmetics and skin care. They are eye and skin irritants. DEA is easily absorbed through the skin and accumulates in body organs including the brain. Animal tests show that some of them cause damage to the liver, kidney, brain, spinal cord, bone marrow and skin. Contact with the eyes can cause impaired vision. In 1998, the National Toxicology Program (NTP) in the USA did a research study showing an association between cancer in laboratory animals and diethanolamine (DEA) and certain DEA-related ingredients, when applied topically. DEA, when in the presence of nitrate preservatives and contaminants, can form the nitrosamine NDELA (nitrosodiethanolamine). In 1991, two surveys were conducted which found that of 29 products tested, 27 were found to contain NDELA and in 1980 the FDA analyzed 335 cosmetic products and found that 42% were contaminated with NDELA. Again, the concentration of nitrates in these products is as much as 50% - 100% higher that in nitrate-processed bacon.

## Phthalates

Phthalates, called "plasticizers," are a group of industrial chemicals used to make plastics like polyvinyl chloride (PVC) more flexible or resilient and also as solvents. Phthalates are nearly ubiquitous in modern society, found in, among other things, toys, food packaging, hoses, raincoats, shower curtains, vinyl flooring, wall coverings, lubricants, adhesives, detergents, nail polish, hair spray and shampoo.

Phthalates have been found to disrupt the endocrine system. Several phthalate compounds have caused reduced sperm counts, testicular atrophy and structural abnormalities in the reproductive systems of male test animals, and some studies also link phthalates to liver cancer, according to the U.S. Center for Disease Control's 2005 National Report on Human Exposure to Environmental Chemicals. Though the CDC contends the health hazards of phthalates to humans have not been definitively established, for some years, the U.S. Environmental Protection Agency has regulated phthalates as water and air pollutants.

Source: Environmental Working Group

## Parabens

Parabens are preservatives that inhibit microbial growth to extend shelf life of product. May cause allergic reactions, skin rashes and kill the intestinal flora so vital to the cleanliness of the intestines. They may damage health by inhibiting the vital action of natural enzymes in your cells. Recent research suggests parabens could act as a foreign hormone-like substance and cause a host of problems, including cancer.

**Propylene glycol, propylene oxide, polyethylene glycol** -- Listed on the FDA government website as a known carcinogen. This is a common ingredient in many moisturizers and lotions. It has also been connected with kidney and liver damage in scientific testing.

Propylene glycol has also now been connected with common skin rashes and skin damage.

**Sodium lauryl sulfate, sodium laureth sulfate** -- A common ingredient in shampoos and liquid soaps. SLS may be the most dangerous ingredient used in personal care products. SLS is the active ingredient in garage floor cleaners, engine degreasers and industrial strength soaps. This is a very corrosive chemical used to clean industrial and greasy surfaces.

**Sodium Fluoride** -- The fluoride that is added to drinking water is hydrofluoric acid. This is a compound of fluorine, which is actually a chemical byproduct of aluminum, steel, cement, phosphate, and other assorted ingredients. Fluoride in this form has no nutritional value and is one of the most caustic industrial chemicals. Fluoride is also an active ingredient in rat and cockroach poisons.

**Mineral Oil, Petrolatum and Coal Tar** -- Used in many moisturizing products. Mineral oil is a petroleum by-product that interferes with skin's ability to eliminate toxins. Because of this it promotes acne and other skin disorders. Mineral oil has also been associated with premature aging. Any product that contains mineral oil may be contaminated with cancer causing Polycyclic Aromatic Hydrocarbons.

Source: NaturalNews

Common Chemicals found in the following skincare products:

## Diaper cream

- ☐ BHA which has been banned in other countries because it may cause skin depigmentation.
- ☐ Boric Acid / Sodium Borate has been banned for unsafe use
- ☐ Fragrance, or phthalates linked to hormonal disruptions

## Lotions & Moisturizers

- ☐ DMDM Hydantoin which may cause "cancer-forming contaminates"
- ☐ Frangrance, or phthalates linked to hormonal disruptions

☐ Cetearetn / PEG Compounds these are petrol chemicals that may contain cancer-causing agents

## Sunscreen

☐ Oxybenzole which can produce cancer causing chemicals

☐ DMDM Hydantoin which may cause "cancer-forming contaminates"

☐ Triethanolamine which may cause "cancer-forming contaminates"

## Body Wash & Liquid Soap

☐ Triclosan which has been linked to thyroid disruption

☐ DMDM Hydantoin which may cause "cancer-forming contaminates"

☐ Fragrance, or phthalates linked to hormonal disruptions

Source:   Cosmetics Database

## Baby Bottles

Plastics to avoid:

☐ **Number 3 Plastics**
V (Vinyl) or PVC
Found in: Cooking oil bottles, clear food packaging

☐ **Number 6 Plastics**
PS (polystyrene)
Found in: Disposable plates and cups, meat trays, egg cartons, carry-out containers

☐ **Number 7 Plastics**
BPA
Found in: Baby bottles, three- and five-gallon water bottles, certain food containers

Source: The Daily Green

## Bedding

Typical baby mattresses contain the following chemicals:

- ☐ Polyvinyl Chloride (PVC)
- ☐ Polyurethane Foam
- ☐ Fire Retardant Chemicals
- ☐ Unsanitary Ingredients

Fortunately many companies have begun making natural mattresses free of these chemicals. Natural bedding and mattresses can be found easily online. You can refer to our resources for a listing.

## Diapers

Commercial diapers contain chemicals such as polypropylene which is found in the liner and polyethylene found in the backing. They also contain bleached materials. Wonderful alternatives are cloth diapers, or bleach and chemical free disposal diapers such as Seventh Generation.

## Detergents

Avoid detergents containing the following:

- ☐ optical brighteners
- ☐ fabric softeners.
- ☐ synthetic fragrances

Many natural baby friendly detergents are available online, at Whole Foods, or your local natural food store.

## Toys

For ecotimetoys.com, their definition of eco-friendly toys involves various pre-defined categories. To be considered an eco-friendly toy, a toy must fall into at least multiple categories listed below. While all of their toys fall within some categories, many of their toys fall within all categories!

These categories are as follows:

**1)    Toys manufactured from Natural Materials**

This includes **natural wood and organic cotton**. Wood is a natural occurring material in our environment. Organic cotton is grown without the use of various pesticides and other harmful chemicals.

2)  **Non-Toxic Paint Coatings**
This includes the use of **water-based** and **lead-free paints**.

3)  **Phthalate-Free Plastics**
Phthalate is a chemical which is used to soften plastics. In general, we stay away from plastic toys as much as possible. However, if there are any plastics in a toy, we use toys that are **100% phthalate-free**.

4)  **Toys manufactured from Recycled or Sustainable Materials**
Many of the toys we carry are manufactured from **recycled, sustainable and renewable materials** such as **recycled wood, recycled plastic, rubberwood** and **bamboo**.

5)  **Toys that are Hand-Made or Made in Small Production Batches**
Many of our toys come from smaller manufacturers who spend countless hours handcrafting their toys. For example, this process may include: finely crafting and intricately painting a **wooden toy**, or carefully hand-stitching an **organic cotton toy**.

6)  **Toys manufactured using High Quality Materials & Fabrics**
All of our toys are made using very high quality materials and fabrics. You can feel the quality of the materials in every toy we carry; from the solid feel of our wooden toys to the soft touch of our **plush toys**.

7)  **Must pass American and/or European Testing Standards**
The European standard for **toy safety** is referred to as **EN71**, which is very stringent. **ASTM**, also known as the American Society for Testing and Materials, monitors toy safety in the United States. All of our toy manufacturers meet either EN71 standards, ASTM standards, or even both standards.

For more information visit: <u>http://www.ecotimetoys.com</u> or email: help@ecotimetoys.com

## Home Environment

In the same way that nutrition plays a significant role for a woman and her baby's health during and after pregnancy, environment plays an extremely vital role to health and safety of moms and babies. There are many factors to consider when assessing a family's unsafe exposure to potentially harmful substances around the home, especially in preparation for a baby: lead, mold, indoor air quality, pesticides, furniture, carpets, household cleaning products, nursery, toys, plastic, and paint. When using paint use low VOC paint. Use eco-friendly and natural household cleaning products. Avoid using pesticides and other harsh chemicals. If purchasing a new computer or laptop look for ones that are lead and PVC free. There are an abundance of resources available. Below are a few:

## The Complete Organic Pregnancy by Deirdre Dolan and Alexandra Zissu

While being pregnant is thrilling, the responsibility of a growing baby can provoke anxiety about what is and isn't safe. In *The Complete Organic Pregnancy*, Deirdre Dolan and Alexandra Zissu address how you can minimize your exposure to the invisible toxins that surround us–in everything from food, cleaning products, and cosmetics to furniture, rugs, air, and water.

## Super Natural Home by Beth Greer

Beth Greer had been living what she considered a healthy lifestyle when a medical crisis prompted her to reevaluate everything—from the food she ate to the personal-care products she used and the environment she lived in. Now, in *Super Natural Home*, she shows the alarming extent of the dangerous chemicals we unwittingly expose ourselves to every day. As she did in her own life, she invites readers to put their lives under a microscope—to scrutinize what Americans put in and on their bodies and bring into their homes—and to make personal choices that will enable them to "live clean" in a toxic world.

## Additional Resources:

http://www.thegreenguide.com/home-garden

http://www.thedailygreen.com/green-homes/

http://greenhomeguide.com/

http://planetgreen.discovery.com/home-garden/

## Clothing

Organic is always best. Here are ten reasons why provided by BestBabyOrganics.com:

**Top 10 reasons to buy Organic Cotton Clothing and Toys for your Baby**

1) About 25% of the world's insecticides and 10% of the world's pesticides are used in producing cotton.

   Organic cotton has low environmental impact by replenishing and maintaining soil fertility, reducing the use of toxic agents, and building up biologically diverse agriculture. (For more facts and details on this, visit the Organic Trade Association)

2) Certified Organic Cotton uses only low-impact dyes, which contain no heavy metals and use less water in the dyeing process.

3) Chemicals used in Conventional Cotton Crops contaminate groundwater systems. Growing Organic Cotton eliminates this type of contamination, therefore protecting and improving the quality of our water.

4) Organic Cotton field workers are NOT exposed to toxic chemicals that endanger their health.

5) Organic Cotton Clothing is often associated with FAIR LABOR practices. Best Baby Organics only works with providers who practice FAIR TRADE or FAIR LABOR principles. This ensures that all workers are paid a fair wage for their labor. No sweatshop clothing for our babies!

6) Clothing made from Organic Cotton is softer and free of Formaldehyde.

7) Babies are more vulnerable to toxic agents that come in contact with their skin and respiratory system. Therefore Organic Cotton Clothing is gentler on the skin and healthier for baby.

8) No more worrying when babies play with organic cotton toys or chew on organic cotton teethers. They are not toxic!

9) Supporting the Organic Cotton Industry helps to protect our children's future by reducing the levels of pollution in our planet.

10) The peace of mind and good feeling of knowing that your baby is getting the best of the best and knowing that you are making the right choices to protect our environment.

## Food

I cannot stress enough the value of a woman's nutrition in relation to her baby's health and development, especially after the baby is born. There is no better time than during a woman's pregnancy to nourish the body with the finest and most nutrient dense foods. Studies have shown that the nutritional value of Organic food outweighs conventional food by far. Organic food is also free of pesticides and herbicides, and irradiation. According to the National Academy of Sciences, pesticides have been linked to cancers, headaches, and even birth defects. Low levels of pesticides can be significantly more toxic to fetuses and children because of their less developed immune systems. For pregnant women, pesticides can add a toxic load to their already taxed body.

The EWG has a great shopper's guide to pesticides listing the fifteen best foods lowest in pesticides and the worst foods that are best to buy organic. You can download the guide by visiting here: http://www.foodnews.org/

## Organizations and people worth knowing:

Campaign for Safe Cosmetics

The Campaign for Safe Cosmetics is a great resource.

They are a national coalition of nonprofit health and environmental organizations. Their collective goal is to protect the health of consumers and workers by requiring the personal care products industry to phase out the use of chemicals linked to cancer, birth defects and other serious health concerns, and replace them with safer alternatives.

The Campaign for Safe Cosmetics is working with more than 100 endorsing organizations, responsible businesses and thousands of citizen activists to shift the cosmetics market toward safer products and to advocate for smarter laws that protect our health from toxic chemicals and encourage innovation of safer alternatives.

They provide information on:
- ☐ Fragrance
- ☐ Lead in Lipstick
- ☐ Contaminants in Bath Products
- ☐ Nail Products and Salons
- ☐ Natural and Organic Products
- ☐ EWG's Skin Deep Database
- ☐ Nanotechnology

http://www.safecosmetics.org

## Healthy Child Healthy World

Healthy Child Healthy World has a very informative parenting guide educating new and expecting parents on toxic exposures, breastfeeding, healthy immunity, holistic medicine, and much more. A more detailed description of their organization can be found in our Product Basics chapter.

http://www.healthychild.org

## Environmental Working Group/ Kid-Safe Chemicals

Environmental Working Group has established the Kid-Safe Chemicals Act Interactive Magazine as an online science information and discussion forum to foster an exchange of ideas for reforming the nation's toxic chemicals policies. The site will feature articles by scientists, lawmakers, regulators, industry officials, community activists, policy analysts, journalists and others interested in environmental health issues.

A major focus of the forum will be the emerging debate over overhauling the Toxic Substances Control Act of 1976 (TSCA). This site is aimed at stimulating conversation about the Kid-Safe Chemicals Act, a measure designed to supplant TSCA and expected to be introduced later this year, and other legislative proposals. As well, commentators will discuss alternative approaches to toxics reform.

Environmental Working Group is a research organization based in Washington, D.C. that uses the power of information to protect human health and the environment.

Environmental Working Group has established the Kid-Safe Chemicals Act Interactive Magazine as an online science information and discussion forum to foster an exchange of ideas for reforming the nation's toxic chemicals policies. The site will feature articles by scientists, lawmakers, regulators, industry officials, community activists, policy analysts, journalists and others interested in environmental health issues.

A major focus of the forum will be the emerging debate over overhauling the Toxic Substances Control Act of 1976 (TSCA). This site is aimed at stimulating conversation about the Kid-Safe Chemicals Act, a measure designed to supplant TSCA and expected to be introduced later this year, and other legislative proposals. As well, commentators will discuss alternative approaches to toxics reform.

Environmental Working Group is a research organization based in Washington, D.C. that uses the power of information to protect human health and the environment.

For more information visit: http://www.ewg.org/kid-safe-chemicals-act-blog/

My favorite networking group thus far is EcoMom™

EcoMom is a global network of women working together to create a healthy and sustainable future. They believe *"that one of the strongest forces in nature is a network of women and our greatest hope for a better world lies in the maternal instinct to nurture and protect. If you doubt it, you've never met a momma bear alone in the woods."*

By inspiring and empowering women and utilizing a business model that answers the growing demand for social justice, ecological protection and economic innovation, they seek to illustrate a model of doing good, doing well, and living according to a new paradigm that can help change the course of history and create a sustainable future.

Women represent a tremendous power as both role models and a major market force. Every day, businesses adapt to the changing demands of women... and every day, children learn by watching their mothers. American women control over $7 trillion dollars and influence over 85% of all purchasing decisions in the world's largest democracy – the United State's economy. The lifestyle and shopping choices women make every day impact the lives of millions of people around the world via the example they set for their children, and the sourcing, production, marketing, and distribution of the goods they choose to purchase and use. We believe that the world is in the midst of a great turning point and opportunity exists to leverage the historically proven power of women to help create an environmentally, socially, and economically healthy future for all.

For more information visit http://ecomom.com

## Super Natural Mom, Beth Greer

Beth Greer, Super Natural Mom™, is an award-winning journalist, holistic health advocate, impassioned champion of toxin-free living, and radio talk show host, who busts open the myth that our homes are safe havens. Her bestselling book, *Super Natural Home: Improve Your Health, Home and Planet...One Room at a Time* (Rodale, 2009), endorsed by Deepak Chopra, Ralph Nader, Peter Coyote and others, shows how food, cosmetics, personal care products, household cleaners and furniture are making us sick.

Beth is a testament to how making small lifestyle shifts can make a huge difference in one's health. By using alternative methods of healing, eating a diet free of pesticides and avoiding hazardous chemicals in her personal care and household products, Beth eliminated a tumor without drugs or surgery.

For more information visit http://supernaturalmom.com/

The wonderful news is that there are also many companies committed to providing products that are completely safe and toxic free.

## ErbaOrganics is one such example.

Erbaorganics was born out of a desire to make available the purest eco-friendly organic skincare to those who need it most: mommys-to-be and babies. Concerned over the chemicals used in traditional skincare, husband and wife Robin Brown and Anna Cirronis started making organic products when they had their first son. They soon realized that others were just as concerned about the harmful chemicals in mother and baby products. Erbaorganics is an effective high quality organic alternative to many products on the market still using harmful ingredients. Erbaorganics is proud to launch a full line of mother and baby products as high in organic ingredients as is possible to make, with food grade preservatives and organic anti-oxidants.

Over the years they have sought out the finest organic ingredients and combined them into unique blends that nourish the body and the soul. This new line is designed to be made available to as many people as possible, as we believe it is everyone's right to be able to use clean, safe, organic skincare particularly for mother and baby.

Erbaorganics is based in Southern California and it is here where the line is manufactured by a dedicated staff who take special care and pride every step of the way. They feel that Erbaorganics products will improve the lives and health of those who use them, as well as that of the environment, bringing the benefits of choosing organic to the forefront of the public consciousness.

For more information visit: http://www.erbaorganics.com/

## Below are some more of my favorite product lines:

ErbaOrganics

Aubrey Organics

Dr Bronner's

Yes to Carrots

Peacekeeper Cause-metics

Ecco Bella

Dr Hauschka

Burt's Bees

Earth Mama Angel Baby

California Baby

Mama Mio

Priti Nails

## Some of my favorite books:

"Super Natural Home" by Super Natural Mom, Beth Greer

"The Complete Organic Pregnancy" by Deirdre Dolan and Alexandra Zissu

"The Safe Shopper's Bible: A Consumer's Guide to Nontoxic Household Products" by David Steinman and Samuel S. Epstein

"Gorgeously Green" by Sophie Uliano

"Green Babies Sage Moms" by Lynda Fassa

# Fertility Basics

A Baby Planner is more commonly known to help a woman throughout her pregnancy, but can also offer a lot of support when parents-to-be are facing fertility issues. The process toward conception can be very time consuming and daunting. There are many options available both medical and natural. Below are a few:

On the medical side you have:

☐ Fertility drugs

☐ Surgery

☐ Artificial insemination

☐ In vitro fertilization (IVF)

☐ Gamete intrafallopian transfer (GIFT)

☐ Zygote intrafallopian transfer (ZIFT)

☐ Intracytoplasmic sperm injection (ICSI)

☐ Donor eggs and embryos

☐ Gestational carriers (also known as surrogate mothers)

On the natural side you have:

☐ Homeopathy

☐ Acupuncture

☐ Chinese Medicine

☐ Nutrition

☐ Yoga

☐ Meditation

All though most people dealing with infertility may opt for drugs, studies have shown that many natural methods can be just as effective. For example: with proper nutrition or by reducing ones' stress levels, couples have been able to successfully conceive a baby.

Here is an article by an international leading fertility specialist, Gabriela Rosa:

**How To Create Your Own Natural Fertility Breakthrough, Reclaim Your Fertility And Create The Healthy Baby Of Your Dreams** by Gabriela Rosa

It's easy to become overwhelmed when trying to conceive—especially if you are challenged with unexpected circumstances including unexplained, recurrent miscarriages and/or infertility.

What you need to know is that your fertility isn't "out there," a magic cure to be given to you by the doctor or other practitioner treating you. It is inside, tucked within your body's own internal wisdom, waiting to be released when coaxed properly.

And right now, all you really need to know is that you can!

## Are You Doing Your Part?

Your objective is to optimize your fertility and the chances of creating a healthy baby but the real question to ask yourself is this: "Am I doing absolutely everything I can to change my results?"

I hear you cry out: "What ELSE could I be doing?"

And that's the point. The answer is not to do more but instead to do it differently, smarter, and more effectively. Clarity about your self-help options and a sense of direction on your trying to conceive (TTC) journey are paramount, to release you from feeling desperate, unsure, frustrated, angry, sad, despairing... which although with good reason, things do not need to be this way.

Often because of not being sure of what effective steps to take, most people use a scatter gun approach and adopt unreasonable regimens that eventually only lead to further disappointment.

## The Challenges Of Today

There are so many challenges when trying to conceive in this modern day. Since our parent's time much has changed… much indeed.

Our environment is no longer the same; chemicals and endocrine disruptors rule the day, the nutrient levels in our food are much decreased. There are far more egg, sperm and embryo toxins (e.g. chemicals, radiation, stress) than ever before.

"Hoping for the best", "not fussing", keeping your "fingers crossed" is resulting in 1 couple in 6 being infertile; 1 pregnancy in 4 miscarrying; 1 baby in 17 being malformed; 1 in 11 babies having low birth weight, 1 baby in 13 ending up in intensive care units, 1 in 4 children developing learning difficulties and 1 in 5 being diagnosed with eczema and asthma 1.

It is crucial to understand that today's average lifestyle is not "foeto-friendly". It's now our job to make it become so. This is no longer something we can afford to take for granted including those not diagnosed with fertility problems—if for no other reason than the health and fertility of the child in the long term.

Vague optimism isn't good enough anymore.

Unfortunately, these are the facts: Most prospective parents aren't healthy enough; The average diet is not good enough; The intake of pollution, medication, alcohol, coffee etc is too high; As many as 50% of couples have genito-urinary infections and 1 in 6 has an allergy or parasites 1. Almost everyone I see in the clinic has nutritional deficiencies and many are overloaded with heavy metal toxicity.

## Is There A Solution?

Absolutely! The key to optimizing your fertility in the 21st century isn't total avoidance of the things that can negatively impact one's fertility—this is impossible, instead the ideal approach is a conscious reduction of all known negative exposures.

Most people believe this is a fair enough goal and in clinical practice, I have seen it work but there is one problem… Most couples lack the complete education required to make the choices that are going to turn things around for them—on their own.

## The Answer?

An effective and all encompassing fertility alignment with a specialized practitioner is a must if you want to give you and your family the best possible start in life.

Proper education is the only road to true empowerment. You can take control of your fertility but only when you understand what you are protecting yourself and your partner from—in specific detail. A careless, haphazard, "cross-your-fingers-and-hope-for-the-best" approach puts your dream of becoming a proud parent at risk.

Only a targeted, comprehensive analysis of your specific circumstance will get you closer to your desired outcome.

## 3 Areas You Must Address

If you want to boost your natural fertility or improve the odds of assisted reproductive therapy (ART) such as ICSI or IVF there are 3 major areas you must address in order to create the results you are looking for.

These areas encompass the triad of health and require emotional, physical and biochemical balance to ensure an effective and truly holistic approach to becoming pregnant and having a healthy baby.

Implementing the 11 Pillars of Fertility (which rest upon the triad of health as its solid foundation) is essential to help you create the healthy baby of your dreams—fast.

Remember this quote? "Do your part and the Heaven's will come to you aid". What a lovely reminder…

Leading natural fertility specialist and naturopath, Gabriela Rosa (BHSc, ND, Post Grad NFM, DBM, Dip Nut, MATMS, MNHAA) has gained international recognition as an expert in her field. Gabriela devotes herself to natural fertility treatment, the management of women's health issues (puberty to menopause) and men's health—via the web and through her busy private practice in Sydney. Gabriela is the author of three books on natural fertility and she is a sought-after expert contributor on topics of holistic health and natural fertility.

For more information or a FREE subscription to the Natural Fertility Booster please visit http://www.NaturalFertilityBreakthrough.com

**Acupuncture & Fertility** by Chalita Photikoe

Acupuncture is a natural and effective method dating back thousands of years to enhance fertility and treat infertility. By inserting tiny needles into specific points, acupuncture restores the body's balance of energy or qi (chee). Acupuncture helps regulate the endocrine system, which thereby regulates hormone levels, ovulation, and menstrual cycles. It also promotes relaxation and increases blood flow to the reproductive organs, which increases the chances of conception. In men, acupuncture can improve sperm motility, volume and concentration as well as increase libido.

Acupuncture and Chinese medicine can be used for women trying to conceive naturally or for those undergoing Assisted Reproductive Technologies such as IUI or IVF. In fact, a study from the British Medical Journal found that among women who received acupuncture and IVF, the pregnancy rates were 65% higher and the rates of live births were nearly twice as high than among women who received IVF with sham acupuncture or no acupuncture.

For more information visit: http://chalitaacupuncture.com/

## Fertility Resources

http://www.NaturalFertilityBreakthrough.com

http://www.naturalbabypros.com

http://www.natural-fertility-prescription.com/

http://www.chalitaacupuncture.com

# Birthing Basics

There are some key decisions your client will have to make in the very beginning stages of her pregnancy which will change the entire approach from that point forward. As a baby planner, being well versed in the area of birthing for your business is crucial. You may have a lot of knowledge about products, but if you do not know the difference between a Lamaze class and The Bradley Method, or if you are not aware of the various options your clients have for giving birth, you're definitely missing one of the most important parts of a woman's pregnancy....Who is going to deliver the baby, and where?

This brings up the following questions: Where would they prefer to deliver their baby? (At home, a hospital, or birthing Center?) Will they deliver naturally or use drugs? If given the option, would they choose to have a cesarean? What about circumcision?

Many clients are not even aware that they have options, so I highly recommend that you become well-versed in this area. Not only will your clients be impressed, but they will also understand the level of professionalism you are bringing to the table.

To get started I would like to begin by introducing you an article originally published in the Huffington Post that every childbirth professional and expecting parent in the U.S. would benefit from:

## Peaceful Revolution: Motherhood and the $13 Billion Guilt
by Melissa Bartick

Since this month's publication of my paper "The Burden of Suboptimal Breastfeeding in the United States" in Pediatrics with Arnold Reinhold, I'm often asked by reporters what the US can do better to improve our breastfeeding rates. I've also gotten quite a few comments asking if this research just makes moms feel guilty if they couldn't breastfeed.

The answers to both these queries are intimately related, and are best illustrated by the following Tale of Two Births. As you will see, if you compare what should happen when a woman gives birth, versus what actually happens, you can appreciate how tough it can be for US women to breastfeed, but how much easier it could be if only things were a little different around here.

## Birth number 1: Having a baby in the ideal, family-friendly United States:

You give birth with the help of a birth doula. She helps you avoid a c-section or vacuum assisted birth, which is why your hospital hired her. Your baby is wiped off, then put directly onto your chest, skin to skin, with his head between your breasts. The nurse puts a blanket around you both, and then your partner cuts the cord. The nurse evaluates his initial transition to life outside the womb as he rests on your chest. As you lay semi-reclining, happy and exhausted, your baby uses his arms and legs to crawl over to your breast and he starts nursing. You and your partner are left undisturbed for an hour to enjoy your new baby, who has now imprinted the proper breastfeeding behaviors thanks to this initial breastfeeding. You are then transported to your post-partum room with your baby on your chest.

The nurse returns and weighs, measures, and examines your baby right there in your room. You are with him as she gives him his vitamin K shot and antibiotic eye ointment. Your baby is handed back to you, and again placed on your chest skin to skin. He stays in your room with you until you go home. From your prenatal class, you knew in advance to ask most of your visitors wait until you go home, so that you can get some rest, and you turn the ringer off your phone, so that no phone calls will wake you. Before you leave the hospital, your baby's routine heel-stick blood test is done while he is nursing, and you are amazed to see he doesn't cry at all. You are discharged with clear instructions around breastfeeding, and phone numbers to call if you need help. You are not given samples and "gifts" from a formula company.

Two days later, you see your pediatrician, who is a little concerned about the baby's weight, but your baby otherwise looks healthy. He quickly refers you to a licensed International Board Certified Lactation Consultant, and all you pay is your standard co-pay. She does a careful assessment and advises increasing the frequency of nursing for a few days, and that does the trick.

You enjoy three months paid maternity leave, at 80% of your usual pay. Your baby sleeps within arm's reach of you, and because you taught yourself how to breastfeed lying down in the dark, you awake fairly refreshed every morning.

When you return to work, your employer allows you flex time. Your employer has a policy that allows new parents to bring their infants to work, so often you bring your baby with you. As in other companies with such policies, your coworkers enjoy having a baby around, and you feel happy, calm, and productive.

When your baby gets more active, you put him in the daycare near your worksite so you can nurse him during lunch, and you can pump milk in the lactation room at work. You bought a nice pump with your insurance's Durable Medical Equipment allowance. After 6 months, you introduce solids. A few months later, you really don't need to pump any more and you and your baby enjoy breastfeeding for another year. Your baby is so healthy that you've never had to miss a full day of work.

## Does that sound like your birth experience, or does this? Birth number 2: Having a baby in the real United States:

Your give birth to a healthy baby, and you've never heard of a birth doula. The umbilical cord is clamped and cut before anyone can say, "It's a boy!" Immediately, your baby is whisked across the room to the warmer where Apgar scores are assigned, he's given a shot of Vitamin K, and antibiotic eye ointment is slathered in his eyes, clouding his vision. He's placed on a cold scale and weighed and measured. He is examined by his nurse, who takes him to a different room to do her evaluation. He is bathed, washing off his mother's scent. At last, he's professionally swaddled into a nice tight parcel and handed to you to hold, cradled sideways in your arms.

He's not skin to skin, and he can't move his arms and legs to crawl to the breast. Before you know it, an hour has passed since his birth, and since he's missed the window of "alert time" after birth, he slips into a deep sleep without having spontaneously breastfeed. You attempt to interest him in the breast, but he is really too tired to try very hard. Because he's wrapped up and has been given a bath, he can't use his sense of touch and smell to crawl his way over to find your breast. You don't know enough to unwrap him and feed him immediately after birth, because your prenatal class didn't stress the importance of skin to skin contact during the first 3 days of life. That was all discussed in a separate breastfeeding class and you didn't really have time or money to take two classes.

Just as you're getting to know your new bundle of joy, the staff decides to check his temperature and his blood sugar. His glucose level is 45 -- normal for a newborn, but low for an adult. His temperature is a little low, too -- all that time in the bath, the cold scale, the swaddling, and the time away from his mom's body heat has led to hypothermia.

Hypothermia and hypoglycemia can be signs of a serious infection, so immediately he is taken from your arms down to the nursery, where he gets what's known as a sepsis evaluation. Lying under a warmer down the hall from you, he gets his blood drawn, and then is left in his bassinet in the nursery to be observed for a few hours so you can't spend time with him as you recover from giving birth. He gets a 2 ounce bottle of formula, most of which he vomits, since the stomach of a five-hour-old baby is no bigger than a teaspoon, the perfect size to digest the colostrum your breast secretes for him in the first few days.

Finally, your baby's brought back to you, swaddled in a nice package. He's more alert, but never imprinted breastfeeding very well, and he's very stressed from all the day's events. He might be full from the formula he's given, and doesn't breastfeed well. He tries later in the day. The nurses try to help you, but it feels like they all give you different advice, much of it conflicting. Little do you know, their advice is based on their personal experiences rather than any scientific evidence because they haven't had much training in breastfeeding. You don't know what to believe. Finally, your baby goes to the nursery for the night "so you can sleep," and he is brought in for you to feed him. He doesn't like it in the nursery, so he cries, and you don't get much sleep either.

You have some pain when he latches on, and you're told that's normal. You're so excited about his birth that you talk to everyone by phone, and lots of people come to visit. They pass him around. Maybe someone wants to give him a bottle, and you figure, ok, why not. He's chewing on his fist, but no one ever told you that means he's hungry, so you give him a hospital-issued pacifier to suck on instead of his hand. You don't know that giving formula and pacifiers in the hospital will undermine your efforts to breastfeed. It's surprising the nursing staff doesn't inform you of this, and you didn't learn it in your prenatal class. You're too embarrassed to feed him with everyone there. Finally, your guests leave, but by this time, your baby's frantic, and nursing doesn't go well as a result.

Overnight, as he stays in the nursery, he gets weighed, and he's lost more weight than he should have. The doctor says it's because your milk isn't in yet, and recommends more bottles. He still sucks happily on a pacifier and sleeps in the nursery despite his alarming weight loss, and no one suggests that you nurse him more often, room in with him, get rid of the pacifier, or see a lactation consultant, all of which would help put him back on track with breastfeeding.

An hour before you're due to go home, the lactation consultant comes in briefly to check on you, but because her department is so understaffed, she couldn't see you earlier when you needed it most, and she has little time to spend addressing your problems. On your way out, a nurse hands you a marketing bag from a brand-name formula company, complete with free samples of formula and information on breastfeeding that makes it sound a little hard and scary. She tells you if you have any questions, to just call your pediatrician.

The first night at home, things don't go well. It's the middle of the night, and your baby won't stop crying when you try to breastfeed. You wonder if you should just give up. You reach for that ready-made bottle and his crying mercifully stops. The problem is solved, at least for now.

You are really motivated to breastfeed, so in the morning, you try to find a lactation consultant. You talk to someone you find in the yellow pages called a "lactation counselor" who is willing to help, but your insurance won't pay. You find someone else called a "lactation consultant." You have no idea what the difference is between a "lactation counselor" and a "lactation consultant." Since these professionals aren't licensed in any state, you have no way of knowing if they know what they are doing.

You meet with the lactation consultant, but have to pay out of pocket. She helps you. Afterwards, you have to file a claim with your insurance company and hope they reimburse you, all while caring for your newborn. The lactation consultant recommends pumping with a double electric pump to help you build up your milk supply, which is now threatened because of all the formula the baby got, and because his breastfeeding technique is not really good enough yet to extract milk well, since he didn't learn properly right from the beginning. Your insurance won't allow the breast pump to come out of your Durable Medical Equipment allowance, and you try to pay for it with your Flexible Spending benefit card, but it's denied. You pay $250 out of pocket. Good thing you had a gift card to pay for all that!

You go to your pediatrician for follow up. Since your pediatrician got very little training on breastfeeding, he doesn't know how to help you, but is concerned that your baby has lost too much weight, and advises giving some formula. You don't know what to do because the lactation consultant's advice was different.

Ugh!!! This is really hard, you think. Eventually, things miraculously end up working out, just because you persevere through thick and thin, and your partner and family and friends are very supportive. By about 4 weeks, your baby is now exclusively breastfeeding, and gaining well. And you are enjoying what time is left of your unpaid leave under the Family Medical Leave Act. But, you have only two more weeks before you go back to work. You can't afford any more time off.

You start pumping to build up a stash of frozen milk for your return to work. You arrange with your employer a place to pump -- how lucky you are that it won't be a bathroom! You go back to work, and before long you discover your milk supply is dwindling and now your baby wants to nurse all night long. You are exhausted.

You call the lactation consultant who tells you that it's common to see a drop in milk supply when moms go back to work. She explains that pumps aren't as efficient at removing milk as your own baby is, so your milk supply may drop, and your baby makes up for it by nursing more when you are with him -- it just so happens that that's at night. "It's called reverse cycle feeding," she tells you. You wonder why you never heard about this before, in any of your follow-up visits with your pediatrician or OB.

You want to see the lactation consultant again, but your insurance will only reimburse you for visits during the newborn period. Well, you think, at least my insurance paid for something -- my friend's insurance doesn't reimburse anything for lactation help.

You nearly fall asleep at the wheel driving to work. "This is crazy," you think. "My baby needs me to be alive, more than he needs me to be breastfeeding." Finally, you give up. You just can't do this anymore. You are very sad and disappointed.

You become a statistic: one of the 41% of US mothers who wean before 3 months. You feel guilty as hell, especially when all you ever hear is how great breastfeeding is, and now how that new study shows it could save the US economy $13 billion/year, and how everyone says it saves lives and how it will make you healthier too. You just wish all these people would just shut the heck up.

So, now that you've heard the difference between what your experience could have been like, and what it was actually like, you tell me:

Do you feel guilty for not breastfeeding? Or do you feel angry because it didn't have to be this way?

And if you answered "angry," then take that anger, and write to your hospital -- tell them you want them to become a Baby-Friendly hospital, so that no one else will have to go through what you did just to feed your child. Write to your state and federal legislators -- tell them to support laws that make breastfeeding easier, like licensing of lactation consultants, and the requirement that insurance companies reimburse for lactation care and services. And write to your US representatives and senators, and tell them you want tax-credits for onsite childcare, and that you don't want the US to continue being the world's only developed country without paid maternity leave.

Yes, I'm a researcher and a physician, but I'm also a mother. Since I live in the United States, you can probably guess what my birth experience was like. Maybe you've heard me on the news saying that moms shouldn't feel guilty. I've been there. So take that guilt and turn it inside out, and do something positive so that other moms don't have to go through what you did. We all deserve better.

Melissa Bartick, MD is an internal medicine physician in Massachusetts, as well as a mother. She is also chairs the Massachusetts Breastfeeding Coalition. She practices hospital medicine.

*A Peaceful Revolution is a blog about innovative ideas to strengthen America's families through public policies, business practices, and* *cultural change. Done in collaboration with <u>MomsRising.org</u>, read a new post at <u>http://HuffingtonPost.com</u> each week.*

One of my favorite organizations who has gone above and beyond to help women make informed decisions is Choices in Childbirth.

**Choices in Childbirth** helps women make well informed maternity care decisions. Their mission is to improve maternity care by providing the public, especially childbearing women and their families, with the information necessary to make fully informed decisions relating to how, where, and with whom they will give birth.

Their website provides "The National Guide to a Healthy Birth", which you can download or request by mail. Their guide provides you with many facts and options relating to the birthing process.

Below I have included a useful and practical questionnaire provided by Choices in Childbirth that you may want to use, or at least introduce to your client when deciding on a care provider.

## Questions To Ask Your Care Provider

Here are some suggested questions to encourage dialogue and to help you get a sense of your care provider's approach. It is a good idea to interview at least 2 or 3 providers. It is never too late to change provider if you are not comfortable with the answers you receive.

## PRENATAL-

1. How much time do you allow for each prenatal visit?
2. How do you handle routine phone calls between visits?
3. Are you part of a high risk practice?
4. Under what circumstances do you recommend the following prenatal tests or procedures?
   - ☐ Ultrasound (number and stage)
   - ☐ Maternal serum alpha-fetoprotein screening (AFP)
   - ☐ Chorionic villus sampling (CVS)
   - ☐ Amniocentesis
   - ☐ Gestational diabetes screening

- ☐ Group B streptococcus screening
- ☐ Prenatal rhogam
- ☐ Other

5. Is there a limit to the number of people who can accompany me during my birth?

6. How do you feel about a labor support professional such as a doula or massage therapist joining my birth team?

7. Will I be able to eat and drink in labor?

## -FIRST STAGE OF LABOR (DILATING)-

8. If I were interested in having a natural, unmedicated birth, how would you feel about it?

9. What non-pharmacological comfort measures do you support?
   - ☐ Freely changing positions and walking around
   - ☐ Water therapy (shower/tub)
   - ☐ A birth ball
   - ☐ A doula
   - ☐ Other

10. Under what circumstances would you recommend an epidural/narcotics?

11. When would you like me to come to the birth center/ hospital?
    - ☐ When my water breaks
    - ☐ When my contractions are _ minutes apart for _ long

12. What are your recommendations if my water breaks before contractions have begun?
    - ☐ Call and stay home until contractions start
    - ☐ Come to office/hospital/birth center to monitor baby and then return home
    - ☐ Come immediately to hospital/birth center

13. How long after my water breaks would you recommend induction if my labor doesn't start on its own?

14. What are your protocols regarding my due date, i.e. inducing labor?

*cultural change. Done in collaboration with <u>MomsRising.org</u>, read a* which synthetic prostaglandin do you recommend?

☐ Cytotec (generic name: misoprostol)

☐ Cervidil

☐ Other

16. Do you believe in active management of first stage, i.e. progress less than 1 cm perhour will call for artificial rupture of membranes (AROM) or Pitocin? If everything isfine with me and my baby, will I be able to labor at my own pace and for as long as Ineed?

17. What non-medical ways of stimulating labor do you recommend?

☐ Herbs

☐ Nipple stimulation

☐ Castor oil

☐ Intercourse (before spontaneous rupture of membranes (SROM))

☐ Enema

☐ Acupuncture

☐ None

18. What is your protocol regarding the following procedures and how often do you perform them?

☐ IVs

☐ Continuous versus intermittent fetal monitoring

☐ Internal fetal monitoring

☐ Artificial rupturing of the membranes (AROM) at _ cm

☐ Epidural

☐ Assisted vaginal delivery (forceps/ vacuum)

☐ Episiotomy

19. What is your cesarean rate? What factors do you believe contribute to that rate?

20. Are you supportive of vaginal birth after cesarean (VBAC)?
What is your VBAC rate?
What are your standard protocols for VBAC mothers?

## -SECOND STAGE OF LABOR (PUSHING)-

21. What percentage of women under your care give birth in the lithotomy position (on their backs with legs raised)? Will I be able to choose the position in which I will give birth such as side lying, all fours, squatting?

## -POSTPARTUM-

22. Can my baby remain with me at all times from the moment of birth? Do you support skin to skin contact between me and my baby immediately after birth? Can I delay newborn procedures such as vitamin K shot, eye ointment, until the first feeding is accomplished?

23. Will you or someone on your staff support me in establishing and maintaining breastfeeding?

24. What percentage of women under you care are given Pitocin following the birth of the baby? Under what circumstances do you recommend this practice?

25. How long will I stay in the hospital/birth center after the birth?

26. (For home birth midwives) How long will you stay with me after my baby is born?

## -BACK UP-

27. If you are in a group practice:
    ☐ Can I meet your partner(s)?
    ☐ What is their perspective on routine hospital interventions?
    ☐ How likely is it that one of your partners will be the one to attend my birth?

28. (For home birth midwives) What is your rate of transfer to hospital? Who is your consultant obstetrician? Will I be able to meet or interview them?

For further resources on interviewing care providers, visit their website:

http://www.choicesinchildbirth.org

Here are a few additional organizations worth knowing about:

## Coalition for Improving Maternity Services

The Coalition for Improving Maternity Services (CIMS) is a coalition of individuals and national organizations with concern for the care and well-being of mothers, babies, and families. Their mission is to promote a wellness model of maternity care that will improve birth outcomes and substantially reduce costs. This evidence-based mother-, baby-, and family-friendly model focuses on prevention and wellness as the alternatives to high-cost screening, diagnosis, and treatment programs.

The evidence-based Mother-Friendly Childbirth Initiative (MFCI) evolved from the collaborative effort of many individuals and more than 26 organizations focused on pregnancy, birth and breastfeeding during meetings spanning nearly three years in the 1990's. The MFCI - the cornerstone of our mission - is the first and only consensus document on U.S. maternity care. The MFCI is recognized as an important instrument for change both in this country and abroad. Acknowledging the need to ensure the ongoing education and promotion of the Mother-Friendly childbirth model of care defined in the MFCI, CIMS was established as a non-profit corporation in 1997.

CIMS is at an exciting time in its development. As CIMS moves forward in its second decade, their focus is on supporting both "bottom-up" and "top-down" advocacy for Mother-Friendly Care. From the powerful work of the Grassroots Advocates Committee's The Birth Survey project, which is mobilizing mothers and volunteers across the country, to the significant contributions of research on the evidence basis for Mother-Friendly Care, CIMS remains committed to providing the guidance and collaboration needed to support the maternity care community and ensure that mothers receive the care they deserve.

CIMS' membership in the National Quality Forum (NQF), a public-private partnership created to develop and implement a national strategy for health care quality and measurement, reflects our commitment to bring about national change. Through the NQF's Consumer Council, CIMS lends its voice to the needs of birthing women in the ongoing national debate about how best to improve maternity care.

CIMS is also an active member of the U.S. Breastfeeding Committee (USBC), a collaborative partnership of organizations dedicated to improving the nation's health by protecting, promoting, and supporting breastfeeding

For more information visit: http://www.motherfriendly.org/

## Childbirth Connection

Childbirth Connection is a national not-for-profit organization founded in 1918 as Maternity Center Association. Their vision is a world in which well-informed pregnant women choose to receive and supportive caregivers and institutions provide safe, effective and satisfying maternity care. Their mission is to improve the quality of maternity care through research, education, advocacy and policy. Childbirth Connection promotes safe, effective and satisfying evidence-based maternity care and is a voice for the needs and interests of childbearing families.

For more information visit: http://childbirthconnection.org

## Natural Baby Pros

NaturalBabyPros.com is a website, resource and directory built to educate about the natural and alternative options in creating healthy, natural babies and moms. It was created with the purpose of educating women and couples on the many natural health care options available for preconception through postpartum and baby care, and to help connect them with the best therapies and professionals for them and their families.

*Think of it as a place where like-minded families and practitioners can find each other, collaborate, and share information about fertility, pregnancy, birth, postpartum and baby care and services.*

Their deepest desire is to create opportunities for families to meet other families and practitioners in a *non-judgmental, educative and supportive environment*, whether online or in the community. We want to build a strong referral network between professionals and each individual profession in an effort to provide the best, most well-rounded resource available for fertility, pregnancy, birth, postpartum and baby care.

To them, ***informed choice = empowerment,*** no matter what that choice may be. It is time for the benefits of natural, holistic perspectives on conception, pregnancy, birth and parenting to be become a viable option for more families, and we would like to provide the place and resource for that to become reality.

**Education without Judgment**

At NaturalBabyPros.com, they understand the uniqueness of each individual person and their experiences, and know that circumstances are not always the same for all of us. They want to promote the education of natural therapies and support those who practice them without discarding the importance of many other conventional medical professionals and practices or judging those who must use them. Through education, communication, and experience, they and their professionals guide you and inspire you, so that you can come to your own educated conclusions about how you feel most comfortable in proceeding with your fertility, pregnancy, birthing, and baby concerns and care.

For more information visit: http://www.naturalbabypros.com

## Sage Femme

Sage Femme produces documentaries about natural birth, sponsors the Motherbaby International Film Festival, and distributes information and films through symposiums, conferences and its website. Their goal is simply to increase everyone's awareness about their options for birth. You'll choose the right way for you.

http://www.sagefemme.com

## EcoBirth

EcoBirth is the study of and practice in Deep Womb Ecology. It links and relates the environments of Birth and Earth. EcoBirth recognizes that the mental and physical care surrounding Birth is an indicator of how we care for the Earth. Since our primary provider and first home is the Earth, EcoBirth advocates cherishing her as a means of protecting our mother's wombs, our baby's births and our children's futures. EcoBirth promotes sustainability and natural processes in all aspects of life, especially at birth.

http://www.sagefemme.com/ecobirth.html

## Circumcision

Circumcision is a very hot topic amongst parents and childbirth professionals and a very important one to understand. Attitudes toward circumcision are changing because of new awareness. As a result, there is growing concern about this often misunderstood genital surgery. It is important that expecting parents are educated about circumcision and know their options. Please note that regardless of a baby planner's personal opinion, they should respect each client's decision.

The Circumcision Resource Center is a nonprofit educational organization with the purpose of informing the public and professionals about the practice of male circumcision. Their mission is to raise awareness and facilitate healing. The Center is a valuable source of male circumcision information for parents and children's advocates; childbirth educators and allied professionals; medical, mental health, and academic people; Jews; and others. Their Directors (majority is Jewish*) and Professional Advisory Board members (one-third is Jewish*) consist of researchers and clinicians in the fields of medicine, mental health, and social science.

Here is a Summary of General Circumcision Information provided from their website. For more details visit: http://www.circumcision.org:

1.  **Worldwide prevalence:** The U.S. is the only country in the world that routinely circumcises most of its male infants for non-religious reasons. Over 80% of the world's males are intact (*). No national medical organization in the world recommends routine circumcision of male infants. (See Circumcision Policies in English-Speaking Countries.)

2.  **Pain:** According to a comprehensive study, newborn responses to pain are "similar to but greater than those observed in adult subjects." Circumcision is extremely painful and traumatic. Some infants do not cry because they go into traumatic shock from the overwhelming pain of the surgery. No experimental anesthetic has been found to be safe and effective in preventing circumcision pain in infants (*). (See Infant Responses During and Following Circumcision.)

3.  **Behavioral response:** Various studies have found that short-term effects of circumcision include changed sleep patterns, activity level, and mother-infant interaction, more irritability, and disruptions in feeding and bonding. Long-term effects have not been studied. Changes in pain response have been demonstrated at six months of age. (*). (See Infant Responses During and Following Circumcision.)

4.  **Circumcision risks:** The rate of complications occurring in the hospital and during the first year has been documented as high as 38% and includes hemorrhage, infection, surgical injury, and in rare cases, death (*).

5.  **Cleanliness:** The American Academy of Pediatrics (AAP) says that "there is little evidence to affirm the association between circumcision status and optimal penile hygiene." "The uncircumcised penis is easy to keep clean. . . . Caring for your son's uncircumcised penis requires no special action. . . . Foreskin retraction should never be forced." (*)

6.  **Sexually transmitted diseases:** According to the AAP, "Evidence regarding the relationship of circumcision to sexually transmitted diseases in general is complex and conflicting. . . . Behavioral factors appear to be far more important risk factors." (*) (See Explaining Claims of Medical Benefits.)

7.  **Matching friends:** The national circumcision rate is 56%, less than 25% in some states. Though past circumcision rates were higher, there is no documented emotional harm to intact boys. To the contrary, there are growing reports from men who have disliked being circumcised since they were boys, even though they were in the majority (*). (See Circumcision to Look Like Others.)

8.  **Adult circumcision:** The medical need for circumcision in adults is as low as 6 in 100,000. Adults, unlike infants, receive anesthetics (*). (See Men Circumcised as Adults.)

9.  **Foreskin function and size:** The foreskin protects the head of the penis, enhances sexual pleasure, and facilitates intercourse. Men circumcised as adults report a significant loss of sensitivity. Men who have restored their foreskin report much increased sensitivity and sexual pleasure. The foreskin on the average adult male is about 12 sq.in. of highly erogenous tissue (*). (See Functions of the Foreskin.)

10. **Jewish circumcision:** A growing number of American Jews are not circumcising their sons. Circumcision among Jews in Europe, South America, and Israel also is not universal (*). (See Jewish Circumcision Resource Center

11. **American origin:** Routine infant circumcision started in the U.S. in the 1870s when it was promoted as a preventive cure for masturbation (*).

12. **Male attitude:** Male satisfaction with circumcision depends on lack of knowledge about circumcision. The more men know, the more likely they are to be dissatisfied. They wish they had a choice (*). (See Why Most Circumcised Men Seem Satisfied, Psychological Impact of Circumcision on Men, and Discovering Circumcision Feelings.)

13. **Professional Protest:** Some aware doctors and nurses refuse to perform or assist with circumcisions because of ethical considerations (*). (See Circumcision, Ethics, and Medicine.)

## NOTES

1. Wallerstein, E., +Circumcision: The Uniquely American Medial Enigma,+ *Urologica Clinics of North America* 12 (February 1985): 123-32.

2. Anand, K. & Hickey, P., +Pain and Its Effects in the Human Neonate and Fetus,+*New England Journal of Medicine* 317 (1987): 1326; Romberg, R., *Circumcision: The Painful Dilemma* (South Hadley, MA: Bergin & Garvey, 1985), 321, 325; Stang, H. et al., +Local Anesthesia for Neonatal Circumcision,+ *Journal of the American Medical Association* 259 (1988): 1507-11.

3. Anand & Hickey, +Pain and Its Effects,+ 1325; Taddio, A. et al., "Effects of Neonatal Circumcision on Pain Response During Subsequent Routine Vaccination," *The Lancet* 349 (1997): 599-603.

4. Kaplan, G., +Complications of Circumcision,+ *Urological Clinics of North America* 10 (1983): 543-9

5. American Academy of Pediatrics, *Newborns: Care of the Uncircumcised Penis* (pamphlet for parents), Elk Grove Village, IL: author, 1999; American Academy of Pediatrics, Task Force on Circumcision, "Circumcision Policy Statement," *Pediatrics* 103 (1999): 686-693.

6. American Academy of Pediatrics, Task Force on Circumcision, "Circumcision Policy Statement," *Pediatrics* 103 (1999): 686-693.

7. National Center for Health Statistics, 6525 Belcrest Rd., Hyattsville, MD 20782; Hammond, T., "A Preliminary Poll of Men Circumcised in Infancy or Childhood," *BJU International* 83 (1999): 85-92.

8. Wallerstein, E., *Circumcision: An American Health Fallacy* (New York: Springer Publishing, 1980), 128.

9. Taylor, J., Lockwood, A., & Taylor, A., +The Prepuce: Specialized Mucosa of the Penis and Its Loss to

Circumcision,+ *British Journal of Urology* 77 (1996): 294; Ritter, T. and Denniston, G., *Say No To Circumcision* (Aptos, CA: Hourglass, 1996), 18-1; Morgan, W., +The Rape of the Phallus,+ *Journal of the American Medical Association* 193 (1965): 223; Bigelow, J., *The Joy of Uncircumcising!* (Aptos, CA: Hourglass, 1995), 17; Denniston, G., +Unnecessary Circumcision,+ *The Female Patient* 17 (1992): 13-14.

10. Silverman, J., +Circumcision: The Delicate Dilemma,+ *The Jewish Monthly*, November 1991, 31; Meyer, M., +Berit Milah within the History of the Reform Movement,+ in L. Barth, ed., *Berit Mila in the Reform Context* (Berit Milah Board of Reform Judaism 1990), 149; Goldman, R., *Questioning Circumcision: A Jewish Perspective* (Boston: Vanguard Publications, 1998), 53; Karsenty, N., +A Mother Questions Brit Milla,+ *Humanistic Judaism* 16 (Summer 1988), 21; Eichner, I., +Every Circumcision is Unnecessary,+ *Yediot*, 6 May 1997, 23.

11. Kellogg, J., *Plain Facts for Old and Young* (Burlington, IA: F. Segner, 1888).

12. Hammond, T., "A Preliminary Poll of Men Circumcised in Infancy or Childhood," *BJU International* 83 (1999): 85-92.

13. Easthouse, K., +Nurses: Circumcision Consent Form Should Alert Parents to Downside,+ *The New Mexican*, Feb. 3, 1993; Pugh, L., +Santa Fe Nurses Reject Circumcisions,+ *Albuquerque Journal*, June 13, 1995, 1.

## Birth Doula

Hiring a Birth Doula can be very beneficial to your clients. Below are frequently asked questions and answers about birth doulas provided by DONA International:

## 1. What is a birth doula?

A birth doula is a person trained and experienced in childbirth who provides continuous physical, emotional and informational support to the mother before, during and just after childbirth.

## 2. Where does the word "doula" come from?

The word "doula" comes from ancient Greek, meaning "Woman's servant." Throughout history and in much of the world today, a cadre of women support, a woman through labor and birth, giving back rubs and providing continuous emotional support. Like their historical counterparts, DONA International birth doulas know how to help a woman in labor feel better. However, today's doulas are much more diverse than their predecessors. DONA International membership includes men and women from a wide range of ages and cultural backgrounds.

## 3. What effects does the presence of a doula have on birth outcomes?

Numerous clinical studies have found that a doula's presence at birth:

- ☐ tends to result in shorter labors with fewer complications
- ☐ reduces negative feelings about one's childbirth experience
- ☐ reduces the need for pitocin (a labor-inducing drug), forceps or vacuum extraction
- ☐ reduces the requests for pain medication and epidurals, as well as the incidence of cesareans

## 4. What effects does the presence of a doula have on the mother?

When a doula is present during and after childbirth, women report greater satisfaction with their birth experience, make more positive assessments of their babies, have fewer cesareans and requests for medical intervention, and less postpartum depression.

## 5. What effects does the presence of doulas have on babies?

Studies have shown that babies born with doulas present tend to have shorter hospital stays with fewer admissions to special care nurseries, breastfeed more easily and have more affectionate mothers in the postpartum period.

## 6. How can I find a doula in my area?

Use DONA International's online doula locator.

## 7. How do doulas practice?

Doulas practice in three ways: privately hired directly by clients, as hospital employees, and as volunteers in community or hospital programs.

## 8. Does a doula replace nursing staff?

No. Doulas do not replace nurses or other medical staff. Doulas do not perform clinical or medical tasks such as taking blood pressure or temperature, monitoring fetal heart rate, doing vaginal examinations or providing postpartum clinical care. They are there to comfort and support the mother and to enhance communication between the mother and medical professionals.

## 9. Does a doula make decisions on my behalf?

A doula does not make decisions for clients or intervene in their clinical care. She provides informational and emotional support, while respecting a woman's decisions.

## 10. Will a doula make my partner feel unnecessary?

No, a doula is supportive to both the mother and her partner, and plays a crucial role in helping a partner become involved in the birth to the extent he/she feels comfortable.

For more information please visit http://www.dona.org

There are also some very powerful movies and organizations that I recommend you become familiar with and suggest to your clients.

## The Business of Being Born

Birth is a miracle, a rite of passage, a natural part of life. But birth is also big business.

Compelled to explore the subject after the delivery of her first child, actress Ricki Lake recruits filmmaker Abby Epstein to question the way American women have babies.

The film interlaces intimate birth stories with surprising historical, political and scientific insights and shocking statistics about the current maternity care system. When director Epstein discovers she is pregnant during the making of the film, the journey becomes even more personal.

http://www.thebusinessofbeingborn.com/

## Labor Under An Illusion: Mass Media Childbirth vs The Real Thing by Vicki Elson, MA, CCE

Anthropologist Vicki Elson explores media-generated myths about childbirth. As a childbirth educator for 25 years, she observes daily how our culture affects our birth experiences. In this documentary film, she contrasts fiction with reality. The result is hilarious, engaging, and enlightening. "To understand what it's really like to have a baby, we have to debunk the silly and scary images served up by the profit-driven media. In reality, birth is hard work, sometimes simple, sometimes complicated, but always miraculous and unforgettable."—Vicki Elson

http://www.birth-media.com/

## Pregnant in America

*Pregnant in America* is a motivational, and inspirational documentary made by film maker Steve Buonagurio about the birth of his daughter Bella. Shocked by the greed of U.S. hospitals, insurance companies and medical organizations, Steve and his wife Mandy set out to create a natural home birth in a world where everything is anything but natural. The film is as much educational as it is entertaining and prepares excepting parent for their uncertain journey of being pregnant and having their baby.

http://www.pregnantinamerica.com/

## Babies

Directed by award-winning filmmaker Thomas Balmès, from an original idea by producer Alain Chabat, *Babies* simultaneously follows four babies around the world – from birth to first steps. The children are, respectively, in order of on-screen introduction: Ponijao, who lives with her family near Opuwo, Namibia; Bayarjargal, who resides with his family in Mongolia, near Bayanchandmani; Mari, who lives with her family in Tokyo, Japan; and Hattie, who resides with her family in the United States, in San Francisco. Re-defining the nonfiction art form, *Babies* joyfully captures on film the earliest stages of the journey of humanity that are at once unique and universal to us all.

http://www.babiesthemovie.com/

## BirthDay

Birth Day is a documentary exquisitely capturing the beauty of a natural home birth in the lush mountain countryside of Xalapa, Veracruz, Mexico. Taped by the baby's grandfather, Georges Vinaver and narrated by the baby's mother, midwife Naoli Vinaver Lopez, we are treated to the birth of this family's third child and first daughter, Tamaya Okumura Vinaver.

http://www.homebirthvideos.com/birthday_dvd.asp

## What Babies Want: An exploration of the consciousness of infants

What Babies Want is an award winning documentary film that explores the profoundly important and sacred opportunity we have in bringing children into the world. Filled with captivating stories and infused with Noah Wyle's warmth as narrator, the film demonstrates how life patterns are established at birth and before. The documentary includes groundbreaking information on early development as well as appearances by the real experts: babies and families. This film is narrated by Noah Wyle, and the director is Debby Takikawa.

**DEBBY TAKIKAWA** DC. is the founder and director of the non-profit organization, Beginnings Inc. A Resource Center for Children and Families, a clinic for infant centered family therapy. In 2001 she set out on a project to make a short educational video to help families understand the issues involved with infant relationship development. Four years later she has produced and directed, not a short educational video, but rather a film of great power and consequence. Debby says, "I started out on an innocent little walk and ended up in a spellbinding flight into the human psyche.

http://www.whatbabieswant.com/

## Additional Resources

http://www.birthcenters.org/

http://www.waterbirth.org/

http://www.midwiferytoday.com/

http://mana.org/

# Breastfeeding Basics

Breastfeeding can be a very intimate and challenging experience for a new mom. At times she may feel alone and embarrassed that she's not enjoying her experience. As a baby planner you are welcome to provide her support and encouragement (non-therapeutic) along with factual information, such as the benefits of breastfeeding. There are also many local support groups and educational classes available. If your client is undergoing more serious issues, you should refer her to a lactation consultant or her midwife/doctor who can assist her further.

Below is a list of the benefits of breastfeeding from the US Department of Health & Human Services:

## Benefits for Babies, Moms, and Families

- ☐ Breastfeeding is normal and healthy for infants and moms.
- ☐ Breast milk has disease-fighting cells called antibodies that help protect infants from germs, illness, and even SIDS. Infant formula cannot match the exact chemical makeup of human milk, especially the cells, hormones, and antibodies that fight disease.

**Breastfeeding is linked to a lower risk of these health problems:**

| In Infants: | In Moms: |
|---|---|
| ☐ Ear infections | ☐ Type 2 48H49Hdiabetes |
| ☐ Stomach viruses | ☐ Breast 49H50Hcancer |
| ☐ Diarrhea | ☐ 50H51HOvarian cancer |
| ☐ Respiratory infections | ☐ 51H52HPostpartum depression (PPD) |
| ☐ Atopic dermatitis | |
| ☐ Asthma | |
| ☐ Obesity | |
| ☐ Type 1 and type 2 diabetes | |
| ☐ Childhood leukemia | |
| ☐ Sudden infant death syndrome or SIDS | |
| ☐ Necrotizing enterocolitis, a disease that affects the 47H48H gastrointestinal tract in pre-term infants | |

Studies are still looking at the effects of breastfeeding on osteoporosis and weight loss after birth.

- ☐ Breast milk is different from infant formula. Colostrum, the thick yellow first breast milk that you make during pregnancy and just after birth, will give your baby the best start at life. It is known as "liquid gold." It is very rich in nutrients and antibodies to protect your baby as he or she first enters the world. Although your baby only gets a small amount of colostrum at each feeding, it matches the amount his or her tiny stomach can hold. A newborn stomach is only the size of a large marble at first!

- ☐ Your milk changes over time to meet your baby's needs. Your breast milk that begins to be made by the third to fifth day after birth has just the right amount of fat, sugar, water, and protein that is needed for a baby's growth. It will be a thinner type of milk, but just as full of all of the nutrients and antibodies for your baby.

- ☐ For most babies, breast milk is easier to digest than formula. It takes time for their stomachs to adjust to digesting the proteins in formula because they are made from cow's milk.

- ☐ Premature babies do better when breastfed compared to premature babies who are fed formula.

- ☐ When you breastfeed, there are no bottles and nipples to sterilize. Unlike human milk straight from the breast, infant formula has a chance of being contaminated.

- ☐ Breastfeeding makes your life easier. You do not have to purchase, measure, and mix formula. There are no bottles to warm in the middle of the night!

- ☐ Breastfeeding can save you between $1,160 and $3,915 per year, depending on the brand of formula.

- ☐ A mother can satisfy her baby's hunger right away with breastfeeding.

- ☐ Breastfeeding requires a mother to take some quiet relaxed time for herself and her baby, helping them bond. Physical contact is important to newborns and can help them feel more secure, warm, and comforted. Breastfeeding mothers may have increased self-confidence and feelings of closeness and bonding with their infants.

☐   Breastfeeding during an emergency can save lives.

## Benefits for Society

☐   Breastfeeding saves on health care costs. Total medical care costs for the nation are lower for fully breastfed infants than never-breastfed infants since breastfed infants typically need fewer sick care visits, prescriptions, and hospitalizations.

☐   Breastfeeding contributes to a more productive workforce. Breastfeeding mothers miss less work, as their infants are sick less often. Employer medical costs also are lower and employee productivity is higher.

☐   Breastfeeding is better for our environment because there is less trash and plastic waste compared to that produced by formula cans and bottle supplies.

## The U.S. Surgeon General Recommends Breastfeeding

The U.S. Surgeon General recommends that babies be fed with breast milk only for the first six months of life. This means not giving your baby any other food or drink — not even water — during this time. Drops of liquid vitamins, minerals, and medicines are, of course, fine, as advised by your baby's doctor. It is even better if you can breastfeed for your baby's first year or longer, for as long as you both wish.

Solid                              iron-rich foods, such as iron-fortified cereals and  pureed vegetables and meats, can be started when your baby is around six months old. Before that time, a baby's stomach cannot digest them properly. Solids do not replace breastfeeding. Breast milk stays the baby's main source of nutrients during the first year. Beyond one year, breast milk can still be an important part of your child's diet.

Learn more about the  HHS Blueprint for Action on Breastfeeding and policy   statements   in   support   of   breastfeeding   from   the American Academy  of  Pediatrics, College  of  Obstetrics  and Gynecologists (PDF, 18 Kb), and the  American Academy of Family Physicians.

## Breastfeeding vs Formula

This is a very heated topic especially amongst childbirth professionals and mothers. I have observed a lot of guilt and judgment of mothers who have not felt they lived up to their expectations of breastfeeding and some have even suffered from depression as a result.

A baby planner has the opportunity to play a supportive role in being objective and empathetic when breastfeeding become a great challenge for some new mothers. If moms have been educated and know about the risks of formula feeding, but exclusive breastfeeding is not an option, providing them with alternative options, and respecting their decision is part of our professional duty as baby planners.

Below are a few websites with information on breastfeeding and formula:

http://www.mercola.com

http://www.westonaprice.org

## Additional Resources

## GotMom.org

GotMom.org was created by the American College of Nurse-Midwives to provide breastfeeding information and resources for mothers and families. It contains information on why breast milk is best, dispels common misunderstandings about breastfeeding, and it provides a list of resources that can help women and families with breastfeeding.

http://www.gotmom.org

## La Leche League

La Leche League was founded to give information and encouragement, mainly through personal help, to all mothers who want to breastfeed their babies. While complementing the care of the physician and other health care professionals, it recognizes the unique importance of one mother helping another to perceive the needs of her child and to learn the best means of fulfilling those needs.

LLL believes that breastfeeding, with its many important physical and psychological advantages, is best for baby and mother and is the ideal way to initiate good parent-child relationships. The loving help and support of the father enables the mother to focus on mothering so that together the parents develop close relationships which strengthen the family and thus the whole fabric of society.

LLL further believes that mothering through breastfeeding deepens a mother's understanding and acceptance of the responsibilities and rewards of her special role in the family. As a woman grows in mothering she grows as a human being, and every other role she may fill in her lifetime is enriched by the insights and humanity she brings to it from her experiences as a mother.

http://www.llli.org

## KellyMom.Com

KellyMom.com is an internationally recognized website providing breastfeeding and parenting information to professionals and parents

http//www.kellymom.com

## ProMom

Promotion of Mother's Milk, Inc. (ProMoM) is a nonprofit organization dedicated to increasing public awareness and public acceptance of breastfeeding.

 http://www.promom.org

## The Academy of Breastfeeding Medicine

The Academy of Breastfeeding Medicine is a worldwide organization of physicians dedicated to the promotion, protection and support of breastfeeding and human lactation.  Our mission is to unite members of the various medical specialties with this common purpose.

http://www.bfmed.org/

# Sleeping Basics

Getting the proper amount of sleep both during and after pregnancy can be very challenging. A woman's body undergoes many changes. The size of her abdomen increases; she may experience shortness of breath, or back pain, and even have insomnia. She should avoid sleeping on her back and on her stomach. If your client's sleep continues to be major problem beyond your scope of practice, refer them to specialist such as a sleep consultant or parent educator that can help.

Lack of sleep weakens the immune system, compromising a pregnant woman's health. It is linked to hormonal disruption, depression, and weight gain. As a result, your client's cravings may increase, her mood may change often, and her energy will be low. Taking naps throughout the day as needed, can be very helpful. If your client works all day, then make sure she takes a few minutes to relax and unwind upon arriving home. The following are factors that can inhibit proper sleep:

- ☐ Poor Diet
- ☐ Stress or Anxiety
- ☐ Bad positioning
- ☐ Overworking
- ☐ Lack of a consistent routine

Here are some tips for your client's to prepare for a restful evening:

## Sleep as close between 10pm and 6am as possible

The body has a natural circadian sleep cycle that occurs between the hours of 10pm and 6am. When disrupted your body does not receive the full repairs necessary to function optimally. Pregnant women need lots of rest and repair, so make sure they try to do so.

## Turn the TV off at least two hours before bed

This gives your eyes and your mind a chance to relax and prepare for bed.

## Play soothing music

Soothing music allows the body to unwind and stay at ease.

## Dim the lights once the sun sets

By dimming the lights, the brain sends a signal to the body that it is time to rest.

## Take a bubble bath

A bubble bath eases tense muscles, and allows the mind to quiet down.

## Participate in an evening prenatal yoga class

A prenatal yoga class is a wonderful way to de-stress the body, meditate, and quiet the mind.

## Use a body pillow that is appropriate for you.

As your client's belly grows, using a body pillow will help to ease lower back tension and even leg cramps.

## Eat your last meal at least 2-3 hours before bedtime

Digestion takes up a lot of your body's energy. If you eat right before bed time, your body will have a difficult time unwinding because it is too busy digesting.

## Your last meal should be light

If you must have something keep on the light side. Decaffeinated tea such as chamomile is also very helpful.

## Avoid fluids before bed

Drink all of your fluids throughout the day and empty your bladder before going to bed. This will help to minimize frequent urination throughout the night.

Below is an article by Dr. Catherine Darley discussing the hormone cortisol, and how it can affect sleep.

## Your Cortisol Rhythm and Sleep

by Dr. Catherine Darley

Cortisol is an intrinsic hormone we all have. It is secreted by the adrenal glands on a regular daily basis. There is a daily fluctuation in levels, called it's circadian rhythm. Cortisol should be low at night while we sleep. It rapidly rises in the early morning, helping us have the energy to start our day. Cortisol also can increase due to acute stress, such as an auto accident, or can be chronically elevated due to a chronic stressor. It is thought that after long periods of chronic stress the adrenal glands get fatigued, so that cortisol is abnormally low. Cortisol is typically elevated in depression, and low in Chronic Fatigue Syndrome (CFS).

So how does our cortisol levels affect our sleep?

Cortisol is a wake-promoting hormone, so it can contribute to insomnia when it is high. In my naturopathic sleep medicine practice we evaluate cortisol when the patient reports high stress levels and difficulty sleeping in the middle of the night. Salivary cortisol levels are typically tested at four time points throughout a day – 7am, noon, 4pm and midnight. The patients results are then compared to the normal profile.

What will help normalize cortisol levels?

Many nutrients are needed by the adrenal glands to function well. These include vitamins C, B6, and zinc and magnesium. Some botanical medicines will also support adrenal function. When the 24 hour cortisol profile is abnormal, supplements are typically recommended for 3 months, then levels are re-tested. As always, it is equally (or more) important to address the underlying reason that the cortisol has gotten out of balance. Behavioral approaches to decreasing stress include deep breathing, progressive muscle relaxation, good diet with avoidance of caffeine and alcohol, and good relationships. If you suspect your cortisol levels may be affecting your ability to sleep consult with a physician for evaluation and treatment if necessary.

## About Dr. Catherine Darley

In 2003 Dr. Darley originated the new field of Naturopathic Sleep Medicine by opening The Institute of Naturopathic Sleep Medicine in Seattle Washington. Dr. Darley's interest in founding Naturopathic Sleep Medicine arises from the belief that since sleep is so basic and essential to health, it makes sense to use the most natural, least invasive therapies to help people obtain the sleep they need. The mission of The Institute of Naturopathic Sleep Medicine is to provide patient care, public education about sleep health, and research on natural treatments for sleep disorders.

Currently, Dr. Darley focuses her efforts on providing excellent naturopathic care for patients with sleep disorders. She works with people of all ages, and especially enjoys working with children and their families. She also provides education about sleep health to many public and professional audiences, as this is a poorly understood base of health. In the future, Dr. Darley will continue her work developing the field of Naturopathic Sleep Medicine by conducting original research on naturopathic treatments for sleep, and providing specialist training for other doctors.

For more information about Naturopathic Sleep Medicine go to

 http://www.naturalsleepmedicine.net

## Infant Sleep

Sleep takes on a whole new challenge for new parents once the baby is born. Below is an article by Sleep Consultant and Parent Educator, Angelique Millette.

## Infant Sleep Development and Challenges: How is it Working for the Whole Family?

Working as a sleep consultant, parent coach and infant-toddler-child therapist intern, I am always struck by how often I hear questions— that cross cultural and demographic lines—related to infant/toddler sleep issues and how infants and young children are affected by sleep challenges. Many parents report they are confused by conflicting suggestions and opinions in the various sleep books. A meta-analysis looking at 40 different books not only found conflicting information on how to treat sleep problems, including contradictory recommendations about co-sleeping and acceptable crying methods, but also that many books (approximately half of those in the study) had a first author with no professional credentials at all. What, then, is a sleep-deprived parent to do?

One of the first questions I ask families when we begin working together is: "How is it working for the whole family?" How is the sleep method or location of the infant or young child working for each member of the family? New research shows that sleep challenges for infants and young children may be related intrinsically to their ability to adapt to information from their caregivers, specifically their mothers, to help them to learn to settle and fall sleep. When mothers are sleep deprived, depressed or anxious, they may be less able to respond to their infant's need to sleep and have more difficulty "reading" their infant's sleep cues. Alternatively, research shows that some babies of sleep deprived, depressed and anxious mothers may develop less organized sleep cycles.

When babies aren't sleeping well, parents aren't sleeping well either, but this may be only half of the picture. In my practice, I want to find all the possible reasons why the baby or young child isn't sleeping well before we look for the solution. Otherwise, it is likely the sleep problem will resurface.

## Why "It" Happens?

One of the most common reasons babies aren't able to "sleep well" is that the part of the brain that organizes sleep is just beginning to form in the first three to six months. This includes the development of *circadian rhythms*, those interesting little biological temporal rhythms that help our bodies "know" a 24-hour day and the difference between day and night. Babies are born without fully developed circadian rhythms and actually are dependent on their environment, *vis-à-vis* their caregivers, to provide *Zeitgebers,* environmental cues necessary to the development of rhythms. Parents can help their babies cue their circadian rhythms by bringing them outside, opening the shades in the nursery and other rooms where the family spends time, feeding frequently during the day and playing actively afterwards and instilling sleep and other routines.

## Can We Fix "It?"

When establishing sleep schedules, I want to be clear that this is not an absolute by-the-clock program. I ask parents to commit to the following: (1) try to keep track of when your child last napped and when the next feeding might take place, (2) learn a little bit about a baby's developmental sleeping milestones and, finally, (3) become aware of your own baby's sleep cues, which are the cluster of non-verbal signs that alert you to your baby entering a *sleep window*.

Common sleep cues include yawning, eye or ear rubbing, red eyes, *gaze avert* (when a baby looks into space for extended periods of time), disorganized or jerky movements and sleep-crying (or *sleep grousing*). Babies use sleep cues to communicate that they are not only tired and over-stimulated, but are entering into a sleep window, and if you start the nap or bedtime routine, your baby or young child will be able to fall asleep much more easily than if you wait and, consequently, miss the window. It's paramount for parents to aid in healthy sleep pattern development by ensuring that during the first months of an infant's life they follow a consistent pattern of routines and thoroughly watch and understand their baby's sleep and other cues. This combined effort can help lead to critical brain development that facilitates greater self-soothing in infants and young children.

But what if it doesn't? What happens when the combination of following consistent routines and observing your infant's sleep cues doesn't result in the development of organized sleep? Because *sleep imprinting* (or an infant's sleep associations) begins on day one, a baby who needs a lot of rocking, movement, *shhhing*, patting and bouncing to fall sleep will likely continue to need those sleep associations, even though he or she could become more capable of self-soothing, using techniques like sucking hands, fingers or a blanket, rolling onto the stomach or making going-to-sleep sounds to settle down. As their baby approaches ages four to six months, parents can do a little less rocking, patting and bouncing to help the baby develop new self-soothing skills for settling down to sleep.

## If So, How?

Parents use a myriad of techniques to try and help their babies to sleep, and when they don't work, they look for help. When I work with parents, I make suggestions that bear in mind parenting philosophy, parental overwhelm, depression and anxiety, along with infant temperament, development and age. While the sleep books will have you believe you either can be a co-sleeping, no-cry parent or a crib-sleeping, cry-it-out parent, the real truth—and studies confirm this—is that most parents are doing combinations of all of the above, just to help their babies and young children to sleep.

Which brings us back to the question: "How is this working for the whole family?" A "sleep problem" for one parent may not be for another parent. All parents have their own threshold, as well as level of willingness to try to solve the problem. The essential difference between using crying-it-out (versus non- or low-crying) methods is that they tend to work very quickly, approximately three to 14 nights, while the non- or low-crying solutions can take two to 12 weeks or more. However, leaving one's baby to cry is often a big departure from one's parenting style. If the sleep solution does not feel right to the parent, it likely won't work. It's important to note that limits to all successful sleep solutions include illness, teething, developmental milestones, growth spurts, travel and consistency.

Parents will see they can help their babies to sleep well by responding to their sleep cues, building positive associations with sleep, being consistent and following sleep routines and a schedule. Ultimately, babies learn best how to slow down their bodies from activity with the help of their parents. There are many solutions for helping parents and babies to get the sleep they need, and parents can feel good about making sleep changes while still following their parenting philosophy.

## About Angelique Millette

Angelique Millette (PhDc, PCD/CD [DONA]) is a parent coach, sleep consultant, infant/toddler sleep and postpartum mood disorder researcher, lactation educator, DONA-certified birth and postpartum doula, and infant-child therapist intern who has worked with families across the Bay Area, the United States and Europe for the past 15 years. She specializes in infant/child development and how parents can meet their own sleep needs while helping their young ones meet theirs. Angelique does not follow one specific sleep program, but rather helps families by taking into account family schedule, infant/toddler/child development, temperament, and parenting philosophy, all while keeping an eye on sleep deprivation, parental overwhelm, depression and anxiety. Angelique's doctoral research addresses the correlation amongst infant sleep locations/methods, maternal postpartum depression/anxiety, and maternal attachment. Angelique teaches sleep workshops at Day One in San Francisco, The Parents Center in Marin,

Birthways in Berkeley, professional conferences and parents groups across the country, and works with families in their homes, on the phone and also via Skype © to provide individual and unique sleep methods and solutions for parents and their infants and young children. Check out http://www.angeliquemillette.com to find out more.

## Co-Sleeping

I really feel that once parents are presented with the facts on cribs vs co-sleeping, it is up to them to decide what works best for them. Some parents may decide to only use a crib, co-sleep, or to use both. Below is a very informative article on co-sleeping and suffocation by Dr James McKenna, of the Mother-Baby Sleep Laboratory, University of Notre Dame.

## Co-sleeping and Overlaying/Suffocation: Is there a chance I'll roll over and crush my child?

To claim that there is NO chance of an adult overlaying a baby would be irresponsible, but so would it be irresponsible to claim that an infant could never be killed while traveling in an automobile, or while sleeping alone in a crib which has an overly soft mattress, or crib slats which do not prevent the infant's head from passing between them. In each case, the dangers are significantly reduced - and the potential benefits of car travel or infants sleeping alone (where this is what parents want) can be realized -- when the safety precautions unique to each choice of behavior are regarded. In the case of automobile travel, strapping infants correctly into a consumer safety approved car seat, and not driving while under the influence (of drugs or alcohol) makes car transportation worth the relatively small risk such travel imposes.

No infant sleep environment is risk free. As regards to co-sleeping (in the form of bed-sharing) what we know to be true scientifically is that for nocturnal infant breast feeding and nurturing throughout the night both mothers and babies were designed biologically and psychologically to sleep next to one another. And while beds per se did not evolve, mother-infant co-sleeping most assuredly did-and not maximize infant and maternal health and infant survival! Infant-parent co-sleeping with nocturnal breast feeding takes many diverse forms, and it continues to be the preferred "normal" species-wide sleeping arrangement for human mother-baby pairs. In the worldwide ethnographic record, mothers accidentally suffocating their babies during the night, is virtually unheard of, except among western industrialized nations, but here there are in the overwhelming number of cases, explanations of the deaths that require reference to dangerous circumstances and not to the act itself.

Let me expand a bit on what we know to be true scientifically. Anthropological and developmental studies suggest that mothers and infants are designed to respond to the presence of the other, and no data have ever shown that among mother-baby pairs who co-sleep for breast feeding in a safe co-sleeping/bed-sharing environment that mothers are unable to sense the proximity of their babies in order to avoid smothering them. Our own laboratory sleep studies of co-sleeping/bed-sharing mother infant pairs (2 to 4 month olds) reveal that both breast feeding mothers and their infants are extremely sensitive throughout their night - across all sleep stages - to the movements and physical condition of the other. The healthy infant, which includes most infants, are able to detect instances, where for example, their air passages are blocked. They can respond very effectively to alert the mother to potential danger, and they have the physical skills to maneuver out of danger, under normal circumstances. That being said, modern societies and the objects on which we sleep and the social and physical conditions within which bed-sharing can and often does occur especially among the urban poor forces professionals to be very guarded when discussing bed-sharing and/or co-sleeping. The truth is that there is no one outcome (good or bad) that can be associated with co-sleeping in the form of "bed-sharing, but rather a range of outcomes (from potentially beneficial to dangerous and risky) depending on the overall circumstances within which the co-sleeping takes place.

For example, the condition of the sleeping surface - the bed (in Western cultures) and the condition and frame of mind of the adult co-sleeper (s), and the purposes for co-sleeping --are very important in assessing the relative safety, dangers or potential benefits of sleeping with your infant or child. During my many years of studying infant-parent co-sleeping/bed-sharing, I am unaware of even one instance in which, under safe social and physical conditions, a mother, aware that her infant was in bed with her, ever suffocated her infant. But just as is true for other aspects of infancy or childhood important precautions need to be taken if families elect to bed-share For example, bed-sharing should be avoided entirely if the mother smokes (either throughout her pregnancy or after) as maternal smoking combined with bed-sharing increases the chances of SIDS.

While there is evidence that accidental suffocation can and does occur in bed-sharing situations, in the overwhelming number of cases (sometimes in 100% of them) in which a real overlay by an adult occurs, extremely unsafe sleeping condition or conditions can be identified including situations where adults are not aware that the infant was in the bed, or an adult sleeping partners who are drunk or desensitized by drugs, or indifferent to the presence of the baby. In these cases often the suffocation occurs while the parent and infant sleep on a sofa or couch together.

In my own work I stress that a distinction must be made between the inherently protective and beneficial nature of the mother-infant co-sleeping/breast feeding context, and the conditions (of the mother and the physical setting including equipment) within which it occurs - which can range from extremely safe to unsafe and risky.

While mother-infant co-sleeping evolved biologically, it is wise to recall that beds did not; whether sleeping in a crib or in the adult (parental) bed, the mattress should be firm and it should fit tightly against the headboard so that an infant cannot during the night fall into a ledge face down and smother. Since contact with other bodies increases the infant's skin temperature, babies should be wrapped lightly in the co-sleeping environment especially, and attention should be given to the room temperature. Obviously if the room temperature is already warm (say above 70 degrees F, the baby should not be covered with any heavy blankets, sheets or other materials A good test is to consider whether you are comfortable; if you are, then the baby probably is as well.

I would avoid co-sleeping with a baby on a couch as too many that I know of slipped face down into the cracks between the pillow seats and were compressed against the back wall of the couch, or fell face down into the back part of the couch and suffocated. Personally, I would also avoid co-sleeping on waterbed, although there may be some instances they are firm enough and lack deep crevices (around the frame) that could be deemed safe.

Under no circumstances should the baby sleep on top of a pillow, or have its' head covered by a blanket. Moreover, if another adult is in the bed, the second adult should be aware (made aware of) the presence of the baby, and it should never be assumed that the other adult knows that the baby is present. Parents should discuss with each other whether they both feel comfortable with the baby being in the bed and with them. I always suggest that if parents elect to co-sleep in the form of bed-sharing each parent (and not just one) should agree to be responsible for the baby. Such a decision, by both sleeping adults, maximizes attention to the presence of the infant.

Toddlers or other little children should not be permitted to sleep in the adult bed next to an infant as toddlers are unaware of the dangers of suffocation. Moreover, it is safer not to permit an infant and a toddler to sleep alone together in the same bed.

Finally, it is not a pleasant thought to consider, but I always think that it is important to consider if, by chance, an infants died from SIDS while sleeping next to you, would you assume that you suffocated the infant, or would you know that you did not, that the infant died independently of your presence? If you are unable to believe that a SIDS could occur independent in the bed-sharing or bed-sharing/breast feeding context, just as it can under perfectly safe solitary sleeping conditions, then perhaps it might be best to have the your infant cosleep next to you on a separate surface, rather than actually in your bed. Regardless of what you decide, it is important to consider the possibility, no matter how remote and unlikely such a scenario may be. That SIDS can, indeed, occur, where safe bed-sharing, breast feeding and complete nurturing and care for the infant has occurred, makes this question worth discussing amongst you and your partner.

Let me end on a positive note: all else being safe, bed-sharing among nonsmoking mothers who sleep on firm mattresses specifically for purposes of breast feeding, may be the most ideal form of bed-sharing where both mother and baby can benefit by, among other things, the baby getting more of mother's precious milk and both mothers and babies getting more sleep - two findings which emerged from our own studies.

**Learn more about co-sleeping** at the following websites:

The Natural Child Project, co-sleeping articles:
http://www.naturalchild.org/articles/sleeping.html

Mothering Magazine, articles on the family bed:
http://www.mothering.com/search/node/co-sleeping

Attachment Parenting International, co-sleeping information and advocacy:
http://www.attachmentparenting.org/support/resources.php#night

Co-sleeping on Wikipedia:
http://en.wikipedia.org/wiki/Co-sleeping

# SIDS

## What Every Parent Should Know About SIDS

By OneStepAhead.Com

Every new parent needs to learn about SIDS, or Sudden Infant Death Syndrome. And while the numbers are decreasing, about 2,500 infants in the United States still die from SIDS each year. Scientists don't yet know how to prevent it, but there are specific precautions you can take to reduce its risk.

## What Is SIDS?

Experts define SIDS as the sudden, unexplained death of an otherwise healthy infant under the age of one. It occurs when babies are sleeping, which is why it is also referred to as "crib death." It is the leading cause of death in infants under age 12 months, and occurs most often in infants between the ages of 2-4 months, according to the American Academy of Pediatrics.

## What Causes SIDS?

Although it's been the subject of many studies, researchers still don't know what causes SIDS. One thing we do know: back-sleeping babies are at less risk of SIDS than babies who sleep on their tummies or sides. The incidence of SIDS deaths has declined by more than 50% since 1994, when America's first "Back to Sleep" campaign was launched.

There are several theories regarding the possible causes of SIDS. One is that bedding around babies' faces can limit air supply, forcing them to re-breathe exhaled air, which is low in oxygen and high in carbon dioxide, a toxin. Another is that SIDS babies may not have the ability to wake themselves when their air is limited, due to a deficit in a part of the brain called the arcuate nucleus.

While the research continues, most experts agree that it may be a combination of factors—rather than a single cause—that contributes to SIDS. That's why it's important to take every precaution when laying your baby down to sleep.

## Steps You Can Take Against SIDS

There are a number of precautions you can take to make baby's sleep environment safer, including these recommendations offered by the American Academy of Pediatrics (AAP), National Institute of Child Health and Human Development, and the American SIDS Institute:

- ☐ ALWAYS place your infant on his or her back to sleep, even for a short nap. Make sure baby's caregivers also follow this practice. A baby who sleeps on its back at home, but on its stomach elsewhere (a practice known as "unaccustomed tummy sleeping") is at a much greater risk of SIDS, according to the AAP.

- ☐ Make sure baby is sleeping on a firm crib mattress, not in an adult bed or on cushioned furniture.

- ☐ Remove all soft and loose items from the crib, including blankets, pillows, and stuffed animals.

- ☐ Do not allow baby to become overheated. Keep the room at a temperature that's comfortable for a lightly-clothed adult. Do not over-bundle baby.

- ☐ Place the crib in an area that's always smoke-free. Better yet, make baby's world smoke-free. According to the American SIDS Institute, the greater an infant's exposure to tobacco smoke, the greater the risk of SIDS.

- ☐ Have baby sleep in your room, secure in his cradle, bassinet, or co–sleeper. Sleeping in the same room as a parent reduces an infant's risk of SIDS. However, babies should not sleep unprotected in adult beds.

- ☐ Breastfeed. Studies suggest that breastfeeding may reduce the risk of SIDS, possibly by helping protect babies from infection.
- ☐ Offer baby a pacifier at bedtime. Some studies show a lower rate of SIDS among babies who suck on pacifiers.
- ☐ Don't rely on products that claim to prevent SIDS. Products like monitors will alert you to baby's noises and movements, but don't eliminate the risk of SIDS. It's important for parents to remain vigilant.

## Don't Forget Tummy Time

There is one drawback to back-sleeping: it can lead to positional plagiocephaly, or the development of a flat spot on the back of baby's head. To avoid this problem, experts recommend plenty of supervised tummy time, which also helps build neck and torso strength. They also suggest changing babies' position during waking hours, and varying the angle of baby's head while lying on his back.

## The Risk is Real

As heartbreaking as it is, a parent can take every possible precaution and still lose a child to SIDS. Sometimes it is simply unpreventable. It is not in any way the parent's fault.

It is hard to imagine a more devastating tragedy, or one that's harder to come to terms with. That's why SIDS support groups and organizations are so important. To find a support group near you, visit the First Candle/SIDS Alliance or The SIDS Network.

## More Information

These are excellent resources for more detailed information about SIDS:

- ☐ American Academy of Pediatrics – http://www.aap.org
- ☐ National Institute of Child Health & Human Development – www.nichd.nih.gov/sids
- ☐ American SIDS Institute – www.sids.org

☐ The National SIDS/Infant Death Resource Center – www.sidscenter.org

☐ First Candle/SIDS Alliance – www.sidsalliance.org

☐ The SIDS Network – www.SIDS-network.org

One Step Ahead supports SIDS research and is a long-time sponsor of First Candle/SIDS Alliance. In time, medical researchers will unlock the mystery of SIDS. But until that day comes, it's important for parents to educate themselves and take every precaution to protect their babies. For more information visit http://www.onestepahead.com or email customerservice@onestepahead.com

## Summary

Luckily our industry has been blessed with a variety of parent educators and sleep consultants whose mission is to help expecting and new parents obtain quality sleep, especially after a baby is born. Take the time to get to know all the sleep consultants and parent educators in your client's community. Keep track of all the local class offerings on sleep and do your best to attend them. Additionally you should inform your clients of all their sleeping options. Sleep is one area that a large percentage of your clients will request more education on.

## Resources

**Institute of Naturopathic Sleep**
http://www.naturalsleepmedicine.net

**Angelique Millette, Parent Coach and Sleep Consultant**
http://www.angeliquemillette.com/

**Additional Online Education**
http://internationalsleep.org
http://maternityinstitute.com
http://www.helpguide.org/life/sleeping.htm
http://www.sleepfoundation.org/
http://www.sleepeducation.com/

# Health, Fitness,
# and Nutrition Basics

I am extremely passionate about holistic health, fitness, and nutrition during and after a woman's pregnancy. It is the foundation of my business, and what continues to be the driving force behind The Baby Planner. Health for me is truly a luxury. It is priceless. As a mom, certified personal trainer, yoga, pilates, and wellness coach, I fully understand the value and priority of a women's health and self-confidence during her pregnancy.

Pregnancy is actually a wonderful opportunity to get healthy. It can be a catalyst that pushes a woman into healthy habits that are long lasting—habits that may last for the rest of her life. It is common for a woman during pregnancy to feel physically and emotionally drained due to the requirements of the body during this special time of growth. As a result, health and nutrition demands special attention during pregnancy, and throughout the months of nursing.

Here are the basics, but I encourage you to learn as much as you can. You may even decide to get certified as a professional in a variety of fields that exist in the Health and Fitness Industry. It would be a huge asset to your baby planning career as the health of the baby is the most popular and primary concern of most of your clients.

## Stress

We all know stress is bad, but until recently we didn't exactly know why it harms the baby. In October of 2009, The UK Times reported on new research which shows exactly how stress can harm a baby's development and how it can lead to long-term problems.

According to research by a professor of perinatal psychobiology, Vivette Glover, maternal anxiety affects the placenta by reducing the activity of the main barrier enzyme that hinders the hormone cortisol from reaching the fetus. The babies of women who were stressed had a lower birth weight, lower IQ, slower cognitive development and more anxiety than those born to the other women in the studies.

Research by Sir Michael Rutter, a leading child psychologist, has produced evidence that mental health is worse in children today than in the past. This may be because women are more stressed during pregnancy, more likely to be single, and less likely to be supported by their families.

Taking care of ourselves during pregnancy could be the most important thing for our children's health going forward.

Here are some key recommendations from scientists and doctors:

- ☐ Eat foods containing B vitamins to increase your levels of the anti-stress hormone serotonin.
- ☐ Adequate sunshine during the day also greatly increases seretonin levels.
- ☐ Exercise is proven to ease tension. Swimming is perfect, as your bump is supported by the water. Walking barefoot in the grass is also very calming.
- ☐ Ask your employer if you can avoid rush hours by starting and finishing work earlier. Midwives say commuting is a big source of stress.

Some new research from the Harvard Medical School in Boston was also just made public. They presented their findings of a study done on a group of urban moms and their babies. They surveyed more than 387 mothers with a questionnaire about stress levels to assess the following areas of their lives:

* financial stress
* health and well-being
* relationships
* home environment
* community safety

The research found that the babies born to stressed out mothers had more immunoglobulin E (IgE) in their blood at birth than babies who are born to mothers with normal stress levels. IgE is an immune system antibody that indicates an immune system response. Research suggests that these babies are more likely to have asthma or allergies because Immunoglobulin E (IgE) is an antibody involved in allergic and asthmatic reactions.

## Exercise

Exercise and Nutrition help to reduce stress levels for mom as well as support the healthy development of the baby. Natural and simple reminders such as staying hydrated, taking walks, and getting at least 20 minutes of sunlight every day, are tips you can pass on to your clients. Highly qualified fitness trainers and nutritionists can provide safe and effective programs and tailored advice for your clients. I highly recommend finding the top fitness trainers and nutritionists in your area to network with so you can refer your clients when the time comes. Remember to inform your client's midwife or obstetrician if she starts on either program.

Below are some benefits of exercise during and after pregnancy:

## Benefits of Exercise

- ☐ Reduction in stress levels
- ☐ Increase of energy
- ☐ Alleviates discomforts of pregnancy
- ☐ Enhances mood and self-image
- ☐ Helps you quickly return to your pre-pregnancy weight
- ☐ Provides good preparation for labor
- ☐ Makes sleeping easier

Below are contributions from industry top experts in pre and postnatal yoga, pilates, and diastasis recti.

## PreNatal Yoga

**Prenatal Yoga May Result in Less Labor Pain, Shorter Labor**
by Debra Flashenberg CD(DONA), LCCE, E-RYT 500

For years I have been asked to substantiate with a clinical study the idea that prenatal yoga helps pregnant women during labor. So you can imagine my excitement when I was reading from the *Journal of Perinatal Education* and found this article doing just that. Please read and enjoy the article. This may help remind you, each time you step on your mat, that you are not just taking care of your body in the present, but you are benefiting yourself in the future.

*Chuntharapat, S., Petpichetchian, W., & Hatthakit, U. (2008). Yoga during pregnancy: Effects on maternal comfort, labor pain and birth outcomes. Complementary Therapies in Clinical Practice, 14(2), 105-115. [Abstract]

Summary: In this trial conducted in Thailand, nulliparous pregnant women without previous yoga experience were randomly assigned to practice prenatal yoga (n=37) or to usual care (n=37). The yoga group attended a series of six 1-hour yoga classes every two weeks in the final trimester and were given a booklet and audio tape for self-study, which they were encouraged to practice at least three times per week. Daily diaries kept by participants and weekly phone contact from researchers helped ensure compliance. Participants in both groups completed a prenatal questionnaire to assess anxiety and collect demographic data.

Once in labor, pain and comfort were assessed every 2 hours in the first stage of labor (for a maximum of three measurements) and again 2 hours postpartum using multiple pain-measurement instruments that have previously been validated for use in laboring women. The researchers controlled for maternal age, marital status, education level, religion, income, and maternal trait anxiety.

Data were available for 33 of 37 women assigned to each group but the researchers provide no explanation for this attrition. Although this omission limits the reliability of the study, the strength and consistency of the researchers' findings suggest that attrition probably did not significantly alter results. The experimental group (yoga group) had significantly less pain and more comfort than the control group at each of the three measurement intervals during labor and at the postpartum measurement. This finding was consistent and significant across all three pain main measurement instruments used.

The researchers do not present data about mode of birth. However, the length of the first stage of labor and total duration of labor were significantly shorter in the yoga group (mean length of first stage = 520 minutes in yoga group versus 660 minutes in control group; mean total time in labor 559 minutes in yoga group versus 684 minutes in control group). There were no differences in length of second stage of labor, pethidine usage or dose given, augmentation of labor, newborn weight, or Apgar scores. Epidural analgesia was not mentioned so presumably it was not available.

Significance for Normal Birth: This study provides evidence that regular yoga practice in the last 10-12 weeks of pregnancy improves maternal comfort in labor and may facilitate labor progress. The researchers offer several theories for these effects. First, yoga involves synchronization of breathing awareness and muscle relaxation which decrease tension and the perception of pain. Second, yoga movements, breathing, and chanting may increase circulating endorphins and serotonin, "raising the threshold of mind-body relationship to pain" (p. 112).

Third, practicing yoga postures over time alters pain pathways through the parasympathetic nervous system, decreasing one's need to actively respond to unpleasant physical sensations.

Prenatal strategies that help women prepare emotionally and physically for labor may help reduce pain and suffering and optimize wellbeing in childbirth by providing coping skills and increasing self-confidence and a sense of mastery. More research is needed to confirm the findings of this study. However, yoga's many health benefits and the lack of evidence that yoga is harmful in pregnancy or birth provide justification for encouraging interested women to incorporate yoga into their preparations for childbirth.

## Debra Flashenberg, CD(DONA), LCCE, E-RYT 500

Debra is a graduate of the Boston Conservatory of Music with a degree in Musical Theater. She has spent most of her life performing and was introduced to yoga through a choreographer in 1997. After several years as a yoga student, she decided to continue her education and became certified as a Bikram Yoga instructor. In 2001 Debra headed out to Seattle to study with renowned prenatal yoga teacher Colette Crawford, R.N., at the Seattle Holistic Center. Debra has received a certificate for Vinyasa Yoga from Shiva Rea, with whom she continues to study. Debra has also studied the Maternal Fitness Method with Julie Tupler. In 2004, Debra completed the OM Yoga advanced teacher training with Cyndi Lee. Debra currently studies with Cyndi Lee, Genevieve Kapular, and Susan "Lip" Orem.

After being witness to several "typical" hospital births, Debra felt it was important to move beyond the yoga room and be present in the birthing room. In 2003, Debra attended her first birth as a DONA certified labor support doula. In that short period of time, Debra has attended about 75 births. She is continuously in awe of the beauty and brilliance of birth.

In 2006, Debra received her certification as a Lamaze Certified Childbirth Educator. In September of 2007, Debra completed a Midwife Assistant Program with Ina May Gaskin, Pamela Hunt and many of the other Farm Midwives at The Farm Midwifery Center in Tennessee. Most recently, Debra had the incredible experience of helping one of her clients give birth on the bathroom floor. Luckily, the EMS arrived seconds before the baby did!

Drawing on her experience as a prenatal yoga teacher, labor support doula and childbirth educator, Debra looks to establish a safe and effective class for pregnancy and beyond.

http://www.prenatalyogacenter.com

The Prenatal Yoga Center is the first yoga center in New York City to focus on moms and moms-to-be. Over the past 7 years, over 6000 women have come through our door to take classes and workshops. Based on the Upper West Side of Manhattan, we offer Prenatal Yoga, Postnatal Yoga, Mommy and Me, Infant Massage, Baby Sign Language and Music for Babies. We also offer Moms-to-Be and New Moms Support Groups as well as a variety of events and workshops including Childbirth Education, Infant CPR and Safety, Partner Yoga & Massage, Caring for Newborn and Breastfeeding.

## PreNatal Pilates

**About Pilates** by Carolyne Anthony

**Pilates for Pre-Conception, Pregnancy, Birthing, and Beyond**
Are you planning for a natural labor and delivery? Have you considered Pilates as a part of your birthing experience? For many women, the thought of utilizing Pilates as a method to facilitate natural birth never would have crossed their minds. Here are some reasons why they may want to think again.

## What is Pilates?

Pilates is a form of exercise that focuses on whole body integration to strengthen, stretch, and correct the body's natural alignment. It is a combination of fluid movements put together to suit an individual's needs, experience, and goals. Practicing Pilates can involve one or a combination of modalities, which include mat exercises, equipment such as a ball or bands, and Pilates specific machines.

## Why try Pilates?

Pilates can be beneficial for the health and strength of any person, and is especially useful for women before, during, and after pregnancy. It can be specifically tailored to help prepare a pregnant woman for and assist in labor and birth by opening the pelvis and emphasizing optimal pelvic alignment. Not only does Pilates strengthen the physical body, it also strengthens the mind-body connection, which is a vital component to a natural labor and delivery. Utilizing the breath to move the body's energies, Pilates is a great way to release tension and stress, both of which can enhance pain in childbirth, stall labor, and even contribute to infertility for women trying to get pregnant. Pilates can be a great way to rebuild strength from the inside out after birth, and can be started as soon as the baby is born. In fact, the sooner Pilates exercises are taken up after birth, the better the results will be!

Pilates is a very safe and effective form of exercise, which can be started even after becoming pregnant. To find a Pilates instructor who is specially trained in the areas of pregnancy, birthing, and post-partum strengthening and healing, visit our Directory. To find more information about Pilates and how it can help you, view our Articles section, read our Blog, or ask a question in our Forum.

**Carolyne Anthony** has been in the Dance, Fitness and Pilates world for over 30 years. She trained as a professional dancer in London, England in the late 1970's. She obtained her teaching diploma in1982 and went on to dance professionally in Europe, Asia and Africa. She remains a member of the Royal Academy of Dancing and an Associate of The Imperial Society of Teacher of Dance. Carolyne was introduced to Pilates in 1983, at the prompting of her Jazz instructor. She found Alan Herdman and continued to learn from him until she left for the USA.

In the 80's as a newcomer to the USA her focus turned to fitness as the aerobics boom began to hit. Carolyne certified with AFAA and the AEA as a group fitness instructor and went on to study the PACE (People with Arthritis Can Exercise) program. She put all this knowledge to good use as an instructor with the New England Health and Racquet Clubs.

While living in Connecticut Carolyne also joined the faculty of the Hartford Conservatory of Music and Dance, teaching ballet, jazz and pedagogy to the diploma students. She danced with the New England Dance Theater and helped found and became the Artistic Director of the Enfield Civic ballet Company. It was during this time that she became pregnant with her first child.

Carolyne was dismayed to learn that no matter how many certifications or diplomas she had acquired, nothing had given her any information on how to exercise during her pregnancy. Being too scared to do what she was doing, Carolyne opted to stop moving during the pregnancy. Finding herself with a unrecognizable body after the birth of her daughter, she busied herself with designing an exercise program that was both safe and beneficial for pregnant women. Her goal was to prepare the body for the birth, not just to be fit. Through the course of her next two pregnancies, Carolyne refined her skills and knowledge and today you have the highly successful Pre and post natal Pilates Specialist™ programs.

These programs and many of The Center's workshops have been included in international conferences such as Body Mind Spirit and Pilates on Tour.

Carolyne works from a holistic point of view, seeing the body as an amazing instrument that needs the correct attention in order to work properly. Her efforts to make this possible for her clients has led her to study for her Masters in Natural Health, become certified as a Birth Doula and to learn other healing modalities . Currently Carolyne is a level two Reiki practitioner, Level 1 Myofascial release practitioner (John Barnes approach) and an Esoteric Healer. She is certified by Polestar, BasiPilates and PhysicalMInd. Carolyne is on the faculty for Balanced Body University and is part of BasiPilates Advanced Education Course™.

Today TheCenter for women's Fitness has 12 host studios around the world, 10 faculty members and more than 300 certified teachers teaching the method. The Center continues to expand. For more information visit: http://www.thecenterforwomensfitness.com/

## Diastasis Recti by Julie Tupler, RN, CCE

### Checking For Diastasis

A diastasis can be checked both during and after pregnancy. The object is to determine how many fingers will fit in the space between the two recti muscles. You also want to determine the condition of the connective tissue. The deeper your fingers will go towards your spine, the weaker the connective tissue. If you feel a pulsing while you are checking, this is a sign of very weak connective tissue. Start with your middle three fingers. You will also want to measure your waist before you start on the program. This measurement will get smaller as the muscles start coming together.

Lie on your back with your knees bent. Place your fingers in your belly button. Your fingers should be pointing in the direction of your toes.
Relax your abdominal muscles and lift your head. If you are holding your abdominal muscles in as you check it will give you a false reading as this will make the diastasis appear smaller. The muscles will get closer together the higher you lift your head.

To get a more accurate reading, it is important to check yourself when you first start feeling the muscles coming together. You might have to come up and down a few times so you can feel how the muscles work. If you don't feel the two ridges of the muscles with 3 fingers you may have to put more fingers in. If you see the football- like ridge you should start by using 4 to 5 fingers. You may even have to use 2 hands if your diastasis is very large.

### Definition of Diastasis

A diastasis is a separation of the rectus abdominis (outermost abdominal muscles). When these muscles separate the connective tissue that joins them stretches sideways. The more it stretches sideways the thinner and weaker it becomes.

### Cause of Diastasis

Forceful forward pressure on the weak spot (belly button) of the connective tissue from:

1.  Doing crunches

2. Pilates 100's
3. Pregnancy

Beer belly or "guy gut"

## Effect of Diastasis on the Body

The function of the outermost muscle is to support your back and your organs. When the muscles separate this support system is weakened causing low back pain and the "mummy tummy." The mummy tummy is actually your protruding organs. They are protruding because they are being supported by a thin (saran wrap-like) piece of connective tissue instead of your muscles if they were together. If there is trauma to the abdominal area and the connective tissue is torn away from the muscle, a ventral hernia can develop and surgery will be required.

## Effect of Closing Diastasis on the Body

Closing the diastasis will give you a flat belly, a smaller waist and relieve any back problems you are having.

## Time Period to Close a Diastasis

The amount of time it takes to close a diastasis depends on two things:

1. Your particular diastasis
2. Your commitment to doing the 4 step research-based Tupler Technique program

To determine the severity of your diastasis you need to know two things:

1. The distance between the two muscles. The wider the diastasis the longer it takes to close it.
2. The condition of the connective tissue. The further your fingers go into your belly, the weaker the connective tissue. The weaker the connective tissue the longer it takes to heal. As the muscles come together the connective tissue will become shallower.

We recommend making a six week commitment to the program. You may not entirely close the diastasis, but you will definitely see improvement with it getting smaller. Start the program by measuring the diastasis and your waist. After six weeks measure again and you will be pleasantly surprised! Our new *Tupler Technique Guidebook* gives a chart of all the exercises you need to be doing each day and the progression each week for six weeks.

**A diastasis can be closed no matter when or how it was created with the Tupler Technique.**

## Julie Tupler, RN, CCE

Julie is a Registered Nurse, certified childbirth educator and fitness instructor. She developed the *Maternal Fitness*® Program in 1990 and has been working with pregnant women and new moms ever since. She is on the advisory board of *Fit Pregnancy* and the Women's Sports Foundation. She is the author of two books, *Maternal Fitness*® and *Lose Your Mummy Tummy*. She is the producer of the *Maternal Fitness*® and Lose Your Mummy Tummy DVDs and has developed the Diastasis Rehab ™ splint.

She is an expert on diastasis recti and has developed the research-based Tupler Technique to close a diastasis no matter when or how it was created. She trains medical and fitness professionals with her Tupler Technique Training for Treatment of Diastasis Recti. She speaks frequently at conferences throughout the U.S

Dr. Oz calls her an expert on diastasis recti. New York Magazine calls her the guru for pregnant women. She has been featured on many national television programs such as the Today Show, Regis & Kelly as well as in many fitness, medical, and women's health magazines. Elle Macpherson (who pushed her baby out in 20 minutes) is a big fan of her program and wrote the forward for the Lose Your Mummy Tummy book.

For more information visit: http://www.diastasisrehab.com

## Nutrition

The Expectant Mother's Guide states the following:

*"Proper nutrition during pregnancy has been shown to reduce the risk of birth defects in babies and chronic diseases in adulthood such as*

*heart disease, type 2 diabetes, high blood pressure, and high cholesterol. Likewise, babies born to mothers who gain excessive amounts of pregnancy weight are at increased risk for childhood obesity.*

*A healthy diet helps mothers avoid pregnancy complications such as anemia, high blood pressure, and gestational diabetes. Good nutrition may also minimize morning sickness, fatigue, and constipation. And mothers who eat sensibly during pregnancy are more likely to return to their pre-pregnancy weight sooner. "*

Suggestions:

- ☐ Eat a variety of fresh, unrefined foods
- ☐ Supplement with DHA and eat a diet high in fatty fish
- ☐ Supplement with a high quality Pre-natal vitamin from whole-food sources
- ☐ Fresh fruits and vegetables are always better than canned or frozen
- ☐ Stay hydrated
- ☐ The vitamin D produced from sun exposure aids in the absorption of many vitamins and minerals

## DHA

DHA is an important building block of pre-natal nutrition. This fatty acid is often overlooked by mothers and health care providers, and is quite possibly the most important nutrient expectant mothers don't know about. If taken during pregnancy, it may help lower the risks of post-partum depression and pre-mature birth. In a survey of expecting women, more than half of them did not know about the need for DHA, a critical nutrient in the development and health of the baby's brain, heart and eyes. DHA Omega-3 is also important for a woman's health throughout life.

## Sunshine

Vitamin D is produced when sunlight strikes the skin. Vitamin D has been shown to protect against serious health concerns such as: cardiovascular diseases, autoimmune disorders, many types of cancer (including breast, colon and prostate), diabetes, mental health problems (such as depression and bipolar disorder), muscle disorders, and gum health.

Vitamin D's role in muscle function was highlighted in a new study showing that low levels of this nutrient during pregnancy makes a woman four times more likely to have a c-section. The same researchers were also surprised by separate findings showing that seventy-five percent of the women in the study (and their babies) had low vitamin D levels, even though they had been taking prenatal vitamins and drinking vitamin D-fortified milk during their pregnancy. Add this to a new study from Turkey--which found that infants with low vitamin D levels are more vulnerable to developing respiratory infections---and you can see why getting sunshine is critical.

A recent batch of research involving vitamin D, cancer, and UV rays from the sun, showed that vitamin D from the sun was linked to lower levels of colon and breast cancers, as well as ovarian and kidney cancers, and non-Hodgkin lymphoma. It seems that the benefits of sunshine are just beginning to be discovered.

## Pre-eclampsia+ Sunshine

According to a new study conducted by researchers at the University of Pittsburgh School of Health Sciences, pregnant women who are vitamin D deficient have *five times* the risk of suffering a potentially fatal condition known as preeclampsia. This condition occurs in approximately 7 percent of all first-time pregnancies.

Preeclampsia is generally involves high blood pressure combined with elevated protein levels in the urine, and may also involve the swelling of the hands and feet. Preeclampsia can cause damage to the kidneys, liver, and vessels. In some cases, it progresses into eclampsia, a potentially fatal condition that can cause seizures and severe damage to the blood, organs, lungs, and nervous system. Eclampsia may be to blame for 70 percent of all pregnancy deaths in Third World countries. That is a staggering figure.

## Excessive weight gain

We all know some women gain more than others, and you may have observed, often times heavier women have heavier babies. Now, according to a study at the Harvard Medical School, these women may not only have heavier babies, but bigger teenagers, too.

Using data of almost 12,000 children and teenagers, the study found that those whose mothers had put on more than the recommended amount of weight while going through pregnancy had a 42% higher chance of being obese later in life.

Pregnant women who are obese are significantly more likely to give birth to children with birth defects than women who maintain normal weight, according to a study conducted by researchers from Newcastle University and published in the *Journal of the American Medical Association*.

They found that obese women had more than twice the risk of having a child with a neural tube defect, such as spinal bifida, than women with a normal body mass. These obese women also had a significantly higher risk of bearing children with cleft lips and heart defects.

## Caffeine

Drinking as little as ten ounces of coffee per day may double a pregnant woman's risk of miscarriage, according to a new study conducted by Kaiser Permanente researchers. This study was just published in the *Journal of Obstetrics and Gynecology*. Women who never had caffeine only had a 12.5 percent chance of miscarriage, while the women who drank 200 milligrams or more of caffeine per day had a 24.5 percent miscarriage rate.

You can always switch to decaf, but still be careful since even decaf coffee contains fairly high quantities of caffeine. This varies from brand to brand.

## Acupuncture

Below is an article contribution by Chalita Photikoe, who shares with us how acupuncture can be beneficial to treat common problems that occur throughout pregnancy.

## Acupuncture & Pregnancy

Acupuncture is a safe, comfortable and cost effective treatment for many of the problems that commonly develop in pregnancy. Acupuncture is the practice of inserting tiny needles into specific points to restore the bodys' balance of energy or qi (chee). While many medications are not safe to take during pregnancy, acupuncture and herbs are a natural way to maintain health and comfort for both mother and baby. Acupuncture during the first trimester focuses on setting the foundation for a healthy pregnancy. Treatments are given to prevent miscarriage and to address any early pregnancy symptoms, such as nausea and fatigue.

Acupuncture during the second trimester focuses on addressing imbalances that result from the growing fetus such as heartburn, constipation and hemorrhoids. During the third trimester, treatments prepare the body for labor and delivery, but also work to relive conditions such as sciatica, carpal tunnel, and high blood pressure. Treatments for breech presentation and to induce labor are also available near the end of the third term. Studies show that women who receive regular acupuncture during the third trimester typically have shorter and more productive labor.

Chalita Photikoe, L.Ac. is a licensed acupuncturist, herbalist, and yoga instructor with extensive clinical training in fertility, obstetrics and pediatrics. She completed her 4 years master's program in Traditional Chinese Medicine in 2004 from the Academy of Chinese Culture and Health Sciences in Oakland, CA. She teaches pre and post-natal yoga classes, yoga for conception, and workshops on holistic pediatrics and obstetrics. Chalita lives in San Rafael, CA with her husband and daughter Naia.

http://chalitaacupuncture.com/

## Postpartum Depression

As many as 80% of first time mothers experience postpartum blues. According to the American College of Obstetricians and Gynecologists, approximately 10% of women who have just given birth experience postpartum depression.

Many new moms feel happy one minute and sad the next. If your client feels better after a week or so, she probably just had the "baby blues." If it takes her longer to feel better, she may have postpartum depression.

Postpartum depression can make your client feel restless, anxious, fatigued and worthless. Some new moms worry they will hurt themselves or their babies. Unlike the "baby blues," postpartum depression does not go away quickly. Very rarely, new moms develop something even more serious. They may stop eating, have trouble sleeping and become frantic or paranoid. Women with this condition usually need to be hospitalized.

Researchers think that changes in your hormone levels during and after pregnancy may lead to postpartum depression. If you think she has it, refer her to a qualified healthcare professional.

Source: WomensHealth.gov

## What Causes Postpartum Depression?

There are a number of reasons why a woman may develop postpartum depression, although it is generally the result of a number of compounding factors rather than a single cause. Giving birth is a major life event and sometimes the stress of this huge change can be enough to trigger depression. Common causes may include a combination of the following factors:

- ☐ Hormonal changes
- ☐ Previous episodes or family history of depression
- ☐ Little support from family and/or friends
- ☐ Other life stressors such as marital problems or financial concerns
- ☐ Anxiety about the health of the baby
- ☐ Problems or complication during pregnancy or birth
- ☐ Exhaustion and lack of sleep or difficulty adjusting to disrupted sleep patterns
- ☐ Feeling overwhelmed by all the new responsibilities and demands or feeling doubtful of ability to make a good parent
- ☐ Feeling stressed by the sudden changes in home, work and personal routines.

Feeling a loss of identity and definition as the role of mother becomes predominant and may seem all-consuming. This may include feelings of loss for other roles such as the role of the sensual woman, career woman, wife and lover, or the loss of the ability to be spontaneous, independent and "free".

Source: http://www.nativeremedies.com

There are many alternative options to treat postpartum depression. It is not up to you to diagnose or prescribe treatment; however you can refer them to a qualified professional who is suited to attend to their needs. Get to know your client's local postpartum depression resources.

Below are examples of common treatments:

Drugs
Homeopathy
PsychoTherapy
Yoga/Meditation
Nutrition
Light Therapy
Exercise
Acupuncture
Doula Support

## Resources:

## Postpartum Support International

Postpartum Support International (PSI) was founded in 1987 by Jane Honikman and is headquartered in Santa Barbara, California. The purpose of the organization is to increase awareness among public and professional communities about the emotional changes that women experience during pregnancy and postpartum. Approximately 15% of all women will experience postpartum depression following the birth of a child. Up to 10% will experience depression or anxiety during pregnancy. When the mental health of the mother is compromised, it affects the entire family.

The organization has a volunteer coordinator in every one of the United States and in 26 countries. PSI disseminates information and resources through the volunteer coordinators, the website and an annual conference. The goal is to provide current information, resources, education, and to advocate for further research and legislation to support perinatal mental health.

http://postpartum.net/

## Postpartum Progress

Postpartum Progress offers the most comprehensive information available on the latest research, events and resources, as well as an unflinching look at what it is truly like to experience PPD. It features daily news and commentary, as well as a continuously-updated list of support groups around the country, personal stories from moms and fellow sufferers, and links to major support organizations and top treatment programs. Its readers include current sufferers, survivors, and clinicians from such institutions as Massachusetts General Hospital and Johns Hopkins.

Katherine Stone is a nationally-recognized, award-winning advocate for women with perinatal mood and anxiety disorders. In 2001 she suffered a devastating bout of postpartum obsessive-compulsive disorder after the birth of her first child. The feelings of fear, isolation and shame she experienced inspired her to take action to help others. In 2004 she created the blog Postpartum Progress, now the most widely-read blog in the United States on postpartum depression (PPD), postpartum anxiety, postpartum psychosis and other mental illnesses related to pregnancy and childbirth.

http://www.postpartumprogress.com/

# Postpartum
# and Newborn Care Basics

From my experience and research, the fourth trimester is a very critical time for the right support system to be in place. A newborn baby has just arrived is and a new life for expecting parents has just begun. Adjusting is not always so easy, however with the proper support system, the transition into parenthood can be made a lot smoother. As Beth Salerno explains below, preparing an after-birth plan can alleviate a lot of unnecessary stress.

## After-Birth Plan (Preparing For Postpartum)
By Beth Salerno, CPD

By the time most parents leave the hospital with their newborn, they are shocked and scared. In the rest of the world, families receive help and guidance during this process. Somehow, we fall short in preparing parents for life AFTER BIRTH.

How can we make the transition to motherhood easier? Realistic expectations are a good place to start. Learning to feed, soothe and care for your baby takes time. In the first days and weeks after birth, most moms are exhausted and emotionally raw. Recovering from childbirth, mastering breastfeeding and baby care is no small feat. But, with some preparation and help, you can alleviate a lot of unnecessary stress.

**Step one:** Build Your Support Network. You need to know other moms. Moms who have been where you're going and came out the other side. Moms who will be happy to discuss the color of your baby's poop! Make friends with the moms in your prenatal yoga class, childbirth class, and go to at least one La Leche League, Dar a Luz Network, or New Moms' Group while you're pregnant.

**Step Two:** Know your Resources! Even if you don't think you'll ever need them, it's much easier to gather the information before you find yourself in a crisis. Have the contact information on two breastfeeding professionals that do home visits in your area.

**Step Three:** Prepare your home. I'm not talking about the latest baby gadgets. I'm talking about staples and necessities. Think about all that you might use in a two-week period. Stock your freezer and start collecting Take-Out menus. Chances are, you'll be ravenous and have less than 20 minutes to prepare any meal! If you're only going to have limited help, check out laundry services and possibly housecleaning services.

**Step Four:** Scope out your team. Even if you're lucky enough to have a partner with family leave, you're going to need help. If you have a friend or relative who you communicate well with, figure out how much help they can offer. Delivering a few casseroles and helping with laundry, groceries, and giving you a break can be a lifeline. If no one you know fits the bill, consider hiring a Postpartum Doula. (Most Postpartum Doulas will also help you complete steps 1-3!)

**Step Five:** Take care of yourself! There will most likely be days when you don't get to shower or even brush your teeth. But, you have to make time to address your basic needs. You need to sleep more than you need a clean house. You need to get out for a walk, or visit with a friend, or do whatever makes you feel good. If you don't take care of yourself, you can't take care of your baby.

**Step Six:** Pace yourself. This is the biggest key and potential pitfall to postpartum recovery. Life After Birth is a marathon. If you push yourself too far, it could be days or weeks until you can get caught up again. This is NOT the time to test your limits. Take it slow. It's okay to ask for help. Eventually, you'll feel in control again. Right now, it's best to let go and try to accept life as it comes.

**Step Seven:** ENJOY! Your baby will only be this small for a short time. If you watch closely, you can almost see them growing! Motherhood is a learning process. You will make mistakes. You will learn on the job. If you can relax your expectations and pace yourself, you can truly enjoy your baby's first weeks.

Beth Salerno is a Certified Postpartum Doula, Breastfeeding Counselor, and mother of two. She co-leads the NJ Chapter of Dar a Luz Network (pregnancy/birthing/mothering support group). www.daraluznetwork.com Beth is happy to answer questions-so don't be shy! Send emails to: DoulaInfo@yahoo.com or visit her website: www.doula-care.com

## The First 8 Days of Being a Mom

One of my favorite postpartum books and a great resource for both baby planners and their clients, is a book by Gea Meijering, called *The First 8 Days of Being a Mom*. Gea's book is an absolute gift and provides every expecting, new mom, their loved ones, as well as all childbirth educators with valuable and practical information in a simple and easy to read format. Additionally, her book supplies a wealth of education and support not only on newborn care but also on new mom care. This is truly what makes her book unique. I also appreciate Gea's knowledge and honesty, and am excited to share her book with everyone.

*The First 8 Days of Being a Mom* is very useful for every woman who is going to have a baby! Whether they deliver their baby in the hospital, at home, or in a birthing center, with either a vaginal delivery or with a cesarean, it doesn't matter. Every new mother with a newborn baby can use the information. It is also educational for fathers and other family members.

Most importantly baby planners, can use it as a resource to help their clients prepare an after-birth plan.

For every woman's experience:

- ☐ Deliveries in the hospital or at home
- ☐ Vaginal birth or C-section
- ☐ Breast or bottle feeding

## About Gea

Gea Meijering gave birth to two sons on two different continents within twenty months. While going through that, she discovered that maternity care and recovery was organized totally different in the United States as compared to the Netherlands. Actually she was amazed that most new moms in the U.S. are on their own again very soon after their delivery. No time to recuperate from the delivery, or to learn and get used to the newborn. And no one to teach them the tricks of the trade. In the Netherlands every new mom gets a specialized nurse at home for the first 8 days after delivery.

Gea realized that the Dutch approach she experienced with her oldest son was very special. And that the book she used then, and used again the second time, would be a great help to all the moms in the US, as it was for her. It took her some time because she was busy with diapers, park days, painting, Spanish, and other very important stuff being a

New mom. But she is proud to announce the birth of The First 8 Days of Being a Mom.

And while in the process of making the book she discovered that publishing it herself would give her much more flexibility. Gea founded iCare Press, LLC to realize her goal and get this valuable information available to new moms in the US.

The past 7 years Gea has lived in the US busy with her mommy career. That gradually evolved from nursing to applying band-aids to volunteering in the classroom to starting up her own company. She grew up in the Netherlands, obtained a bachelor degree in tourism and recreation studies and worked as a marketing professional for more then 10 years at a national insurance company and international bank.

She moved to the US together with her husband for his new job.

Gea takes painting classes to satisfy her artistic drive, loves to travel and tries to work out on a regular basis. But most importantly she is committed to steering her two children through childhood, with bumps and bruises, laughs and joy along the way.

For more information visit http://www.thefirst8days.com

# Child Proofing Basics

Safety is truly a top concern and priority for expecting parents and providing them with general information, even in the form of a tip sheet, would be very valuable. You should get to know the baby proofers in your area, or may even consider getting certified as a baby proofer if you feel moved to get more involved in this area with your clients. Visit The International Association for Child Safety to learn more about how to obtain a child proofer certification or to find a certified child proofer at http://www.iafcs.org

The City of Mill Valley website provides an absolutely wonderful basic guideline contributed by the Mill Valley police department for Child Proofing, which I share with you below.

You can also find this guideline directly on their website at: http://www.cityofmillvalley.org/

**Child Proofing**

Many parents worry about how to protect their children from stranger abduction and violence, but they overlook one of the biggest threats to their child's safety and well-being - their own home. The Baby Center Medical Advisory Board reports that children ages one to four are more likely to be injured by fire, burns, drowning, choking, poisoning, or a fall (in that order) than by a stranger's violence. The following information is offered to assist in child proofing your home. But, as child proofer consultant and expert Anne Altman states: "The best child proofing device is supervision."

**Before Your Baby Arrives**

There is a lot to think about even before your child is born. Use this checklist to help prepare for your newborn:

- Install carbon monoxide detectors if you use gas or oil heat, or have an attached garage.
- Install and maintain smoke detectors, and check them monthly.
- Keep a fire extinguisher in the kitchen.
- Plan a fire escape route.
- Assemble a first-aid kit for babies. You may also want to take an infant CPR class.
- Post the emergency numbers for police, fire, and poison control next to your telephones.

- If you have flaking and peeling paint and suspect it may contain lead, have a professional remove or seal it.

- Put non-slip pads under area rugs that don't have non-skid backs.

- Set your water heater no higher than 120 degrees Fahrenheit.

- Purchase an infant bathtub with contours or other features that make it slip-resistant.

- Make sure your baby's bassinet has a sturdy bottom and a wide, stable base; the surfaces are smooth with no protrusions; the legs lock securely; and the mattress is firm and fits snugly.

- Purchase a changing table that has a safety strap. Place baby wipes and other toiletries within your reach but out of baby's. Make sure there is carpet or rug below the table in case of a fall.

- Purchase a car seat specifically for infants. Install it properly, in rear-facing position and in middle of back seat, if possible. Car seat installation checks are provided for free at your local Police Department.

**Before Your Baby Crawls**

On average, babies crawl at eight months, which means many get moving even earlier. A crawling baby will soon start pulling up, too, which means counters and other surfaces are no longer beyond reach. Use this checklist to help you prepare for your quick-moving youngster, and then crawl around on your hands and knees to see if you've missed anything:

- When bathing your child, fill the tub just enough to cover baby's legs (two or three inches of water); use warm, not hot water (96 to 100 degrees Fahrenheit is recommended); do not put your baby into a tub when the water is still running (the water temperature could change or the depth could become too high); never leave your baby unsupervised in the tub - not even for a few seconds (children can drown in less than an inch of water and in less than sixty seconds); and use a non-slip mat in the tub and covers for the spout and knobs.

- Install a toilet lock, as children are curious and top-heavy - if they lose their balance and fall in head first, they cannot get out.

- To prevent burns (the second leading cause of child injuries) don't carry hot food or drink and your baby at the same time; keep hot food and drink away from edges of tables and counters; don't hold your baby while cooking; turn pot handles toward the back of stove; secure the oven door with an appliance latch; and use a plastic stove guard that blocks access to burners and knob covers.

- Keep your baby in a rear-facing car seat until at least one year old AND 20 pounds.

- Don't use clothing with drawstrings, loose buttons or small beads and adornments.

- Keep drop side of crib up and locked when you are not in the room; don't leave toys in the crib when baby is sleeping; when baby pulls up, remove the bumper pads and put the mattress in lowest position; when baby gets up on hands and knees, remove mobiles and hanging toys.

- Replace electrical outlet plates with safety plates that automatically cover the outlet when the plug is removed (childproofing experts don't recommend outlet plugs since they are mouth-sized and can end up choking a child), or block the outlet with furniture; hide electrical cords behind furniture or use a hide-a-cord devise; and keep blow dryers, toasters and other often used appliances unplugged and out of reach.

- Use doorstops and door holders to protect your baby's fingers.

- To prevent falls never leave your baby alone on beds or sofas, in a bouncy chair or a high chair, on a changing table, or in any other spot from which a fall could occur. Use

- window guards and safety netting on windows, decks, and landings. If stair or landing railings have openings wider than four inches, block with plastic garden fencing, Plexiglas, or other material.

- Install gates to block stairways at bottom and top. Look for gates that your child cannot dislodge but that you can easily open and close. Choose a gate with a straight top edge and a rigid mesh screen. If the gate is constructed using vertical slats, make sure the spacing between each slat does not exceed 2 3/8 inches (a canned soda should not fit between the slats). Install a gate that screws to the wall instead of one that stays put by using pressure. Never use an expandable accordion-style gate that opens to form diamond-shaped spaces as this kind of gate can trap a child's head. Make sure the gate you purchase displays a seal from the Juvenile Products Manufacturers Association (JPMA).

- Install a fireplace grill and keep it in place; move gas fireplace keys, logs, matches, and fireplace tools out of reach.

- In the kitchen, keep knives, breakables, heavy pots, and other dangerous items locked up or out of reach. Put locks and latches on accessible cabinets and drawers that house unsafe items. Don't leave even small amounts of water, cleaning solutions, or other liquids in buckets or other containers. Keep trash cans in inaccessible cupboards or use ones with child-resistant covers. Secure the refrigerator with an appliance latch. Don't use tablecloths or placemats because a baby can pull them and what's on them down.

- Distract your baby from forbidden places by keeping one cupboard unlocked and filled with lightweight, baby-safe items.

- Cover or block access to hot radiators and floor heaters.

- Keep small fingers out of VCRs with a lock.

- Attach corner and edge guards on furniture; secure furniture that can topple and large and/or heavy objects (bookcases, chests of drawers) to the walls using L-brackets; keep television sets on low furniture, pushed back as far as possible against a wall; secure tall and easily tipped lamps behind furniture.

- Survey your house and move cleaning agents, medicines, vitamins, toiletries, mothballs, and other potentially toxic and harmful items out of reach or lock them away. Not all hazardous substances are obvious - for children under six, the number one killer is iron pills, followed by pesticides, kerosene, and lighter fluids.

- Remember that your purse or a visitor's purse can hold medicines, vitamins, and other toxic substances, so keep it from your baby's reach.

- Keep both ipecac and activated charcoal on hand in case of accidental poisoning, but don't use either without advice from your pediatrician, an emergency room doctor, or an expert at a poison control center.

- The safest toys are securely put together and in good condition; have no buttons, eyes, beads, ribbons, or other pieces that pull off and could cause choking; have no strings or cords longer than 12 inches; are appropriate for the child's age, size and physical skills; and can't be hung around the child's neck.

Source: Source: Mill Valley Police Dept;
http: //www.cityofmillvalley.org

## Crib Safety Standards recommended by American Academy of Pediatrics

In addition, make sure your crib meets these safety standards, as recommended by the AAP:

- Make sure that the spaces between the slats are no wider than 2 ⅜" apart.
- Choose a firm mattress, not a soft one. Never place baby on a water bed, sofa, or other soft surface.
- Avoid gaps between the mattress and crib walls. Try the " two fingers" test: if you can fit two fingers between the mattress and crib, it's not safe to use.
- Ensure the corner posts are level with the height of the end panels (or much higher, as on canopy-style beds). Otherwise clothing can get caught on the post.
- Don't choose a crib with decorative cutouts—a trapping hazard— on its end panels.
- Check the distance between the height of the crib sides and the mattress. When lowered, the crib sides should be at least 9" above the mattress. When raised, they should be at least 26" above the mattress in its lowest position.
- Make sure the drop sides can't be released by a child. The sides should feature a locking, hand-operated latch.
- Examine your crib frequently for hazards: loose parts, off-kilter joints, splinters, chipped paint. If you spot a problem, fix it immediately.
- When buying a new crib, look for Juvenile Product Manufacturers Association (JPMA) certification.

**Additional Resources**

**International Association for Child Safety**

The International Association for Child Safety (IAFCS) is a worldwide network of child safety professionals. IAFCS Members are recognized childproofing experts and are ready to help you make your home a safe place for your little one. You can search for a child proofer or pool installer in your town through their website. You can also obtain a professional certification through them.

http://www.iafcs.org/

**US Consumer Product Safety Commission**

The US Consumer Product Safety Commission offers a downloadable pdf file showcasing 12 safety devices to protect your children. You can download the file by visiting:

http://www.cpsc.gov/CPSCPUB/PUBS/252.pdf

**Safe Kids**

Safe Kids Worldwide is a global network of organizations whose mission is to prevent accidental childhood injury, a leading killer of children 14 and under. More than 450 coalitions in 16 countries bring together health and safety experts, educators, corporations, foundations, governments and volunteers to educate and protect families.

http://www.safekids.org/skwHome.html

**Safe Beginnings**

Safe Beginnings offers an abundance of baby proofing products

http://www.safebeginnings.com/

# Child Care Basics

An important part of your job may involve helping your clients find the proper care for their babies upon arrival or when they decide to return back to work. Most clients will not know the major differences between a baby nurse, post-partum doula, and a nanny. It is your job to understand each of these roles and educate your clients accordingly. It is also your job to develop strong relationships with childcare providers who will suit your client's needs and whom your client's can trust. Before you decide to fully take on the responsibility of hiring a doula, nanny, or baby nurse, you should consider all the legalities involved. You should also carefully think about involving your clients in each interview and have them make the final decision. This protects both you and your client. You'll definitely want to perform a background check for In-Home Child Care.

For example, in the state of California, if you place a caregiver in a family's home, you are required to ensure that the caregiver is either already registered with Trustline, or has applied to register at Trustline. Please note that Trustline supplements a separate background check, but should not be relied on as the sole source for background check information.

Partnering or working with a reputable staffing agency can be a tremendous asset for you. One such example of a distinguished agency here in the Bay Area is Town & Country Resources. They have been in business for the last twenty five years and have successfully matched more than 100,000 childcare and household staff with San Francisco Bay Area families. They provide a very helpful resource for conducting a thorough interview featured below. You can find more helpful tips by visiting their website at http://www.tandcr.com/

## Nanny Interviewer Guidelines

Town and Country Resources has developed the following list of questions for its' clients to help them conduct a thorough and thoughtful interview.

## Personal Background:

- ☐  What brought you to the area?
- ☐  What are your goals for the future?
- ☐  What do you enjoy doing in your spare time?

- [ ] What are your strengths and weaknesses?
- [ ] Tell me a little bit about your family background and childhood.
- [ ] Is there anything else you wish to tell me about yourself?

## Professional Experience:

- [ ] Tell me about your experience working in this field.
- [ ] How did you originally become interested in this work?
- [ ] What is your education or training in regards to this type of work?
- [ ] What were your responsibilities in your last position?
- [ ] What did you like most about your last position? What did you like least?
- [ ] Tell me about your relationship with your last employer.
- [ ] If asked for a reference, what would your last employer say about you?
- [ ] Do you have any special talents or interests to share with us?
- [ ] Have you ever been confronted with an emergency situation at work?

   -If so, how did you respond?

## Childcare Background:

- [ ] What is your education or training with regards to childcare?
- [ ] What ages of children have you worked with?
- [ ] What were your responsibilities in your last position?
- [ ] What kinds of activities did you do with the children in your last position?
- [ ] What did you like most about your last position? What did you like least?
- [ ] If asked for a reference, what would your last employer say about you?
- [ ] Do you have any special talents or interests to share with children? (e.g. do you play an instrument or sing?)
- [ ] What would a typical day be like for you and an infant/toddler etc.?

&#9633;    Discuss specifically what you expect the employee to do with your child(ren).

&#9633;    Discuss your child(ren)'s daily schedule.

&#9633; How have you set limits with child(ren) with whom you've worked?

&#9633; What is your philosophy on discipline?

   &#9633;    Discuss your family's thoughts on discipline and boundary setting.

&#9633; How would you reward a child for positive behavior?

&#9633; What do you see as your most important responsibility with a child this age?

   &#9633;    Discuss your own family's philosophy of raising children.

&#9633; Are you comfortable driving children?

   &#9633;    Discuss proper car safety such as car seats and seat belts.

## Household Duties:

&#9633; Are you comfortable cooking meals for the household? Child(ren)-only meals?

&#9633; Would you be comfortable running errands? Household errands? Child(ren)-only errands?

&#9633; Are you comfortable working around pets?

   &#9633;    Describe your housekeeping expectations.

## For Live-In:

&#9633; How do you anticipate spending your free time?

&#9633; Do you consider yourself a morning person or a night person?

&#9633; What is the longest stretch of time you have cared for children at one time?

&#9633; How much time each week do you spend watching television? On the internet?

&#9633; How do you spend your time on the weekends?

   &#9633;    Discuss if there will be a household curfew.

   &#9633;    Will this apply to the employee's days off?

## Hours, Salary and Benefits:

- ☐ How do you feel about working weekends? Evenings? Holidays?
    - ☐ Discuss the required hours of the position and any flexibility that is needed.
    - ☐ Discuss vacation, sick days and holidays.
- ☐ Are you open to travel? If yes, what limit might there be on the duration of travel?
- ☐ Do you have any evening commitments? If so, what time?
- ☐ If the employee is taking classes: Will the class schedule stay the same next quarter/semester?
- ☐ What length of commitment are you expecting?
    - ☐ - Discuss the official start date.
- ☐ What hourly, weekly or monthly salary is agreeable?
    - ☐ How often would it be paid?
    - ☐ Discuss which taxes are being withheld.
    - ☐ Discuss any benefits to be provided. (e.g. health insurance, car insurance, cell phone)
- ☐ Are you comfortable driving for work-related tasks?
    - ☐ Discuss whose car will be used.
    - ☐ If the employee's car is to be used, discuss mileage reimbursement policy and insurance coverage.
    - ☐ If a car is provided for the employee's personal use, discuss frequency, cost and restrictions.

Source: Town & Country Resources

## Some additional questions for parents to consider:

- ☐ What training does the staff have in infant/toddler development?
- ☐ Does the caregiver use straightforward, simple words to talk with my child?
- ☐ Are activities and schedules explained to my child?

- ☐ Are toys and materials well organized so my child can choose what interests him/her?
- ☐ Is this caregiver able to accommodate the special needs of my child?
- ☐ Does the environment accommodate the special needs of my child?
- ☐ Does this caregiver respect the language, culture and values of my family?
- ☐ Do the caregiver and I agree on discipline? Weaning? Toileting? Feeding?
- ☐ Can this person handle conflicts without losing patience, shaming a child or frequently displaying anger?
- ☐ Does the caregiver enjoy children?
- ☐ Am I welcome to drop in at any time?
- ☐ Will my child feel good about coming here?
- ☐ Is the environment sanitary and safe?
- ☐ Is the place appealing with comfortable lighting and an acceptable noise level?
- ☐ Is the program licensed per the state or local government?
- ☐ Is the child care program accredited by the National Association for the Education of Young Children or the National Association of Family Child Care?
- ☐ Are the caregivers certified by the Council for Early Childhood Professional Recognition with a Child Development Associates degree credential for infant/toddler caregivers or an equivalent credential that addresses comparable competencies (such as an associates or bachelor's degree)?
- ☐ Is there a primary caregiver for my child?
- ☐ Are the ratios and group size appropriate for my child's age?

Source: Mill Valley Police Dept;

http://www.cityofmillvalley.org

## Postpartum Doula

Should your client work with a postpartum doula and what do they do?

Postpartum doulas are trained or experienced in providing postpartum care for the new family. Postpartum doulas offer families evidence-based information and support on infant feeding, emotional and physical recovery from childbirth, infant soothing and coping skills for new parents. They may also help with light housework, meal preparation, laundry, breastfeeding, and helping incorporate an older child into the experience while helping parents ease the transition of bringing a new baby home.

Source: Sarah Cohen PCD, CECE; http://www.sleepyfamily.com

Baby Planner and Postpartum Doula, Emily Schaffer (CBP, PCD, CLE, HBE) shared with me the benefits of hiring a doula listed below:

A doula:

- ☐ Can help a new mom feel more secure, cared for, and build self-confidence
- ☐ Can act as a buffer and mediator in family relations.
- ☐ Helps to connect the older sibling(s) with the new arrival
- ☐ Can help to prevent postpartum depression
- ☐ Helps mom have a greater success with breastfeeding
- ☐ Helps mom stay well nourished
- ☐ Is able to make evidence based informed decisions
- ☐ Helps to lower incidence of abuse

http://www.emilyschaffer.com/

## When interviewing a postpartum doula DONA International recommends the following questions:

## Questions to Ask a Doula

The following questions will help you decide if a particular doula is right for your client.

☐ What training have you had? (If a doula is certified, you might consider checking with the organization.)

☐ Do you have one or more backup doulas for times when you are not available? May we meet her/them?

☐ What is your fee, what does it include and what are your refund policies?

☐ Tell me about your experience as a postpartum doula.

☐ What is your philosophy about parenting and supporting women and their families during postpartum?

☐ May we meet to discuss our postpartum needs and the role you will play in supporting us in the postpartum period?

☐ May we call you with postpartum questions or concerns before the birth?

☐ When do your services begin after birth?

☐ What is your experience in breastfeeding support?

☐ Have you had a criminal background check, a recent TB test and current CPR certification?

## Check credentials and references.

If the doula is a DONA International certified doula, you can confirm her certification by using our online doula locator. DONA International certification is a meaningful measure of a doula's commitment and professionalism.

## Conduct an in-person interview.

It is a good idea for both you and your partner to meet doula candidates to decide if they are compatible with your family. Are they kind, warm and enthusiastic? Are they knowledgeable? Do they communicate well? Are they good listeners? Are they comfortable with your choices or do they seem to have their own agenda? Do you feel at ease with them?

The way that you feel with a doula is more important than the number of births that they have attended or how many new families they have nurtured. You may want to interview more than one doula and make comparisons before choosing your doula.

# Resources

## DONA International

With more than 6,995 birth and postpartum doula members and growing, DONA is the largest doula association in the world. They support doulas by providing quality training and meaningful certification. They serve mothers and families by providing access to information and research about doulas, childbirth and the postpartum experience. DONA International certification sets the bar for doula education and professional development. It indicates to families that a doula has achieved a high level of training and professionalism.

DONA International began in 1992, when a small group of some of the foremost experts in childbirth decided that the time had come to promote the importance of emotional support for mothers and their partners during birth and the postpartum period. Convinced by significant evidence of the importance of doulas to a mother's (and consequently to a family's) wellbeing, they created an association for a relatively new group of professionals steeped in timeless tradition – doulas.

What they created is an organization that supports doulas who strive to help women and their partners to have satisfying childbirth and postpartum experiences. Doulas support childbearing families emotionally, and help them feel comfortable and nurtured. Doula care has been studied extensively in scientific trials and the results show remarkably improved physical and psychological outcomes for both mother and baby.

http://www.dona.org/

## International Nanny Association

**The International Nanny Association (INA)**, a nonprofit organization, serves as the umbrella organization for the in-home child care industry. INA members include nannies, nanny employers, nanny agencies, educators and industry service providers. Since 1985, INA has worked to professionalize the industry by setting high standards for industry professionals and nanny agencies. INA leverages the expertise of industry professionals from around the globe to help increase awareness about the industry, to develop the professional skills of nannies, and to educate parents about the benefits of hiring a qualified nanny to care for their children.

http://www.nanny.org/

## The National Association for Family Child Care

The National Association for Family Child Care is a non-profit organization dedicated to promoting quality child care by strengthening the profession of family child care.

The goals of the Association are:

- ☐ To strengthen state and local associations as the primary support system for individual family child care providers.
- ☐ To promote a professional accreditation program which recognizes and encourages quality care for children.
- ☐ To represent family child care providers by advocating for their needs and collaborating with other organizations.
- ☐ To promote the diversity of the family child care profession through training, state and local associations, public education, and Board membership.
- ☐ To deliver effective programs through strong organizational management.

http://www.nafcc.org/

## CAPPA

CAPPA certified professionals aim to empower, connect and advocate for families in the childbearing year. CAPPA seeks to forge positive and productive relationships between organizations that support healthy, informed family choices. The organization consists of a leadership board, regional representatives, trainers, mentors, advisors and its membership. CAPPA is the most comprehensive pregnancy, childbirth and postpartum organization available.
http://www.cappa.net

# Product Basics

This chapter will introduce you to product basics such as what to look for when buying strollers, car seats, high chairs, baby cribs, and mattresses. But before we begin, baby planners should become well acquainted with following organizations (descriptions have been taken directly from each organization's website):

## Consumer Reports

*Consumer Reports Best Baby Products* is the perfect personal baby shopping consultant. Over the years, this invaluable guide has helped thousands of new parents navigate the multitude of complex and sophisticated baby products, pointing them to the best products, and steering them away from the less-than-the-best. *Consumer Reports* buying advice and ratings allows buyers to streamline the selection process, avoid shopping pitfalls, and help keep the baby budget in balance.

Consumers Union (CU) is an expert, independent, nonprofit organization whose mission is to work for a fair, just, and safe marketplace for all consumers and to empower consumers to protect themselves. The organization was founded in 1936 when advertising first flooded the mass media. Consumers lacked a reliable source of information they could depend on to help them distinguish hype from fact and good products from bad ones. Since then CU has filled that vacuum with a broad range of consumer information. To maintain its independence and impartiality, CU accepts no outside advertising and no free samples and employs several hundred mystery shoppers and technical experts to buy and test the products it evaluates.

CU publishes *Consumer Reports*, one of the top-ten-circulation magazines in the country, and ConsumerReports.org, which has the most subscribers of any Web site of its kind, in addition to two newsletters, *Consumer Reports on Health* and *Consumer Reports Money Adviser*. They have combined subscriptions of more than 8 million. All of CU's work is informed by the more than 1 million readers who respond to our Annual Ballot & Questionnaire, among the largest and most comprehensive consumer studies in the world. In 2008, CU also launched several initiatives, including ConsumerReportsHealth.org and the Consumer Reports Health Ratings Center, which serve to educate and empower consumers to make more informed health-care decisions and to help change the market.

To further advance its mission, Consumers Union employs a dedicated staff of lobbyists, grassroots organizers, and outreach specialists who work with the organization's more than 600,000 online activists to change legislation and the marketplace in favor of the consumer interest. The organization generates more than $200 million in revenue, and a staff totaling more than 600 work at CU's 50 state-of-the-art labs and offices in Yonkers, N.Y.; its 327-acre Auto Test Center in East Haddam, Conn.; and our three advocacy offices, in Washington, D.C., Austin, Texas, and San Francisco. Consumers Union is governed by a board of 18 directors who are elected by CU members and meet three times a year.

For more information visit: http://www.consumerreports.org

## Juvenile Products Manufacturers Association

The JPMA is a national trade organization representing 95% of the prenatal to preschool industry. Today, JPMA represents 250 companies in the United States, Canada, and Mexico who manufacture, import and/or distribute infant products such as cribs, car seats, strollers, bedding, and a wide range of accessories and decorative items.

JPMA has been recognized as an organization dedicated to enhancing children's product safety. JPMA's extensive history of leadership in juvenile product safety includes the development of a comprehensive Certification Program to help guide parents and caregivers toward purchasing juvenile products that are built with safety in mind.

JPMA continues to work with government officials, consumer groups, and industry leaders on programs to educate consumers on the safe selection and use of juvenile products. Safe & Sound For Baby and Baby Safety Month are only a few of the programs JPMA sponsors to keep today's safety conscious parents informed.

JPMA has been an asset to the juvenile products industry for more than four decades. Members rely on JPMA for a variety of reasons, including money-saving services, business enhancing programs, product safety input, and networking opportunities. JPMA understands that each company has unique needs and finds value in belonging to the only association solely dedicated to promoting the industry and the safe use and selection of juvenile products.

Retailers can count on JPMA to monitor the juvenile products industry as it relates to the regulatory landscape, work to promote the industry and those involved, and serve as the foremost resource for product safety information. JPMA takes pride in our role of serving as the voice of the industry and is committed to doing our part to ensure the safety of our nation's children.

Expectant parents, baby-store owners, and company presidents alike can trust JPMA as a leading resource for all things juvenile.

For more information visit http://www.jpma.org/

## American Society for Testing and Materials (ASTM)

ASTM International is one of the largest voluntary standards development organizations in the world-a trusted source for technical standards for materials, products, systems, and services. Known for their high technical quality and market relevancy, ASTM International standards have an important role in the information infrastructure that guides design, manufacturing and trade in the global economy.

For more information visit http://www.astm.org/

## US Consumer Product Safety Commission

The U.S. Consumer Product Safety Commission is charged with protecting the public from unreasonable risks of serious injury or death from thousands of types of consumer products under the agency's jurisdiction. The CPSC is committed to protecting consumers and families from products that pose a fire, electrical, chemical, or mechanical hazard or can injure children. The CPSC's work to ensure the safety of consumer products - such as toys, cribs, power tools, cigarette lighters, and household chemicals - contributed significantly to the 30 percent decline in the rate of deaths and injuries associated with consumer products over the past 30 years. Their website includes Recalls and Product Safety News where you can find information on over 4,500 product recalls and recall alerts using the various searches.

For more information visit http://www.cpsc.gov/

## The National Highway Traffic Safety Administration

NHTSA was established by the Highway Safety Act of 1970 to carry out safety programs previously administered by the National Highway Safety Bureau. Specifically, the agency directs the highway safety and consumer programs established by the National Traffic and Motor Vehicle Safety Act of 1966, the Highway Safety Act of 1966, the 1972 Motor Vehicle Information and Cost Savings Act, and succeeding amendments to these laws.

They have a wealth of valuable information and resources on Child Passenger Safety for parents, caregivers, partners, and advocates.

For more information visit: http://www.nhtsa.gov/

## Safe Kids Worldwide/USA

Safe Kids USA is a member of *Safe Kids Worldwide*, a global network of organizations with a mission of preventing unintentional childhood injury. Safe Kids USA is a nationwide network of organizations working to prevent unintentional childhood injury, the leading cause of death and disability for children ages 1 to 14.

They educate families, provide safety devices to families in need and advocate for better laws to help keep children safe, healthy and out of the emergency room.

Safe Kids Worldwide was founded in 1987 as the National SAFE KIDS Campaign by *Children's National Medical Center* with support from Johnson & Johnson. Safe Kids Worldwide is a 501(c)(3) non-profit organization located in Washington, D.C.

For more information visit: http://www.safekids.org

## Healthy Child Healthy World

Is a 501(c)(3) nonprofit inspiring parents to protect young children from harmful chemicals.

They are leading a movement that educates parents, supports protective policies, and engages communities to make responsible decisions, simple everyday choices, and well-informed lifestyle improvements to create healthy environments where children and families can flourish.

Healthy Child Healthy World exists because more than 125 million Americans, especially children, now face an historically unprecedented rise in chronic disease and illness such as cancer, autism, asthma, birth defects, ADD / ADHD, and learning and developmental disabilities. Credible scientific evidence increasingly points to environmental hazards and household chemicals as causing and contributing to many of these diseases.

For the past two decades Healthy Child Healthy World has been the nation's leading organization of its kind. We help millions of parents, educators, health professionals, and the general public take action to create healthy environments and embrace green, non-toxic steps.

## Purpose and Goals

☐ **Expand** awareness and understanding of environmental hazards to children's health

☐ **Help** the public learn about healthier practices, solutions, and products in the marketplace

☐ **Encourage** daily action and informed lifestyle choices

☐ **Create** standards and policies for safer products, foods, materials, and chemicals used in the home – promoting safer options and new alternatives

☐ **Advocate** for and support corporate policies and governmental legislation that protect children from environmental risks

☐ **Engage** communities to make wise choices and responsible decisions so families can flourish

Healthy Child Healthy World was founded by James and Nancy Chuda in 1991 after their daughter Colette died from Wilm's tumor — a rare form of non-hereditary cancer. Healthy Child is a national, non-profit 501(c) 3 organization headquartered in Los Angeles. Healthy Child is governed by an outstanding volunteer Board of Directors and distinguished group of advisors and is strengthened by community and corporate partners. Healthy Child is playing a leadership role in one of the most important public health and environmental movements of the 21st century.

For more information visit http://healthychild.org

## Healthy Stuff Toys

HealthyStuff.org has tested thousands of toys since 2006. These test results are intended to help consumers with the information they need to make better choices when purchasing toys and other children's products. They are based on research conducted by environmental health organizations and other researchers around the country. The Ecology Center created HealthyStuff.org and leads its research and development. The Ecology Center is a Michigan-based nonprofit environmental organization that works at the local, state, and national levels for clean production, healthy communities, environmental justice, and a sustainable future.

For more information visit http://www.healthystuff.org/

As a baby planner, your clients will appreciate when you educate them on what to look for when purchasing the following most used and necessary products. It is highly recommended that you suggest and not recommend products and work closely with a product expert who does this on a full-time basis.

Below are gear guides for Baby Strollers, Car Seats, and High Chairs provided by Charles Schwartz and OneStepAhead.com. These guides are very helpful and provide a general overview with tips, when suggesting essential products to your clients. The guidelines below should not be used as your only source, as changes happen quite frequently in this industry. Make sure to check for updates.

## Car Seats
by Chas Schwartz, CPS

According to the National Highway and Traffic Safety Administration (NHTSA), up to 80% of kids' car seats are not being used properly. Mistakes range from minor errors that are easy fixes to major misuse. The issue is either the way the car seat is installed in the car, or how the child is being fitted into the seat. Here is what you need to know to help ensure children are as safe as possible when being driven in cars.

-State laws

-The different stages of car seats

-Installation

-Side impact protection

-Accessories

-Insurance

## State Laws

State laws dictate how long children are legally required to ride in designated restraints. In California the requirement is until children reach six years of age, or sixty pounds, whichever comes first. What that means is that a child must fit the specifications of your car seat, and the seat must be used according to the manufacturer's instructions of the car and car seat. That is two instruction manuals to reference for proper use.

When a newborn baby is ready to be sent home from the hospital, nurses are instructed to determine whether the car seat has been properly installed, and sometimes come out to the car to check. Children will not be released from the hospital if it is found that the proper arrangements have not been made to safely transport the baby home.

State laws dictate when children are no longer legally required to sit in a car seat. It may seem like a long time, but they should stay in a booster car seat until they reach four feet eleven inches tall.

## The different stages of car seats

There are three main stages of kids' car seats; infant, convertible and booster. It is not a legal requirement that you have your car seat professionally inspected or installed however it is very highly recommended.

Parents don't have to start with a stage one infant only carrier car seat. A newborn baby is okay to start in most stage two bigger convertible longer lasting seats. The convenience of stage one seats makes them worthwhile for almost everyone, every time, as they allow parents to carry the child around in the seat in the sensitive early months. Stage two seats are one piece and stay more permanently mounted in the car.

Stage one consists of a two piece car seat. The base stays mounted in the backseat of the car, and the seat come easily off the base to be carried around and attached to the child's stroller. Most infant car seats fit into a wide variety of strollers. Car seat and stroller brands can often be mixed and matched, allowing the car seat from one manufacturer to fit and be okay to use in another manufacturers stroller.

Babies have somewhat irregular sleeping patterns when first born. The ability to move them in and out of the car while they stay sleeping makes infant car seats a wise investment. Infant car seats are available in small and large sizes, face only backwards in the car, and typically last between six and twelve months.

Children outgrow car seats by exceeding either a height or a weight limit. When the child's legs hang over the edge of the infant car seat, they've most likely reached the height limit. When the seat is so heavy the parent doesn't want to carry the baby in it anymore, they've most likely grown too heavy for it. The specifications of height and weight maximums and minimums can be found on labels on the sides back and bottom of the seat.

Newborn babies face backwards because it is a significantly safer way to ride in the car. It is highly recommended to keep children rear facing in cars as long as possible. It is legally okay to turn kids forward in the car at one year of age, if they weigh at least twenty pounds.

Kids usually graduate out of infant car seats under a year old. They move into the next stage, a convertible car seat, and remain facing backwards for a few more months. The convertible seat then turns forward and re-installs, and typically lasts three to five years.

Stage two convertible car seats are available in small, medium, and large sizes. The large size comes most highly recommended as it lasts the longest. Frequent travelers and those with small cars benefit most from small size.

Eighteen to twenty four months is a realistic goal for turn-around time. Kids are still safest facing backwards, even when their legs bunch against the seatback, so long as they are within the car seats rear facing height and weight limit.

The best method of restraint for a child is a five point harness. Five point harnesses can be found on almost every car seat on the market today. Kids can move out of a five point harness into the third and final stage of car seats, the seatbelt positioning booster stage, as early as three years old, if tall and heavy enough.

Booster car seats use the same type of seatbelt that adults wear. Most boosters do not permanently install in the car. They sit children higher up and position the shoulder part of the seatbelt lower down off the neck, to just above the child's shoulder. Seatbelt positioning boosters are very easy to use, however they do not offer as much protection as a five point harness.

It is safest to keep kids in a harness as long as possible before graduating them into a booster car seat. Realistically four to five years old is an appropriate age to try a booster.

## Installation

The middle of the back seat is the safest place in the car for one child, as long as there are no issues with installation. Compatibility is rarely an issue. Most seats fit in most cars, but require a solid effort to install properly. The driver and passenger vehicle seats may have to be moved farther forward.

For two or more children, make sure their seats are installed properly no matter where in the back seat of the car. Do not put kids in the front of the car, unless it is a two seat car that allows the passenger airbag to be disabled. In that case disable the airbag.

There is often more than one way to properly install a car seat, however there is only one way to properly secure the child into the seat. It requires more work to protect kids in cars than adults, but does not have to be mysterious or confusing.

It has been a vehicle manufacturer requirement that cars come equipped with Lower Anchors and Tethers for Children (LATCH) since September, 2001. No LATCH, no problem. LATCH is an alternative method of installation that does not use the cars seatbelt.

LATCH is not safer than using the cars seatbelt. It is sometimes easier, but not always. Do not use both LATCH and the cars seatbelt to install a car seat. LATCH is often available on only the outer side seats of cars. Car seats serve children better properly installed in the middle of the back seat with the cars seatbelt, rather than with LATCH on the side.

Car seats are tight enough when installed so they move no more than an inch in any direction where the seat is fastened to the car. Infant car seat particularly sit tight from where the seat is attached to the car, yet feel loose and not tight enough in the back of the seat, moving upward and side to side more than an inch.

There are a variety of different brands to choose from. The safest car seats are the ones that parents are going to use properly, that the child fits best into, and that fit best into the car. Some seats are simply easier to use and are a better fit than others, while most seats fit fine in most cars.

Car seats are approved to use on airplanes if they have a label that says "certified to be used in motor vehicles and aircraft." The bigger size seats may not fit on small planes.

Children are not required by airlines to have their own seat until around two years of age. They can be kept on the parents lap. Body harnesses are available for purchase but not provided by or available through the airline, to attach babies to parents. Depending on the length of the flight parents may find it best to purchase an extra seat for their baby.

## Side Impact Protection

Side Impact Protection (SIP) is a feature now available on a variety of models of all stages of car seats. It is an additional safety feature. Far from top priority, it is worthwhile to consider having. The overall protection provided by car seats is quite good without SIP. Parents should sleep comfortably at night knowing their car seat is installed properly, whether it has extra side impact protection or not.

Side impacts account for between a quarter and a third of car collisions, yet pose a much higher threat to children when they occur. In addition to reducing the movement of the head of the child in the event of a collision, the SIP seats are often significantly easier to adjust, with sliding headrests that raise or lower with the twist of a knob or the push of a lever, rather than the re-routing of the harness which usually requires that the seat is taken out of the car, adjusted, and re-installed.

## Accessories

There are a wide variety of accessories available for kid's car seats, however it is not recommended to use anything that did not come with the seat. The main priority is that the car seat is installed properly. If the driver wants an extra mirror in the car to better see the baby, he or she should not spend too much time looking in it. If you really need to check in with the baby, pull over. Mats are available to protect car interiors, and should not be of concern so long as car seat is installed correctly. Car seats mostly have sufficient padding inside them. Extra pads are more useful inside the seat of a stroller.

Insurance replaces car seats in the event of collision. Even in the case of a low speed fender bender, car seats must be replaced. This is due to the materials used, and the fact that you cannot see inside the car seat to assess potential damage.

Car seats in general are okay to use for about six years from the date of manufacturing. They all expire eventually. Dates of manufacture and sometimes expiration are printed on the seat. If unsure, contact the maker of your seat and provide them with the information on the seat labels.

For more information and as best practice call or visit a certified child passenger safety technician in your area.

## About Chas Schwartz, CPS

Chas is a newborn products expert specializing in kids car seats. He's three times certified as a child passenger safety technician by The National Safe Kids Campaign. In the baby business since 2000, certifying first in 2005, again in 2007 and 2009, he has nearly a decade of experience educating expecting parents. He has personally installed over a thousand car seats, participated in local community checkpoints, and spoken at Marin General Hospital on the subject of proper use of baby products. Chas currently advises on, demos, sells, and installs car seats and other baby products at the independently owned Baby News outlet Heller's for Children in San Rafael, CA.

To locate your local car seat inspection station visit: http://www.nhtsa.gov/cps/cpsfitting/index.cfm

Safe Kids Worldwide in partnership with the NHTSA offers a basic child passenger safety awareness online course for a new parent, caregiver, automobile or car seat retailer, called In and Around Cars. The course can be found here: http://www.safekidswebinars.org/

## Baby Strollers

### Strollers
by OneStepAhead.com

Choosing your baby's stroller is one of the most significant purchasing decisions you will make.

Over the next few years, your stroller is going to get quite a workout. You want one that is safe and comfortable for both you and your child...easy to open, close, maneuver, and store...and will hold up to tough everyday use.

But with so many strollers the market, how do you begin to choose?

At One Step Ahead, we've been evaluating strollers for more than a decade – and we're happy to share our experience with you. First, we'll tell you about the different types of strollers available, so you can decide which one (or ones) are right for you. Then, we'll tell you how to choose a high-quality, high-performance stroller that will serve you well, mile after mile.

## Types of Strollers

If you've already begun looking at strollers, your head is probably spinning. These days, there are strollers for virtually every life style, from formal carriages to rugged "all-terrain vehicles." Before you choose, consider where you live-city, suburbs, cold or warm climate – and how you will be using your stroller.

You may find that a single stroller will not meet all your needs. In this case, you may want to select both a primary, everyday stroller, and a secondary stroller (such as a travel stroller or jogger) for special activities.

Although they are marketed under a variety of names, strollers fall under these major categories:

**Carriage Stroller** - This large, heavyweight stroller features a fully-reclining back, padded seat, full canopy, and large basket. It offers large wheels for a smooth, springy ride and may feature a reversible handle. As baby grows, the back adjusts to an upright seat. Ideal for young infants because it offers the greatest support and protection, but it can become cumbersome after the early months. Makes a great first stroller.

**Umbrella Stroller** -Lightweight, portable and inexpensive, it folds easily and fits in tight spaces. It consists of a pouch-like seat slung across a light metal frame, with two umbrella-like handles. It may not offer a canopy or basket. Handy for shopping and travel because it's easy to maneuver and transport, but lacks durability and does not provide baby with much back support. Some models tend to tip easily and should not be weighed down with diaper bags or purses. A good secondary stroller for jaunts and trips.

**Standard Stroller** - For many families, this will be baby's primary stroller. The standard stroller offers a partial or fully reclining seat and a well-padded seat cover for baby's comfort. It feature double wheels for a smooth, stable ride and front swivel wheels for better maneuverability. It may come equipped with a wide range of desirable features, such as a wide, adjustable sun canopy, bumper bar or tray, generous storage basket and adjustable handles.

**Lightweight Stroller** -This cleverly-designed stroller combines the convenience of the umbrella stroller with some of the luxury features of a standard stroller. Constructed of high-tech aluminum, it is at once lightweight and sturdy. Like an umbrella stroller, it is very portable and will fit into an airplane's overhead bin. But it may also offer a reclining seat, nicely-padded upholstery and large sun canopy, plus a bumper bar or tray, double wheels and adjustable handles. Generally, lightweight strollers are more expensive than their standard counterparts, but most parents find the 2-5 pound weight difference more than justifies the higher price.

**Car Seat/Stroller Combos** - These comprehensive "travel systems" feature an infant car seat that locks onto a sturdy stroller frame. Ideal if you live in the suburbs and drive everywhere, because you do not have to disturb baby with every stop. As baby grows, remove the car seat and you have a stand-alone stroller. An excellent choice if you're in and out of the car frequently, or if grow-with-me capabilities are important to you.

**Jogging Strollers** - Truly built for jogging, these lightweight strollers feature three large, bicycle-like tires and an oversized sun canopy. Very smooth rolling with excellent shock absorbers and brakes, but not intended for tight spaces (the front wheel doesn't swivel). A must if you plan on running or jogging with baby.

**Tandem and Side-by-Side Strollers** - If you have twins, triplets, or children close in age, a double or triple stroller is for you! Tandem strollers feature one seat behind the other; side-by-side seats are mounted next to each other on a single, wide frame. Some parents find tandems easier to maneuver, although traditionally, the baby in back has a limited view. (Some new models offer "stadium" seating or reversible seating to solve this problem.) If choosing a side-by-side model, be sure it fits through a standard 30" wide doorway. No matter which type you choose, look for individually adjustable seats and canopy protection for each baby.

**What to Look for In a Stroller**
Regardless of what type of stroller you choose, you'll want to make sure it's safe, comfortable and well-constructed. Look for these characteristics:

## Sturdy, quality construction

- ☐ The metal frame should be strong and stable. Look for neatly welded seams and finished edges.
- ☐ All four wheels should touch the floor evenly – no tipping or rocking.
- ☐ The seat cover should be well-padded and securely stitched. Look for thick, even padding and plush, substantial fabrics. Removable covers/liners are a plus.
- ☐ Look for spring-action shock absorbers for a smooth ride.
- ☐ The canopy should be generously sized to shield baby from sun and other elements.
- ☐ Treaded pneumatic (i.e., air-filled) tires are best if you plan on using your stroller extensively over uneven terrain or city sidewalks.
- ☐ If you will be maneuvering your stroller through narrow aisles or crowded spaces, look for adjustable wheels that offer both swivel and fixed capabilities.
- ☐ All terrain wheels are ideal on all types of surfaces.

## Safety features

- ☐ A reliable restraint system is crucial. We prefer the five-point harness, which secures baby at the shoulders, waist and crotch. (A crotch strap is very important, since it will keep baby from slipping down.)
- ☐ Look for a secondary locking mechanism on the frame. This ensures that the stroller cannot fold while in use.
- ☐ To prevent rolling, check for reliable, rear-wheel brakes.
- ☐ Avoid models with sharp, unfinished edges and small pieces that might come loose.
- ☐ The frame should be tip-resistant, in both the open and folded position

## Easy to use

- ☐ Evaluate accessibility. You should be able to get baby in and out easily. Some models offer bars that open or remove for easy access to baby.

- ☐ An adult should be able to fasten and unfasten the harness quickly.

- ☐ Be sure to consider stroller weight – especially when buying a tandem or side-by-side stroller – because heavyweight strollers can become burdensome. Lightweight strollers (made of aircraft-quality aluminum) are a wonderful choice because they are both light and sturdy.

- ☐ The stroller should fold and unfold easily. Some strollers fold with just one hand-ideal if you're holding baby with the other.

- ☐ How maneuverable is the stroller? Look for dual, swivel front wheels and one-handed steering. (If your stroller has a reversible handle, all four wheels should have swivel capabilities.)

- ☐ How easy is it to adjust the stroller back or activate the brakes? Look for smoothly operating mechanisms.

- ☐ Adjustable handles are a necessity for parents who are tall (or petite). Padded, ergonomic handles are also a plus.

- ☐ Make sure that, when folded, the stroller will fit in the trunk of your car.

## Easy to clean

- ☐ Make sure the seat cover is both removable and machine washable.

## Grow-with-me capabilities

You want a stroller that will comfortably accommodate baby as he or she grows. Look for:

- ☐ A generously sized seating area.
- ☐ A multi-position back that adjusts to recline or to a near-recline.

☐   An adjustable footrest for growing legs.

☐   Weight maximums of 40 lbs. or more.

## Storage Capabilities

☐   Look for a generously-sized storage basket.

☐   Some strollers offer a tray or cup holder located on the stroller handle-a nice convenience for parents. (You can also add these to you stroller later.)

## Other Considerations

Here are some other features you might find desirable:

☐   Some canopies feature plastic viewing windows that allow you to keep tabs on baby.

☐   A play bar or tray that will help keep baby occupied while riding.

## High Chairs

by OneStepAhead.com

Few pieces of baby equipment are subjected to tougher conditions than the high chair!

After all, baby's high chair will be pressed into service at least three times a day for several busy, messy, active years – adding up to roughly a thousand uses in a single year! You will be scrubbing that high chair more times than you can imagine, and moving it countless others. It will undoubtedly receive its share of bumps and bruises along the way.

There are dozens of different high chairs on the market, and they vary widely in terms of quality, durability, safety, features and style. How can you identify quality construction? Safe design? How do you know what features you need? Read on!

At One Step Ahead, we've been evaluating high chairs for more than a decade. Based on our experience – combined with the advice of consumer experts – we recommend that you look for the following characteristics:

## Sturdy, quality construction

1. Look for a wide, stable base (or "footprint") for stability.
2. All four legs should touch the floor evenly – no tipping or rocking.
3. The seat cover, if there is one, should be thick, not flimsy, to hold up to wear and tear.
4. If the seat cover is vinyl, the heat-sealed seams should be smooth and flat, not scratchy against baby's legs.
5. If the high chair legs have folding hinges, make sure they feature a dependable locking mechanism.
6. Look for a large, wrap-around tray that operates smoothly on its tracks.

## Safety features

- A reliable restraint system is crucial. We prefer the five-point harness, which secures baby at the shoulders, waist and crotch. (A crotch strap is very important, since it will keep baby from slipping or sliding under the tray.)
- A molded center post-positioned in the center of the seat between baby's legs-is also a desirable option, since it also prevents baby from sliding.
- The tray should be smooth underneath, with no sharp edges or hanging pieces.
- There should be no small pieces on the high chair (such as plugs for metal tubing) that might come loose and pose a choking hazard.

## Easy to clean

- Look for a removable, easy-to-clean tray with a large lip that helps keeps food contained. (Some trays may even be cleaned in your dishwasher.)

☐ The seat should be easy to clean. A cloth seat cover should be removable and machine washable. A wood or vinyl seat should be easily sponged clean.

☐ Remember, the fewer nooks and crannies in the design, the easier it will be to keep free of debris.

## Easy to use

☐ Evaluate accessibility. You should be able to get baby in and out easily. The tray should slide in and out smoothly, preferably with one hand. An adult should be able to fasten and unfasten the harness quickly.

☐ If the chair is a folding model, find out how simple (or complicated) the folding process is. Also, is there a place on the frame to hang the tray?

☐ If you plan on moving the high chair from room to room, a wheeled high chair is a good choice for you. However, make sure the wheels lock for safety if you elect this feature.

## Grow-with-me capabilities

You want a high chair that will accommodate baby as he or she grows. Look for:

☐ A generously sized seating area.

☐ A seat that is height adjustable. (Eventually, you'll probably want to remove the tray and have baby sit with you at the table.)

☐ An adjustable footrest for growing legs.

☐ Some parents also like a multi-positioned back.

## Style

With so many styles available, you'll want to find one that compliments your own. You may find yourself drawn to a state-of-the-art import that offers luxury features...or a timeless wooden highchair with simple, classic lines. If space is an issue in your home, you'll also want to consider the chair's dimensions, both folded and unfolded.

# Crib Safety: What The Experts Say

By OneStepAhead.com

In the first few years of life, your baby will probably spend more time in his or her crib than any other single place. Naturally, you want it to be welcoming, comfortable, and most of all, safe.

There are a number of steps you can take to safety-proof your baby's crib, including these, as recommended by the American Academy of Pediatrics (AAP), the National Safety Council, and other authorities on child safety.

First and foremost, ALWAYS place your baby to sleep on his or her back. SIDS (Sudden Infant Death Syndrome) rates have dropped by more than 50% since the America's "Back to Sleep" Campaign was introduced in 1994.

In addition, make sure your crib meets these safety standards, as recommended by the AAP:

- ☐ Make sure that the spaces between the slats are no wider than 2 ⅜" apart.
- ☐ Choose a firm mattress, not a soft one. Never place baby on a water bed, sofa, or other soft surface.
- ☐ Avoid gaps between the mattress and crib walls. Try the " two fingers" test: if you can fit two fingers between the mattress and crib, it's not safe to use.
- ☐ Ensure the corner posts are level with the height of the end panels (or much higher, as on canopy-style beds). Otherwise clothing can get caught on the post.
- ☐ Don't choose a crib with decorative cutouts—a trapping hazard—on its end panels.
- ☐ Check the distance between the height of the crib sides and the mattress. When lowered, the crib sides should be at least 9" above the mattress. When raised, they should be at least 26" above the mattress in its lowest position.
- ☐ Make sure the drop sides can't be released by a child. The sides should feature a locking, hand-operated latch.

- ☐ Examine your crib frequently for hazards: loose parts, off-kilter joints, splinters, chipped paint. If you spot a problem, fix it immediately.

- ☐ When buying a new crib, look for Juvenile Product Manufacturers Association (JPMA) certification.

In addition, the National Safety Council offers these suggestions:

- ☐ As charming as they are, don't be tempted to use an antique crib that doesn't meet current safety standards

- ☐ Avoid wrapping the mattress in plastic materials to protect it.

- ☐ Never place baby's crib next to a window. Blind cords, drapery cords, and window screens all pose hazards to kids.

Finally, be ready to modify baby's crib as he matures. The AAP recommends removing mobiles and hanging toys when baby begins to push up on his hands and knees or at five months, whichever occurs first. In addition, as soon as baby stands up, set the mattress at its lowest position and remove any bumper pads, which can be used as stepping stones.

To learn more about crib safety, visit:

American Academy of Pediatrics – http://www.aap.org

National Safety Council – http://www.nsc.org

First Candle/SIDS Alliance – http://www.sidsalliance.org

Consumer Product Safety Commission – http://www.cpsc.gov

## About One Step Ahead

One Step Ahead was founded by two real life parents, Karen and Ian Scott, who wanted the best for their own children.

Frustrated by products that looked terrific in stores and catalogs, but didn't live up to their promises, the Scotts traded in Fortune 500 careers to pursue their vision of a different kind of baby company.

One Step Ahead is a company that subjects its products to tough, hands on testing, by both professional merchandisers and an independent Parents' Panel. One that does the comparison shopping upfront, and then offers only the top performers. One that tracks down innovative, hard-to-find helpers—and when they can't be found, has its Design Team create them from scratch. One that prides itself on outstanding service, so parents can shop with absolute confidence.

For three decades, One Step Ahead has helped new parents navigate the complex baby market. Then in 1989, Leaps and Bounds, a sister catalog geared to children, joined the Chelsea & Scott family. Today, they remain committed to bringing you what parents want: high quality products...ingenious parenting solutions...outstanding service...and the toughest guarantees in the industry.

http://www.onestepahead.com or email: customerservice@onestepahead.com

## A Note about Resale or consignment shopping

If your client wants to go green and purchase all their necessary products from a resale or consignment shop, it is highly recommended that you spend the appropriate amount of time reviewing and testing out each product to ensure that the wear and tear has not compromised the safety or the quality of the product. Although, the manufacturers are ultimately responsible for their products, you may be held liable when recommending an unsafe product. Since this is still a young industry, there are many grey areas around this matter that have yet to be addressed. Therefore, I recommend that you take precaution.

The Consumer Product Safety Commission (CPSC) provides a thrift store safety checklist here:
http://www.cpsc.gov/cpscpub/pubs/thrift/thrftck.html

Baby Planners
share their stories and advice

I am proud to highlight a couple of stories and advice of the following certified baby planners:

## Rachel Macias, DC Baby Planners

Rachel Macias has worked mostly in the communications/marketing fields for the last twelve years. Most recently, she served as a director for the cable television industry's education foundation, Cable in the Classroom (CIC). She represented CIC and served as the primary spokesperson to local cable companies across the US. She promoted understanding and awareness of CIC's resources to cable operators and how to use CIC's resources to connect with the schools and parents in their communities. She also developed marketing materials that cable companies used in their own markets, and has a B.A. in political science. She has been very active in her community including serving on local boards and as a Junior League member. She is married to Paul Macias and has two amazing sons, Alexander and Quinn.

Her inspiration for becoming a baby planner, are her children. She loved being pregnant and planning for the arrival of her two sons. She was forced to learn everything and anything about this new journey. She absolutely loved the entire experience from pregnancy to birth and beyond. She actually never aspired to be a mom-preneur. She was very comfortable working for someone else. However, now that she is a baby planner, she cannot imagine working for anyone else but herself.

The way Rachel discovered baby planning was when she did a nanny share with another mom for their first-born son. The mom, Julie Allen, inspired her to become a baby planner. They talked a lot about the idea of starting their own business and, if so, what they would do. Rachel soon started researching their ideas and realized their ideas were not new. They had a name – "baby planning". Rachel owes Julie a debt of gratitude for encouraging her to become a baby planner. She probably would still be working for someone else if Julie did not put the desire to become a baby planner in her.

What Rachel loves most about being a baby planner is working with expectant parents and sharing in the joy of impending parenthood. The excitement of a child on the way is contagious. She knows what joy the birth of her children brought to her and she very much enjoys helping others through this most important time in their lives. Pregnancy should be a time of joy and celebration and Rachel works to make sure her clients have as stress-free a pregnancy as possible.

Rachel's advice for those interested in a baby planning career is to talk to as many baby planners as possible, take a baby planning course/certification, and put together a solid business plan.

## Isabelle Lacarce-Paumier, Les Fées Du Berceau Baby Planning

Isabelle Lacarce-Paumier is founder and CEO of "Les Fées Du Berceau" located in France and Switzerland.

She has a degree from "Science-Po", a prestigious French political sciences school. She also has a Master in Sciences in marketing of media and spent one year in England studying media studies at the University of Sussex. She started her career as a market research analyst for FMCG and pharmaceutical industries. Because she had a passion for her job, Isabelle dedicated most of her time to her career. Her most recent corporate job was as a Senior Consumer Insight Manager for the food business of a big FMCG company in France.

When she was pregnant with her son, she realized that she did not know much about baby and that a completely new life started for her. She started to meet other expecting mothers in the company and realized that all of them were in the same situation: want the best for their baby but lack support you can trust and time! During her maternity leave, she heard of baby planning industry abroad and become very interested in it. She felt that it was exactly what many women like her needed!

What she loves the most about being a baby planner is understanding and helping expecting mums. In its former company, she was nicknamed "Mum Isabelle" because she has a real passion for listening and supporting other people. Having a baby is the biggest change you have to face in your life. It is also the most wonderful thing that it can happen. Helping people to better know themselves to choose the best for their new life is the greatest reward she can have.

Isabelle resides in Alsace, in the east of France, just next to the Deutsch and Swiss Borders. She is originally from Paris where she continues going there very often to see her family and friends and also visit her clients (it's only from 3 hours from her home). Isabelle's son, "Louis" inspires much in her new career and is a continuing ray of sunshine in her everyday life. Dominique, is beloved husband, is her greatest support in every domains of her life.

# The End to New Beginnings.......

"In my end is my beginning."

-T.S. Eliot

Thank you for taking the time to explore the world of baby planning. It may be your opportunity to empower and enhance the lives of many preconceiving, expecting parents, new parents and their babies on the way. It is a journey where literally every end welcomes a new beginning.

Love and Peace.........

# About the Author

**Mary Oscategui,** *The Baby Planner,* is an international maternity business consultant and holistic educator who specializes in maternal sleep, health, fitness, nutrition and green living. She is the *Founder, CEO,* and *President* of the International Maternity Institute (IMI),  International Academy of Baby Planner Professionals (IABPP), and Co-Founder and Executive Director of the Association of Professional Sleep Consultants (APSC). Additionally Mary also offers health and fitness services through Physical Awakening.com, a holistic integrative approach offering the services of yoga, meditation, pilates, fitness, and nutrition. Mary is a leader in educational development and has been consulting and guiding hundreds of clients for the last 17 years.

She is the author of  "The Baby Planner Profession: What You Need To Know! The Ultimate Guide and Resource for Baby Planner Professionals," and her latest book, "Green Body Green Birth".

Mary enjoys empowering, educating, and supporting expectant and new parents to know all their options so that they may confidently make informed decisions for themselves and their family in the healthiest and safest way. Mary also advises and coaches maternity professionals offering a wealth of knowledge and support. Her enthusiasm, inspiration, creativity, and knowledge has helped launch many maternity start-up businesses in 22 countries around the world. She enjoys helping business owners meet their challenges with clear and direct solutions.

Mary's work in the health, fitness, and maternity industry is backed up by a multitude of prestigious certifications. She is a writer, speaker, educator, coach, baby planner, stress management coach, wellness coach, sleep consultant, certified yoga and pilates instructor, certified personal trainer, holistic nutrition consultant, going green consultant, greenproofer, and birthing options advocate.

Mary introduced a new approach to the baby planning industry by focusing on the needs of her clients through parental education and emotional support and established the first and only certification program in the baby planning industry.

Most recently Mary has been working to raise the bar for the sleep consulting industry by expanding the sleep consultant's role to include working with expecting families, setting forth a formal definition, standards of practice and boundaries to practice for the sleep consulting profession via the IMI Maternity & Child Sleep Consultant Certification.

Mary's greatest joy is to see moms nourish their bodies, bellies, and babies. Mary's daughter, "Bella Luna" is a continuing inspiration for her career and personal development.  Currently Mary is expecting her second child, Taj Orion Sky, whom is due to arrive at the end of the summer. She is also fluent in Spanish and resides in Marin, California.

Founded in 2008, The Baby Planner is your guide and connection to best resources for new and expecting parents. They are focused on helping new and expecting parents ease their transition into parenthood through health and intelligent planning.

Mary also works with a team of experts who serve as advisors and mentors to The International Maternity Institute and International Academy of Baby Planner Professionals. They assist Mary in educating and supporting future baby planners through the certification process in order to help her raise awareness in the baby planning industry. They excel in their fields of practice, and most importantly, they are a joy to work with. Their extended biographies are presented on the next few pages following the list below:

**Green Expert:** Beth Greer, Super Natural Mom and author of "Super Natural Home"

**Small Business and Finance Expert:** Joseph Lizio, CEO of Business Money Today

**Child Safety Expert:** Alison Rhodes

**Natural Childbirth Educator:** Catherine Beier, CBE, MS CCC-SLP/L

**Sleep Consultant and Parent Educator:** Angelique Millette, PhDc, PCD/CD [DONA]

**Diastasis Rehab Expert:** Julie Tupler, RN, CCE

**Nutrition and Fertility Expert:** Cindy Bailey

**Choosing Childcare and Multiples Expert:** Michelle LaRowe

**Childcare Educator and Expert:** Pat Cascio

**Green Daddy:** Tim Ettus, President and Founder, Greeno Bambino

**Childbirth Educator, Film Producer, and Midwife:** Diana Paul

**Pre and Post Natal Yoga Expert:** Debra Flashenberg, CD(DONA), LCCE, E-RYT 500

**Pre and Post Natal Pilates Expert:** Carolyne Anthony

**Infant/CPR Expert & Parent Educator**: Georgia Montgomery, CD, CBE, CLE

**Postpartum Doula and Lactation Expert:** Emily Schaffer, PCD, CLE, HBE

**Clinical Psychologist for new and expecting parents:** Dr. Rama Ronen, PhD

**Acupuncture and Fertility Expert:** Chalita Photikoe, L.Ac.

**Nutrition Expert and Culinary Chef:** Diana Stobo

**Skincare Product Expert:** Robin Brown, Founder of ErbaOrganics

**Household Staffing Expert:** Elizabeth Dameron Drew, of Town and Country Resources

**Child Safety Expert:** Martin Simenc Owner / Founder, Home Safety Services

**Birth Options Expert:** Lisa Malley, Excecutive Director of Choices in Childbirth

**Parenting Community:** Mike Stigliano, CEO Parentville

**Childbirth Educator and Birth Doula:** Stefanie Antunes

**Social Networking Expert:** Dayna Landry, Founder and CEO of CityMommy

**Graphics Expert:** Emily Gevenish

**Online Dad Community and Education:** Khalid Mohammed, Founder of DaddyBluez.com

**Media Mom:** Joy Rose, Founder of MAMAPALOOZA Inc. a woman owned company

**Lactation Consultant and Expert:** Saray Hill IBCLC

## Beth Greer

Beth Greer, Super Natural Mom™, is an award-winning journalist, holistic health advocate, impassioned champion of toxin-free living, and radio talk show host, who busts open the myth that our homes are safe havens. Her bestselling book, *Super Natural Home: Improve Your Health, Home and Planet...One Room at a Time* (Rodale, 2009), endorsed by Deepak Chopra, Ralph Nader, Peter Coyote and others, shows how food, cosmetics, personal care products, household cleaners and furniture are making us sick.

Formerly President and Co-Owner of The Learning Annex, the largest private alternative adult education company in the U.S., Beth has helped thousands see new possibilities and feel empowered to make changes in their lives. Beth currently hosts her own national show "The Super Natural Mom Show" on the Progressive Radio Network, where she shines the light of truth about what goes *in* us, *on* us and *surrounds* us and gives insights on how to live a safer, less toxic, and more natural life.

She's written for the *San Francisco Chronicle's* Home Section and *US* magazine and blogs on her website supernaturalmom.com, intent.com and redroom.com. She has appeared on ABC-TV's The View from the Bay and At Home with Lisa Quinn with segments on

How to Turn your Bedroom into a Safe, Healthy Haven and How to Create a Safe, Healthy Kitchen.

Beth was named a recipient of the "100 Magnificent Marin Women Award" by Search for the Cause, a non-profit organization that investigates how exposure to chemicals in our daily lives increases the risk of cancer.

Beth is a testament to how making small lifestyle shifts can make a huge difference in one's health. By using alternative methods of healing, eating a diet free of pesticides and avoiding hazardous chemicals in her personal care and household products, Beth eliminated a tumor without drugs or surgery.

http://supernaturalmom.com

## Joseph Lizio

Joseph Lizio holds a MBA in Finance and Entrepreneurship and has a strong commercial lending background. In his current venture, Mr. Lizio is the founder of - Business Money Today - a site designed to help business owners find and obtain capital to grow their businesses.

http://www.businessmoneytoday.com/

## Alison Rhodes

Alison Rhodes, also known as The Safety Mom, has exploded onto the national scene as the preeminent voice on kid's safety, wellness and healthy living. She is always on the lookout for the issues facing all children - newborns to teens as well as the entire family.

While Alison's career began as a response to the death of her first child, over the years Alison has expanded her career platform to include the gamut of issues facing children today from the importance of healthy eating and an active lifestyle to cyber bullying and toy safety. Alison believes that a child's parents are their greatest safety advocate and coaches parents that when it comes to dealing with their children, it's important to be parents first and friends second.

Alison provides tips and advice to parents on a broad range of issues. Her ability to connect with parents in a down-to-earth, uplifting and engaging manner while providing important parenting information has made Alison a sought-after guest on many national television shows including The Today Show, Fox & Friends, CNN International, CNBC Squawk Box and The Doctors. Alison has also been featured in a variety of publications and websites including American Baby Magazine, Parents, BabyTalk, The Atlanta Journal Constitution, The Los Angeles Times, The New York Times, Parenting.com, SheKnows.com and Expectant Mother Magazine.

Everyday she offers her insight and tips to readers on her blog, The Safety Chronicles and on other popular parenting sites such as Parenting Weekly and Baby Weekly.

Over the years, Alison has worked as a spokesperson for numerous clients including SC Johnson, Crest, Symantec Technologies, Schlage Locks, Evenflo, Safety First, and Lands End among others.

http://www.safetymom.com

## Catherine Beier, CBE, MS CCC-SLP/L

Catherine Beier has supported and empowered birthing women and families as an independent childbirth educator, author, and webmaster since 2000.

In addition to her work in the birth world, Catherine maintains a small private practice serving children and adults with communication disorders. She is a summa cum laude graduate of Illinois State University with degrees in Speech-Language Pathology and Vocal Performance, is certified by the Amercian Speech-Language-Hearing Association and additionally holds an Early Intervention Specialist credential in both evaluation and treatment for serving children from birth through age 3.

She provides private and telephone consultations, teaches independent childbirth education classes, writes evidence-based articles on natural childbirth and pregnancy, and speaks on childbirth topics to parents and professionals.

Catherine is the owner and webmaster of GivingBirthNaturally.com which provides evidence-based natural childbirth and pregnancy information to parents and professionals. She stays updated on the latest research on childbirth and pregnancy so she can provide parents and professionals with accurate information.

Her book, Birth Outside the Box, was published in 2008. Catherine provides childbirth education classes to clients in her area through individual office visits and group sessions, and works with clients and groups throughout the world through her online childbirth classes. She also writes and publishes guided imagery and relaxation scripts for use in pregnancy, birth and the postpartum period.

Catherine's home and her practice are located in central Illinois, where she resides with her husband, two daughters, Eden, age 7, and Iris, age 5, and their menagerie of pets.

http://www.givingbirthnaturally.com

## Angelique Millette (PhDc, PCD/CD [DONA])

Angelique is a parent coach, sleep consultant, infant/toddler sleep and postpartum mood disorder researcher, lactation educator, DONA-certified birth and postpartum doula, and infant-child therapist intern who has worked with families across the Bay Area, the United States and Europe for the past 15 years.

She specializes in infant/child development and how parents can meet their own sleep needs while helping their young ones meet theirs. Angelique does not follow one specific sleep program, but rather helps families by taking into account family schedule, infant/toddler/child development, temperament, and parenting philosophy, all while keeping an eye on sleep deprivation, parental overwhelm, depression and anxiety. Angelique's doctoral research addresses the correlation amongst infant sleep locations/methods, maternal postpartum depression/anxiety, and maternal attachment.

Angelique teaches sleep workshops at Day One in San Francisco, The Parents Center in Marin, Birthways in Berkeley, professional conferences and parents groups across the country, and works with families in their homes, on the phone and also via Skype © to provide individual and unique sleep methods and solutions for parents and their infants and young children.

http://www.angeliquemillette.com/

## Julie Tupler, RN, CCE

Julie is a Registered Nurse, certified childbirth educator and fitness instructor. She developed the Maternal Fitness Program in 1990 and has been working with pregnant women and new moms ever since. She is on the advisory board of Fit Pregnancy and the Women's Sports Foundation. She is the author of two books, Maternal Fitness and Lose Your Mummy Tummy. She is the producer of the Diastasis Rehab and Lose Your Mummy Tummy DVDs and has developed the Diastasis Rehab ™ splint.

She is an expert on diastasis recti and has developed the research-based Tupler Technique to close a diastasis no matter when or how it was created. She trains medical and fitness professionals with her Tupler Technique Training for Treatment of Diastasis Recti. She speaks frequently at conferences throughout the U.S

Dr. Oz calls her an expert on diastasis recti. New York Magazine calls her the guru for pregnant women. She has been featured on many national television programs such as the Today Show, Regis & Kelly as well as in many fitness, medical, and women's health magazines. Elle

Macpherson (who pushed her baby out in 20 minutes) is a big fan of her program and wrote the forward for the Lose Your Mummy Tummy book.

http://www.diastasisrehab.com

## Cindy Bailey

Through the Fertile Kitchen™ (www.fertilekitchen.com), Cindy Bailey is committed to helping women and couples make a difference in their own fertility through diet/nutrition. In her book, The husband) Pierre Giauque share easy-to-make, flavorful recipes, along with the dietary guidelines and lifestyle changes that helped them succeed against the odds to bring home a baby. The Foreword is written by Philip E. Chenette, M.D. and Medical Director, Pacific Fertility Center in San Francisco.

As a former athlete, Cindy has a passion for good health and nutrition, and a commitment to helping others find natural, holistic ways of healing. She is a member of RESOLVE, the national infertility organization, and is also a freelance writer and award-winning owner of Bailey Communications, a firm that specializes in providing targeted, effective written communications for clients. She is editor-in-chief and co-founder of LitRave.com, a literary webzine, and has written for Glamour, City Sports Magazine, Intercom and other publications. For her firm, clients have included Warner Bros., Mattel Interactive, Los Angeles County, Alexander-Ogilvy Public Relations and many others. Cindy has also taught numerous workshops in creative nonfiction and has read her work at various venues, including San Francisco's LitQuake Festival. She holds a B.A. in Applied Mathematics from U.C. Berkeley and loves to travel, do sports, and hang out with her family.

http://www.fertilekitchen.com

## Pat Cascio

As the founder and director of Morningside Nannies and past president of the International Nanny Association, Pat Cascio has been in the in-home childcare industry since 1983. As the mother of four young daughters she personally experienced the lack of professionalism and top quality screening practices that existed in what was then known as "domestic agencies." As aresult, she founded the first agency in Houston to specialize in the referral of nannies. As a former employer of nannies for her own family, a former Executive Recruiter, and with 27 years in the business of placing nannies, she screens applicants by asking herself this question: "Would I hire this nanny to care for my own children?"

Pat served on the Board of Directors of the International Nanny Association (INA) for ten years, and had the honor of being elected as the President of the INA Board of Directors for eight terms. During her years as president of INA she acted as the spokesperson for the nanny industry and has been interviewed by hundreds of local, national and international media representatives as well as being a guest on various television and radio programs. She is the go-to person for all the major TV channels in Houston. Pat also is one of the Ask The Expert panelists for two industry publications. Morningside

Nannies is located in Houston, Texas and was awarded the honor of "Agency of the Year" in 2008 by the Association of Premier NannyAgencies.

http://www.morningsidenannies.com

## Michelle LaRowe

Michelle LaRowe is the 2004 International Nanny Association (INA) Nanny of the Year and is the author of the Nanny to the Rescue! parenting series, Working Mom's 411: How to Manage Kids, Career and Home and a Mom's Ultimate Book of Lists: 100+ Lists to Save You Time, Money and Sanity.

Michelle is an INA Credentialed Nanny, holds a Bachelor of Science Degree in chemistry, a certificate in pastoral studies and has spent more than 15 years as a professional nanny and parenting consultant. Michelle is an active member of the nanny community and serves as the Executive Director of the International Nanny Association, a 500+ member non-profit association dedicated to improving the quality of in-home child care.

Michelle is regularly called on by the media as a "nanny expert" and has appeared on television (700 Club, NECN, FOX), has been featured in print (USA Today, The Boston Globe, Better Homes and Gardens) and is a regular columnist for several magazinesincluding Families Online Magazine, TWINS Magazine and Today's Pentecostal Evangel. Her writing has been featured in The Experts' Guide to the Baby Years, on modernmom. com and in several national publications. Michelle is a national speaker and has spoken to moms groups across the country on various parenting topics and on the importance of choosing quality child care. Michelle resides in Hyannis, Massachusetts with her husband Jeff and daughter Abigail. You can learn more about Michelle by visiting her website:

http://www.michellelarowe.com

## Tim Ettus, President and Founder, Greeno Bambino

Tim (aka Green Daddy) owns and operates Greeno Bambino, an online retail more thoughtful alternatives.

Tim has a diverse background in e-commerce, marketing, media production, consumer products and business development. He holds a JD from New York University School of Law, an MBA from NYU's Stern School of Business, and a BA from the University of Michigan. He is also a member of the New York State Bar Association.

Born and raised in New York City, Tim is a long-suffering fan of the Jets and Knicks and currently resides in a sometimes leafy-sometimes snowy suburb of Chicago with his wife/college sweetheart, two young children and trusted bulldog.

http://www.greenobambino.com

## Mike Stigliano, CEO Parentville

Mike has a diverse background in digital media and has worked on large consumer-oriented web sites in both technical and business roles. He oversees day-to-day operations and strategic direction of the company. Most recently, he was in online ad sales at the internet division of CondeNast. Prior to that he held technical managerial positions in which he led the due diligence and implementation of mission-critical online systems including ad management and web analytics. Mike holds a B.S. from the University of Delaware and an MBA from the NYU Stern School of Business. As a busy parent of two boys living in New York City, Mike is also an avid user of Parentville.

http://www.parentville.com

## Diana Paul

Diana Paul is the Executive Director of Sage Femme, a non-profit organization that produces documentaries about natural birth, sponsors the Mother Baby International Film Festival, and distributes information and films through symposiums and conferences. Diana owned an independent midwifery practice in Massachusetts for 9 years and is the mother of three children. Diana has a BA in English from Sonoma State University.

http://www.sagefemme.com

## Debra Flashenberg, CD(DONA), LCCE, E-RYT 500

Debra is a graduate of the Boston Conservatory of Music with a degree in Musical Theater. She has spent most of her life performing and was introduced to yoga through a choreographer in 1997. After several years as a yoga student, she decided to continue her education and became certified as a Bikram Yoga instructor. In 2001 Debra headed out to Seattle to study with renowned prenatal yoga teacher Colette Crawford, R.N., at the Seattle Holistic Center. Debra has received a certificate for Vinyasa Yoga from Shiva Rea, with whom she continues to study. Debra has also studied the Maternal Fitness Method with Julie Tupler. In 2004, Debra completed the OM Yoga advanced teacher training with Cyndi Lee. Debra currently studies with Cyndi Lee, Genevieve Kapular, and Susan "Lip" Orem.

After being witness to several "typical" hospital births, Debra felt it was important to move beyond the yoga room and be present in the birthing room. In 2003, Debra attended her first birth as a DONA certified labor support doula. In that short period of time, Debra has attended about 75 births. She is continuously in awe of the beauty and brilliance of birth.

In 2006, Debra received her certification as a Lamaze Certified Childbirth Educator. In September of 2007, Debra completed a Midwife Assistant Program with Ina May Gaskin, Pamela Hunt and many of the other Farm Midwives at The Farm Midwifery Center in Tennessee. Most recently, Debra had the incredible experience of helping one of her clients give birth on the bathroom floor. Luckily, the EMS arrived seconds before the baby did!

Drawing on her experience as a prenatal yoga teacher, labor support doula and childbirth educator, Debra looks to establish a safe and effective class for pregnancy and beyond.

http://www.prenatalyogacenter.com

## Georgia Montgomery, CD, CBE, CLE

Georgia Montgomery is a hospital Perinatal Health Educator and teaches classes in childbirth, newborn care, breastfeeding, infant child/CPR and pediatric first aid at the UCSF Medical Center, and

Kaiser Hospital in Marin. She also taught at the California Pacific Medical Center in San Francisco for 5 years and at Marin General Hospital. She is a member of the Marin Breastfeeding Coalition, and is Founding Director of CPR Family and The Parents Center in San Rafael. She is a Volunteer Health Educator at the Family Service Agency of Marin as well as at the MINT Prison Project as for incarcerated expecting and new mothers. She began her career doing prenatal and postpartum work leading her to teach in hospitals in San Francisco and Marin County. Georgia is the mother of three adult children and is very active in the Childbirth Community as an advocate. She facilitates New Mother Support Groups at The Parents Center in San Rafael California. She teaches classes there as well as other venues in the greater San Francisco Bay Area. Her greatest joy is helping prepare expecting parents through the amazing experience of childbirth and assisting new moms as they navigate the world of parenting.

http://theparentscenter.com

## Emily Schaffer, PCD (DONA), HBE

Emily Schaffer received her B.A. in Holistic Health with an emphasis on the Spanish Language and Women's Studies at Prescott College in Arizona and continued her education to become a certified Postpartum Doula through Doulas of North America. She is a certified Lactation Educator through Evergreen and holds a credential as a Happiest Baby on the Block instructor. Emily is a member of DONA International, La Leche League, Marin, San Francisco and East Bay doula groups. She is very active in the Marin parenting community and holds an Advisory Board position at The Parents Center, San Rafael, CA. She has worked professionally as a nanny, personal assistant and household manager for over 18 years.

Emily currently works as a Certified Postpartum Doula, Lactation Educator and infant sleep specialist. She is committed to help with transition into parenthood with physical and emotional support and education so that new mothers and fathers are better equipped to make informed decisions. Emily offers private newborn care, breastfeeding consulting, sleep solutions, nursery preparation and nanny training. In addition she also teaches Happiest Baby on the Block classes. Emily currently lives in her native town of Mill Valley, CA.

http://www.emilyschaffer.com/

## Lisa Malley, Excecutive Director of Choices in Childbirth

Lisa Malley, Executive Director, joined Choices in Childbirth in November 2009. With nearly ten years of nonprofit experience, Lisa brings extensive fundraising background to the position and a strong dedication to women's health. Her professional experience ranges from reproductive health and rights organizations–including Planned Parenthood Federation of America and the Alan Guttmacher Institute–to university fundraising at Columbia Law School. She has a B.A. from Indiana University and received a Master's degree in Nonprofit Management from Milano Graduate School at the New School University. Lisa lives in Cobble Hill, Brooklyn with her husband Adam.

http://www.choicesinchildbirth.org

## Stefanie Antunes

Stefanie Antunes is a Lamaze® Certified Childbirth Educator and certified birth doula with DONA International. She is the Public Relations Director for DONA International and writes and speaks regularly on the topics of pregnancy, childbirth, and educator and doula roles. After ten years of working in the corporate world in strategy and intelligence, she has turned her focus to the areas of supporting and advocating for young families' health through the founding of her own business, Discover Birth Inc. and a birth advocacy group WiseParent.org

http://www.discoverbirth.com

## Martin Simenc Owner / Founder, Home Safety Services

Martin Simenc has over 20 years of experience in the safety and risk management industry. Martin is regarded as an expert in residential safety, risk management and industrial loss control. He is a frequent public speaker on various topics most commonly those addressing safety in the home. He authors a monthly column entitled "Ask The Safety Guy", was recently recognized in The Wall Street Journal and serves as a consulting expert to various organizations including BabyCenter.com and On The

House with The Carey Brothers. He has also appeared on HGTV's House Detective.

In 1997, Martin founded Home Safety Services, whose purpose is: To Make Home a Safer Place, For Every Generation. Home Safety Services has since become the largest Bay Area residential safety company and has assisted over 10,000 families by increasing their safety, confidence and peace of mind. Prior to founding Home Safety Services, Martin managed the Property Risk Management function for Hewlett-Packard Company on a worldwide basis. Previously, he served as a loss control and risk management consultant to numerous multinational manufacturing companies. It was his father's stroke in 1993 which influenced Martin's change in focus from industrial to residential safety. His father has since recovered extremely well; however, the experience raised the importance of taking practical steps to improve safety in and around the home both prior to and after life changing events.

Martin's education includes a bachelor's degree in Mechanical Engineering from Santa Clara University and a master's degree in Finance and International Business from the University of San Francisco. He is a Licensed Professional Fire Protection Engineer (PE) and Licensed General Contractor. He is a Certified Aging in Place Specialist (CAPS) and has earned the Associate in Risk Management (ARM) designation. He is the Secretary of the International Association for Child Safety and on the Advisory Board of the Safe Kids Coalition. He is a founding member of the California Stop Falls Task Force and the San Mateo County Fall Prevention Task Force. His company's work with Stanford Hospital has recently been recognized as a national model program by the National Council on Aging.

http://www.homesafety.net/

## Dayna Landry, Founder and CEO of CityMommy

Created by a mom for moms, Dayna Landry started CityMommy April 2007 in Los Angeles. Finishing its first year with a membership of approximately 7,500, CityMommy has grown to include 42 areas and currently boasts more than 25,000 members nationwide.CityMommy is a cross between a local social networking site and online community. Members can share photos of themselves and their children and weigh in on everything from pediatricians to preschools. Over a third of members login to the site at least daily. However, for moms who don't have time to scan the active message boards, CityMommy sends out a daily digest of hot topics. Readership is encouraged by invitation--friends invite friends, thus building a strong site community. The CityMommy blog (citymommy.com) offers articles, interviews, and giveaways of interest to members.

http://www.citymommy.com

## Emily Genevish

Emily Genevish is the owner and sole designer of Genevish Graphics. Being a mother of two, she understands the challenges that come with working with young ones at home. Originally from Tampa, Florida and working out of her Jacksonville, North Carolina home, the freelance graphic designer provides graphic design for print and the web to individuals and small businesses across the world. She specializes in unique vector logo design featuring original illustrations and unique typography. Holding a BFA in Digital Design, she is knowledgeable in the most current computer design software to meet any design need.

http://www.genevish-graphics.com

## Dr. Rama Ronen

Dr. Rama Ronen (PSY 23043) is a licensed psychologist and has extensive experience working with individuals, families and children of all ages. She is exceptionally well trained in Cognitive Behavioral Psychotherapy and also incorporates Dialectical Behavioral principles in her practice. Rama works with expectant, new, and experienced mothers, providing support and helping develop useful skills during this transition time. She provides home visits when necessary. In addition, she also has many years of experience working with emotionally and behaviorally challenged children, depression, anxiety, loss and grief.

Dr. Rama Ronen has two areas of specialty:

☐   Prenatal and Postpartum Support

☐   Children and Parenting Consultation

Dr. Ronen's non-judgmental approach helps clients to identify, express and gain clarity about the challenges they face. She guides them to learn and apply creative, effective skills in a supportive and validating environment. She offers expertise on bereavement, and specifically on exploring the role of the continuing bond to the deceased and coping with the death of a loved one. She has extended her focuses to the impact of pet loss.

Dr. Ronen earned her Ph.D. in Clinical Psychology from Pacific Graduate School of Psychology, which is fully accredited by the American Psychological Association (APA).

http://www.entelechywellness.com

## Chalita Photikoe, L.Ac.

Chalita Photikoe is a licensed acupuncturist, herbalist, and yoga instructor with extensive clinical training in fertility, obstetrics and pediatrics. She completed her 4 years master's program in Traditional Chinese Medicine in 2004 from the Academy of Chinese Culture and Health Sciences in Oakland, CA. She teaches pre and post-natal yoga classes, yoga for conception, and workshops on holistic pediatrics and obstetrics. Chalita lives in San Rafael, CA with her husband and daughter Naia.

http://chalitaacupuncture.com/

## Diana Stobo

Culinary artist and raw food enthusiast, Diana Stobo is living proof that her diet and lifestyle works. Once plagued by relentless pain and physical discomfort due to food toxicity, Diana successfully navigated her way through old patterns to discover a healthy way of eating and living that has transformed her own life to one of optimum health, vibrance, and beauty. Passionate about everything in life including her relationships, her family, her health, and especially her food, Diana understands how integral food is to all aspects of nutrition including child development, family patterns, social expectations, and body awareness. As someone who looks and feels younger than she did 10 years ago, Diana's philosophy is to empower the individual with food choices that create a better lifestyle, and a healthier and more energetic way of being in the world. Diana's goal is to design nutritious products that are accessible, filled with familiar foods that have taste and flare, and introduce many exciting and healthful new ingredients. Integrating the whole of her experience from her early teenage tart baking business to training in the Cornell culinary arts division of the Hotel Administration Program, running her own highly successful Signature Catering business, consulting one-on-one with clients to tailor individualized programs, and developing a raw snack line for the "tween" pangs of hunger, Diana's has refined and focused her unique blend of expertise to emerge in the living food movement as a leading innovator and educator. Combining professional expertise with rich personal experience, Diana is dedicated to creating delicious, nutritious recipes that are easy to prepare and satisfying to the senses. Feasting while dropping excess weight, increasing physical and mental energy, and staying young and sexy while developing a new healthier relationship with food—this is the lifestyle that Diana has discovered for herself and wishes to share with you!

http://www.dianastobo.com/

## Robin Brown, Founder of ErbaOrganics

Erbaorganics was born out of a desire to make available the purest eco-friendly organic skincare to those who need it most: mommys-to-be and babies. Concerned over the chemicals used in traditional skincare, husband and wife Robin Brown and Anna Cirronis started making organic products when they had their first son. They soon realized that others were just as concerned about the harmful chemicals in mother and baby products. Erbaorganics is an effective high quality organic alternative to many products on the market still using harmful ingredients. Erbaorganics is proud to launch a full line of mother and baby products as high in organic ingredients as is possible to make, with food grade preservatives and organic anti-oxidants.

Over the years they have sought out the finest organic ingredients and combined them into unique blends that nourish the body and the soul. This new line is designed to be made available to as many people as possible, as we believe it is everyone's right to be able to use clean, safe, organic skincare particularly for mother and baby.

Erbaorganics is based in Southern California and it is here where the line is manufactured by a dedicated staff who take special care and pride every step of the way. We feel that Erbaorganics products will improve the lives and health of those who use them, as well as that of the environment, bringing the benefits of choosing organic to the forefront of the public consciousness.

http://www.erbaorganics.com/

## Elizabeth Dameron-Drew, Vice-President, Baby Nurses

Elizabeth joined Town & Country Resources as a Placement Counselor in 1996. Over the years here she has helped find solutions for a wide range of client and candidate needs. She has this to say of her current focus on Baby Nurse placements, "I'm incredibly satisfied by connecting parents to baby experts who offer much needed support during such a special, but often very challenging time." As a working mom with years of experience having employed a Nanny, she has a first hand understanding of the peace of mind that quality childcare gives parents. She has a Bachelors Degree in Fine Art from California College of the Arts. Elizabeth lives on the Peninsula with her husband and her two sons. Because of her oldest son's heart defect, Elizabeth has a unique understanding of the needs of families with children with health challenges.

http://www.tandcr.com/

## Khalid Mohammed, Founder of DaddyBluez.com

DaddyBluez.com, a web portal dedicated to empowering dads and dads-to-be. The idea of DaddyBluez evolved from personal experience when DaddyBluez.com founder Khalid Mohammed and his wife Renata became parents. They quickly realized that dads needed more focused content and tools to help guide them on their parenting path.

At DaddyBluez.com, visitors find up to date information and expert advice about pregnancy and parenting specifically gearded towards dads. Filled with useful tools, DaddyBluez.com empowers men to play a more active role in their partner's pregnancy and their child's first three years of life. Winner of the Families Online Magazine best parenting website award, DaddyBluez continues to be a one-stop resource for dads and dads-to-be.

http://www.daddybluez.com

## Joy Rose Is The Media Mom & Founder of MAMAPALOOZA Inc. a woman owned company

JOY ROSE has been awarded the Susan B. Anthony Award from NOW-NYC 2009. Joy Rose is President and Founder of Mamapalooza Inc. a company by women, promoting (m)others for social, cultural and economic benefit. She is also acting Executive Director for The Motherhood Foundation working towards the Museum Of Motherhood. Joy was appointed the Susan B. Anthony Award from NOW-NYC in recognition of her grassroots activism and dedication to advancing equality and improving the lives of women and girls in 2009.

Committed a lasting legacy of empowerment and support, while redefining what it means to be a modern mother, Joy has successfully pioneered a new culture of mom-branded art and performance. She's also the founder and lead singer of the rock band, 'Housewives On Prozac'. Inspired by her experiences as a feminist mother in the arts, she works tirelessly with women, and volunteers around the country co-creating events and programming, changing the way women's voices are heard in the media, education and performing arts, impacting the culture of modern mothers and their families.

Day to day operations of Mamapalooza include the inception and production of a series of large-scale festival events across the country each April –June, working in alliance with local government, parks departments and cultural affairs. Each Mamapalooza Festival generates community awareness while highlighting mom-music performers, women-owned businesses, vendors, health education, social services for families and kids activities.

Joy Rose – holds a BFA in Theater from Denison University, was a core team member of the Betsey Johnson organization and opened the first Soho Store in New York City. She has enjoyed success as a recording and video artist, is a Billboard Chart topping performer and MTV Basement Tape Winner. She worked closely with her midwife to form 'Prepared Parenting Classes' post childbirth, and is the proud mother of Brody, Blaze, Ali and Zena.

Her writing has been published in Women's Media Center, The Mom Egg, Hot Moms Handbook and The International Museum Of Women and The Association For Research On Mothering. Her music has appeared on radio stations around the country and she's been profiled on CNN, American Voices, Women In History, NPR, Good Morning America, USA Today, The London Times, The Chicago Tribune, ABC, CBS, NBC, Ladies' Home Journal, Child Magazine and People Magazine to name a few.

She is a featured guest speaker for Women's Events, on Radio, in Hospitals (Highlighting stories of courage and survival), most recently at The Association For Research On Mothering where key delegates agreed on the formation of the IMN (International Mothers Network). She has appeared at The Women's Media Center, NYC founded by Jane Fonda, Robin Morgan and Gloria Steinem, speaking on Art, Feminism and Finances. She was a featured guest speaker at the 'What Women Want' Conference, October 2007, Montana, The MPLZCC Creativity & Lifestyles Conference, NYC, and sits on a special committee for the Westchester Office For Women and The Women's Hall Of Fame. Joy holds the key to Seneca Falls, NY for her work on behalf of Women & Mothers 2005.

Joy is currently blogging and networking through Mamapalooza, Moms Rising.org, Hot Moms Club, Word Press and First Wives World. She works closely with a staff of nearly fifty freelancers & volunteers creating opportunities that involve thousands of artists, educators, and mom and women-owned businesses worldwide.

Joy is currently at work editing a film about 'The Motherhood Movement', capturing the voices of Feminist Mothers of the 21st century, and pioneering the 'Sustainable Women' Initiative for Eco-consciousness and mindful living.

She is also a contributor to ENCYCLOPEDIA OF MOTHERHOOD: A New 3-volume Reference to Be Published by Sage Publications, edited by Andrea O'Reilly due out 2010. This comprehensive work will be marketed and sold to college, public, and academic libraries and includes some 750 articles, covering all aspects of a social science perspective on motherhood, including psychology, gender studies, sociology, education, human development, history, and other fields.

Joy Rose
joy@mamapalooza.com

877.711.MOMS (6667)
O. 914.479.5085
PO Box 210 Hastings On Hudson, NY 10706
www.mamapalooza.com
www.housewivesonprozac.com
www.mamaztv.com
www.motherhoodfoundation.org
www.internationalmothersnetwork.org

## Saray Hill, IBCLC

Saray Hill is an IBCLC (International Board Certified Lactation Consultant), a Lactation Educator and Breastfeeding Peer Counselor, as well as a mom and wife residing in Los Angeles, CA. Born in Ecuador, she is fluent in Spanish and English. Saray holds a Bachelor's degree in Economics from the Universidad Católica Santiago de Guayaquil in Ecuador and completed the Lactation Consultant Training Program at UCSD-Extension. Mom entrepreneur Saray is the President of her own company, Mother's Utopia, where she offers lactation consultations, baby care classes in person and online to support expectant and new parents on their journey of parenthood. Saray is the Lactation Specialist for St. John's Partnership for Families in Santa Monica, CA and previously worked as a Breastfeeding Peer Counselor for BELLAS (Breastfeeding Encouragement Learning Liaison and Support) in Charlotte, NC and WIC (Women Infants and Children) in Los Angeles, CA. These positions put her in contact with families of different backgrounds/ ethnicities, socio-economical and educational levels, with individual and specific needs. She is the founder of El Club de Lactancia en Twitter, a Spanish speaking breastfeeding support group for moms to support one another on their motherhood and breastfeeding journeys. She is also one of the breastfeeding experts at Sixty Second Parent.

Saray believes that empowering parents means giving them evidence based information to help them make their own educated decisions when it comes to feeding and raising their children, along with compassionate and emotional support.

http://www.mothersutopia.org

# Index of Resources

## Baby Planners

http://www.thebabyplanner.com

http://www.weeplanbabyplanners.com

http://www.dcbabyplanners.com

http://www.mindfulmotheringbda.com

http://www.emilyschaffer.com

http://www.babybloom.com.hk

http://www.bforbaby.fr

http://www.sweetexpectationsbabyplanner.com

http://www.thehoustonbabyplanner.com

http://www.bassettbabyplanning.com

http://www.bellytobabyplanners.com

http://www.bellejourbabyplanning.com

http://blossombabyplanning.com

## Birthing Resources

http://www.choicesinchildbirth.org

http://www.birthcenters.org/

http://www.waterbirth.org/

http://www.midwiferytoday.com/

http://mana.org/

http://www.motherfriendly.org

http://childbirthconnection.org

http://www.naturalbabypros.com

http://www.sagefemme.com

http://www.sagefemme.com/ecobirth.html

http://www.givingbirthnaturally.com

http://www.discoverbirth.com

http://www.circumcision.org

## Birth Movies

http://www.thebusinessofbeingborn.com

http://www.birth-media.com

http://www.pregnantinamerica.com

http://www.babiesthemovie.com

http://www.homebirthvideos.com/birthday_dvd.asp

http://www.whatbabieswant.com

## Breastfeeding

http://www.breastfeeding.com

http://www.llli.org

http//www.kellymom.com

http://www.promom.org

http://www.mothersutopia.org

http://www.babyinthefamily.net

http://www.mercola.com

http://www.westonaprice.org

http://www.gotmom.org

 http://womenhealth.gov

http://www.bfmed.org/

## Business

http://www.businessknowhow.com

http://www.bplans.com

http://www.businessmoneytoday.com

US Small Business Administration
 http://www.sba.gov

United States Patent and Trademark Office
 http://uspto.gov

EIN number
 http://www.irs.gov/businesses/small/index.html

Small Business Readiness Assessment Tool
 http://www.sba.gov

LMA Consulting Group
 http://www.lmaconsulting.cc

## Car Seat Safety

http://www.nhtsa.gov

http://www.safekidswebinars.org

## Certifications

Baby Planner Certification

International Maternity Institute
http://www.maternityinstitute.com

Parent Coaching Certifications:

Parent Coaching Institute
http://www.parentcoachinginstitute.com

Academy for Coaching Parents International
http://www.academyforcoachingparents.com

Lactation Consultant:

International Board of Lactation Consultant Examiners
http://www.iblce.org

Lactation Education Resources
http://www.leron-line.com

Lactation Education Consultants
http://www.lactationeducationconsultants.com

Childbirth and Postpartum Professional Association
http://cappa.net

Baby Nurse and Nanny Certifications:

Infant and Childcare Training Center
http://www.infantcaretraining.com

International Nanny Association
http://www.nanny.org

Birth and Postpartum Doula Certifications:

DONA International
http://dona.org

CAPPA
http://cappa.net

International Childbirth Education Association
http://www.icea.org

Child Birth International

http://www.childbirthinternational.com

ChildProofer Certification

International Association for Child Safety
http://iafcs.org

Prenatal Yoga Certification

http://www.prenatalyogacenter.com

Prenatal Pilates Certification

http://www.thecenterforwomensfitness.com

Prenatal Fitness

http://www.healthymomsfitness.com/training.htm

http://www.afpafitness.com/store/prepost-natal-exercise-certification-p-674.html

http://www.afaa.com

Diastasis Rehab

http://diastasisrehab.com

Nutrition Certification

Institute for Integrative Nutrition
http://www.integrativenutrition.com

Bauman College
http://www.baumancollege.org

Global College of Natural Medicine
http://www.gcnm.com

Car Passenger Safety Certification

http://cert.safekids.org

## Childbirth Classes

The Bradley Method
http://www.bradleybirth.com

Lamaze International
http://www.lamaze.org

Birth Works International
http://www.birthworks.org/site

Birthing From Within
http://www.birthingfromwithin.com

International Childbirth Education Association
http://www.icea.org

HypnoBirthing
http://www.hypnobirthing.com

Hypnobabies
http://www.hypnobabies.com

The Leclaire Method
http://www.leclairemethod.com

## Child Care

Town & Country Resources
http://www.tandcr.com

City of Mill Valley Police
http://www.cityofmillvalley.org

Sarah Cohen PCD, CECE
http://www.sleepyfamilyindex.com

Postpartum Doula, Emily Schaffer (PCD, CLE, HBE)
http://www.emilyschaffer.com

DONA International

http://www.dona.org

International Nanny Association
http://www.nanny.org

The National Association for Family Child Care
http://www.nafcc.org

Morningside Nannies
http://www.morningsidenannies.com

Michelle LaRowe
http://www.michellelarowe.com

## Child Proofing

City of Mill Valley
 http://www.cityofmillvalley.org

International Association For Child Safety
http://www.iafcs.org

US Consumer Product Safety Commission
 http://www.cpsc.gov

Safe Kids
http://www.safekids.org/skwHome.html

Safe Beginnings
http://www.safebeginnings.com

## Child Safety

http://www.safekids.org

http://healthychild.org

http://www.aap.org

http://www.nsc.org

http://www.sidsalliance.org

http://www.cpsc.gov

http://iafcs.org

http://www.homesafety.net

http://www.safetymom.com

## Fertility

http://www.naturalbabypros.com

http://www.fertilekitchen.com

http://naturalfertilitybreakthrough.com

http://www.natural-fertility-prescription.com

## Fitness, Yoga, and Pilates

http://www.prenatalyogacenter.com

http://www.thecenterforwomensfitness.com

http://www.diastasisrehab.com

http://www.healthymomsfitness.com/training.htm

http://www.afpafitness.com/store/prepost-natal-exercise-certification-p-674.html

http://www.afaa.com

http://www.PTontheNet.com

## Green Resources

http://www.ewg.org

http://naturalnews.com

http://www.cosmeticsdatabase.com

http://www.thedailygreen.com

http://www.ecotimetoys.com

http://www.BestBabyOrganics.com

http://www.safecosmetics.org

http://www.ecomom.com

http://supernaturalmom.com

http://www.erbaorganics.com

http://www.thegreenguide.com/home-garden

http://greenhomeguide.com

http://planetgreen.discovery.com/home-garden

http://www.alexandrazissu.com

http://www.gorgeouslygreen.com

## Nutrition

http://www.integrativenutrition.com

http://www.baumancollege.org

http://www.gcnm.com

http://www.dianastobo.com

Shopper's Guide to Pesticides

http://www.foodnews.org

## Parenting Communities

http://www.parentville.com

http://www.citymommy.com

http://www.daddybluez.com

## Postpartum Depression

http://www.nativeremedies.com

http://postpartum.net

http://www.postpartumprogress.com

http://www.entelechywellness.com

## Postpartum and Newborn Care

http://www.thefirst8days.com

http://www.emilyschaffer.com

http://www.doula-care.com

http://www.daraluznetwork.com

## Products

 http://www.consumerreports.org

http://www.jpma.org

http://www.astm.org

http://www.cpsc.gov

http://www.healthystuff.org

http://www.onestepahead.com

http://www.greenobambino.com

 http://www.amazingregistry.com

## Sleep

http://www.naturalsleepmedicine.net

 http://www.angeliquemillette.com

http://www.sleepyfamily.net

http://www.internationalsleep.org

http://www.helpguide.org/life/sleeping.html

http://www.sleepfoundation.org

http://www.sleepeducation.com

http://maternityinstitute.com

## Co-Sleeping

The Natural Child Project,
http://www.naturalchild.org/articles/sleeping.html

Mothering Magazine, articles on the family bed:
http://www.mothering.com/search/node/co-sleeping

Attachment Parenting International, cosleeping information and advocacy:
http://www.attachmentparenting.org/support/resources.php#night

Co-sleeping on Wikipedia:
http://en.wikipedia.org/wiki/Co-sleeping